GEORGE CANNING

GEORGE CANNING

Reproduced by the courtesy of the Dean of Christ Church, Oxford, from the portrait by Sir Thomas Lawrence in Christ Church Hall

[Frontispiece

GEORGE CANNING

BY

SIR CHARLES PETRIE, Bt.

M.A. (Oxon)., F.R.Hist.Soc.

Corresponding Member of the Royal Spanish Academy of History

LONDON

EYRE & SPOTTISWOODE

First published 1930
Second edition 1946

Printed in Great Britain for
Eyre & Spottiswoode (Publishers), *Limited,*
15 Bedford Street, London, W.C.2

PREFACE TO FIRST EDITION

To write the life of George Canning in six volumes would be comparatively easy, but to do so in one necessitates the omission of much that is both of interest and of importance, particularly in respect of the earlier years of his career. In the present instance the attempt has been made not only to produce a biography that is of moderate length, but also to let its subject so far as possible speak for himself, in the hope that through Canning's words the reader may be enabled the better to understand the character of the man who wrote or spoke them.

Like every other worker in this field, I must acknowledge my debt to the labours of Professor Temperley, and, in a slightly lesser degree, to those of M. Pierre de la Gorce: where I have ventured to disagree with the conclusions of either, it has only been after the most careful consideration. The two volumes of letters which Captain Josceline Bagot edited some twenty years ago have proved to be a mine of information, hitherto unworked so far as Canning's earlier life is concerned. For advice and information upon various points I must express my gratitude to my friend Professor R. B. Mowat, of Bristol University; the Under Treasurer of Lincoln's Inn; Lieut.-Colonel John Murray, D.S.O.; and a number of other friends and correspondents too numerous to mention individually.

CHARLES PETRIE.

April, 1930.

PREFACE TO SECOND EDITION

THIS book has been completely re-written, and more than one judgment modified, in the light of the fresh matter relating to Canning which has become available during the past fourteen years. In particular I must refer to Miss D. Marshall's *The Rise of George Canning*, and to Professor Aspinall's *The Formation of Canning's Ministry* and *The Letters of King George IV, 1812–1830*; my debt to both is obvious throughout this present work. I should also like to express my obligation to Mr. Fred R. Gale for the contribution which he has made over a number of years in *Notes and Queries* to the elucidation of many obscure circumstances in connection with Canning's life and family.

CHARLES PETRIE.

December, 1945.

CONTENTS

CONTENTS

CHAPTER I

THE EARLY YEARS

GEORGE CANNING was born in London of Irish parents on April 11th, 1770,[1] being thus a few months younger than Napoleon and nearly a year junior to Wellington. In spite of his English birth-place he always considered himself, as he once told Sir Walter Scott, to be first and foremost an Irishman. In this assertion he was undoubtedly right, for although he received the conventional English education, and passed his life in the world of English politics, Canning remained Irish at heart, with all the strength and weakness which that implies; and in this fact is surely to be found the explanation both of his successes and failures. For the most part his victories were in the field of international, and his defeats in that of domestic, politics, and it is difficult to resist the conclusion that one reason for this was that, like so many of his fellow-countrymen, he was liable from time to time to fall into grave errors concerning the working of the English mind, while he found that of the foreigner far more easily comprehensible.

In origin, however, the Canning family was English, for it was a cadet branch that had settled in Ireland. Its first home would appear to have been Bishop's Canynge in Wiltshire, a county to which more than one great statesman owes his origin; from there some member moved to Bristol, where the Cannings were pros-perous merchants in the Middle Ages. In the reign of Henry VI one of them married Agnes Salmon, an heiress, of Foxcote in Warwickshire, and settled there. Later still, a George Canning of this branch in 1618 obtained from James I a grant of the manor of Garvagh in Co. Londonderry, and from him the subject of this biography was descended. These genealogical details have, nevertheless, little bearing upon the career of George Canning, for few British Prime Ministers have owed less to their ancestors; but they do show that he came of a family that did not hesitate, when occasion arose, to pack up its tents and follow whither fortune seemed to beckon.

Stratford Canning, the grandfather of the Prime Minister, was a parent of a singularly harsh and tyrannical disposition. He had three sons, George, Paul, and Stratford, and he quarrelled

[1] The same year that saw the birth of Beethoven, Wordsworth and Hegel.

with the first and last. George's political views were from the
beginning too extreme for his father, and when, in addition, he
fell in love with a girl who did not secure parental approval, he
was cut off with an allowance of £150 a year, and he went to seek
his fortune in England. The third son not only fell in love with a
girl of whom his father disapproved, but he actually married her,
and so met the same fate as his brother. He, too, settled in
England, but, unlike the unfortunate George, he prospered in
business, and in due course became the father of the future Viscount Stratford de Redcliffe. The other brother, Paul, eventually
succeeded to the family property; his son was raised to the
peerage in 1818, and from him the present Lord Garvagh is
descended.

George Canning the elder arrived in London in 1757, and his
career may be dismissed in a few lines. He began to read for the
Bar, and was eventually called by the Middle Temple in 1764,
but as a barrister he was so complete a failure that he finally
abandoned the law for the wine trade, only, however, to be equally
unsuccessful there. He also wrote for the papers, and published
a translation of the *Anti-Lucretius* as well as a collection of poems.
Meanwhile, he was frequenting the company of the more extreme
Whigs, and was a devoted adherent of Wilkes. As none of these
activities was in any way lucrative, it is hardly surprising that he
found his allowance of £150 a year wholly inadequate for his
needs, and was soon heavily in debt. Eventually old Stratford
Canning settled with his son's creditors, but only upon condition
that George consented to the breaking of the entail in favour of his
brother, Paul, and this was duly accomplished. As if he had not
committed imprudences enough, in 1768 George married Mary
Anne Costello, a Connaught girl of eighteen who was as conspicuous for her beauty as for her impecuniosity. This marriage
so enraged Stratford that he cut off his son's allowance, and three
years later George died, just twelve months after he had become
the father of a boy to whom was given his own Christian
name.

Such were the circumstances attendant upon the entry of
Canning into the world in which he was to play so large a part.
He was certainly not born, like so many of his later colleagues,
with the proverbial silver spoon in his mouth, and it was thus
with perfect truth that his friend, John Hookham Frere, could
write:

Born with an ancient name of little worth,
And disinherited before his birth,
A landless orphan, rank and wealth and pride
Were freely ranged around him, nor denied
His clear precedence. . . .

Like many another pretty young woman, Mrs. Canning now determined to make her fortune on the stage, and she appeared at Drury Lane on December 3rd, 1773. She was speedily undeceived in her expectations, and before long was compelled to leave London for the provinces, where she acted a good deal both in Hull and in the West of England. During the course of her wanderings she met an actor-manager named Reddish, with whom she lived for several years, and to whom she bore five children, including two sets of twins; Reddish, however, turned out to be a bad lot, and in due course died of drink. In 1783 she married in Exeter a draper, by the name of Hunn, and five more children, including twins again, were born from this marriage. Mary Anne Canning was, however, doomed to disaster in her relations with the opposite sex, for Hunn failed in business, and for a time actually appeared on the stage with his wife.

Though the deprivation of his father's care was probably no great loss to Canning in view of the unstable character of the elder George, yet his death and the *liaison* of his widow with Reddish meant that the boy had no regular home, and that his education was in the hands of his mother's lover. For such a part Reddish was wholly unsuited, and there is the authority of John Moody, the actor, for the statement that at this stage of his career Canning was " on the road to the gallows ". Moody was, like the Cannings, Irish, though he came from Cork, and in his youth had been implicated in Jacobite intrigues to an extent which made it advisable for him to seek his fortune in the West Indies. He went on the stage in Jamaica, where he prospered, and in due course returned to England with a reputation which he enhanced in London. Moody was a close friend of Garrick, whom he persuaded to help Mrs. Canning in her distress. In the seventies and eighties of the eighteenth century Moody was at the height of his fame, and it was at this time that he proved a benefactor to the young Canning, as well as to his mother.

The Irish actor first of all interested Stratford, the boy's uncle, and through him an appeal was made to the grandfather at Garvagh. The old man, who died soon afterwards, at length consented to allow Canning a sum of about £200 a year, being the income from some property that the family owned at Kilmainham in Co. Kilkenny. Henceforth, Canning was to all intents and purposes adopted by his uncle, and at a later stage of his career he repaid the debt which he thus owed to this branch of the family by the help he gave to his cousin, the younger Stratford. At the same time his first start in life was due to his warm-hearted fellow-countryman, John Moody, whose name surely deserves to be rescued from oblivion for this act alone.

In later life Canning was frequently accused of pride, arrogance, and insensibility to the feelings of others, and to his reputation on this score were due many of the disappointments which he experienced during the course of his career. Nevertheless, with one thing he could never be charged, and that was neglect of his relations. His mother's career was hardly an asset to a rising statesman, but the frailties and misfortunes of Mrs. Canning created no breach between her and her eldest son. As a schoolboy he persuaded his guardians to make her a small allowance out of his own modest income, and when she left the stage in 1801, Canning, who had then been Under-Secretary of State for five years, arranged to have his annual pension of £500 settled on his mother. Mrs. Canning thereafter lived at Bath, and there she died, shortly before her son, at the age of seventy-eight. She exercised little influence over Canning, and circumstances kept the two apart, but in sympathy mother and son remained united throughout life, and he never failed to write to her once a week. In 1816, for example, her nephew, Stratford, is found writing, " Mr. Canning . . . invited me to meet him on the road, and I accompanied him to Bath, where his mother was residing. I found a handsome old lady of commanding presence and much apparent energy, answering to what he had told me, namely that ' I should see a person of high spirit, and spirits also '." [1] Nor was this all, for although Canning never recognized the young Reddishes as his half-brothers, he did all that he could to assist them as soon as his own circumstances permitted, while to his grandmother and to his maternal aunt, who acted as his mother's companion, his attentions never varied.[2]

---

[1] Lane-Poole, S.: *The Life of Stratford Canning*, vol. I, p. 271.
[2] Marshall, D.: *The Rise of George Canning*, pp. 113, *et seq.*: also *Notes and Queries*, Thirteenth Series, vol. CLIII, pp. 129–133 and 147–150, for letters to his Hunn relations.

The first school to which Canning was sent after this improve-
ment in his prospects was Hyde Abbey, Winchester, then kept by a
Dr. Richards, for whom his pupil later secured a prebendary's
stall at Winchester. Holidays were spent chiefly with his uncle,
Stratford, and his aunt, Hetty, who were then living at Putney.
His cousins consisted of Henry, who was about his own age;
William, who was some years younger; Bessy, whose feelings
towards him were one day to be warmer than he realized; and
Stratford, the future ambassador, but a baby during Canning's
earlier school-days. The household was strongly Whig, for
political differences had also played their part in the quarrel
between Stratford and his father, and to Putney came such Whig
leaders as Sheridan and Fox. Canning was greatly influenced by
all he saw and heard; and his boyish enthusiasm was all for the
cause of which these great men were champions. It was, it may
be added, during one of these holidays that the portrait of Canning, at the age of twelve, was painted by Gainsborough.

At Hyde Abbey he made up for any time that had been lost in
the matter of his education, and when he left there, in 1782, for
Eton, to which he was probably sent at the suggestion of Fox, he
had made sufficient progress to be at once placed in the fourth
form. Eton and Oxford were two very important milestones in
Canning's career, for in both places he came under influences, and
formed friendships, which were to affect him for the rest of his
life. At the former he was most successful in his work, and by
the autumn of 1786 he was top of the school. In spite, however,
of his ability and restricted means he did not become a Colleger,
and the reasons which he gave in a contemporary letter for avoid-
ing that situation throw an interesting light upon his character and
views while he was still at Eton:

A Colleger stays at Eton till nineteen; then, if a vacancy
falls out at King's College, Cambridge, while he is first in the
school, he is translated thither, and enjoys the advantage of
upon an average from first to last about £50 per annum till
he dies or marries. When a man goes into the Church the
advantage is greater, as he may chance by very good luck to
get a living. These are the advantages. The contrary is—
a Colleger rises much slower in the school, and is consequently
much later at the top. He stays till nineteen—an Oppidant
till seventeen: two years, or a year even, to a man whose

line is the Bar, is surely an object. A Colleger may, after all, not go to King's if a vacancy does not fall. Where *then* is the advantage? A Colleger, among the boys even, is not looked upon in near so respectable a light as an Oppidant. This was one of my principal reasons for my dislike.[1]

In 1787 Canning was captain of the Oppidans, or, as he spelt it at the time, Oppidants, and at the Montem of that year he was the chief figure.

The friends that a boy makes at school, or a young man at the university, have not infrequently as much influence upon his later life as his scholastic achievements, and such was the case with Canning, for at Eton he laid the foundation of that circle of intimates which was to mean so much to him during the rest of his career.

Foremost among them was John Hookham Frere, who was Canning's senior by one year, and with whom he was to be associated on so many public and private occasions. Frere came of an old Norfolk family, and from Eton he went to Caius College, Cambridge. He had unquestionably a very good brain, but he was both indolent and absent-minded. In middle life he married the widow of the sixteenth Earl of Erroll, a nobleman who had committed suicide at Grenier's Hotel, in Jermyn Street, in a fit of remorse for having, while under the influence of drink, betrayed an official secret entrusted to him by Pitt. Lady Erroll was the sister of the first Lord Wallscourt, and came from Co. Galway, where her ancestral home is said to have given Miss Edgeworth the idea of Castle Rackrent. On her first introduction to Frere at a ball he took her to supper, but became so interested in her that he drank off the glass of wine which he had just procured for her, and then gave her his arm to take her back to the ballroom. They were married in London in 1816, and Frere is said to have gone straight from the church to Albemarle Street to see John Murray, who was publishing one of his poems. Murray asked him to stay to dinner, and it was only then that Frere remembered that his bride was waiting for him to go on their honeymoon. He hurried back, and they went to Hastings, where Frere had characteristically forgotten to bespeak accommodation.[2] Lady Erroll was no

[1] *Some Letters of George Canning*, by the Rev. J. Raven in the *Anglo-Saxon Review*, vol. III, December, 1899, p. 49.
[2] Bagot, J.: *George Canning and His Friends*, vol. I, p. 12–13.

friend of Canning, for she was always jealous of his intimacy with
Frere, but she was rather awed by him, and she once wrote " that
man's eyes see through one ".[1]

Another friendship which Canning made at Eton was that with
Charles Ellis, who was younger than himself by about eighteen
months. Ellis had hereditary connections with Jamaica, of which
his grandfather was Chief Justice, and he inherited a considerable
fortune. For many years Ellis was a fine rider to hounds, but the
nerve he displayed in the hunting-field forsook him when he acted
as Canning's second in the famous duel with Castlereagh. On
that occasion so anxious did he feel for the fate of his friend that
his hand is said to have shaken to such an extent that he was
unable to load the pistol, which had to be done for him by the
other second, Lord Yarmouth. Ellis entered the House of Commons as member for Heytesbury when he was barely of age, and
with one break he sat there until 1826. He was not a brilliant
speaker, and his importance at Westminster rested upon the fact
that he was the acknowledged head of the then powerful West
Indian interest. In 1826 the Prime Minister gave Canning the
nomination of a friend to the peerage, and to the general surprise
his choice fell on Charles Ellis, who duly became Lord Seaford.

Canning seems to have taken little or no part in games at Eton,
and his ignorance of natural history is attested by the fact that
years later, during the course of a country walk, Frere discovered
that his friend was quite unaware that tadpoles turned into frogs.
On the other hand, Canning gave promise of the talents he was
later to display by the part he took, with Frere, Ellis, and others,
in the foundation and production of *The Microcosm*. This was a
weekly paper, produced by the boys themselves and published by
Knight, a Windsor bookseller. Westminster had a rival publication called *The Trifler*, on the frontispiece of which was a representation of a pair of scales in which Westminster greatly out-
weighed Eton. It is recorded that on seeing this Canning dashed
off the following lines :

> What argues this device so rare, ye wits of Eton jealous?
> It proves that we ascend like air and you are heavy fellows.

Unlike so many ventures of its kind, *The Microcosm* not only
made some money for those who produced it, but it also won a
public outside the walls of the school. In the first month of its

[1] Festing, G.: *John Hookham Frere and His Friends*, p. 117.

B

publication, for example, Fanny Burney noted in her diary, " I read once more, in the morning, to the Queen, a paper of *The Microcosm*, which I forget whether I have mentioned; it is a periodical imitation of other periodical papers, and written by a set of Eton scholars. It has great merit for such youthful composers." [1] So early an introduction to Royalty stood Canning in good stead, for his comparatively humble origin would otherwise have postponed for many years his acquaintanceship with the occupant of the throne; as it was, George III never failed to greet him on the occasions when they met. Not long after this entry by Fanny Burney a friend drew Hannah More's attention to the publication, " Have you seen a very extraordinary production of some Eton boys? It is a periodical paper called *The Microcosm*, in one of which, for they are very unequal, the practice of common swearing is treated with a vein of ridicule, not unworthy of Addison in his happiest mood. This is what I should have least expected from a boy. If he had jumbled together all the learning that he could have collected from all the translations and compilations he could get, I should not have been much surprised: but elegant ridicule, and well supported ironical pleasantry is not often found at that age." [2] The author of the article in question was Canning, whose method of approach to his subject was the same as that which was to become so famous a few years later in *The Anti-Jacobin*.

During the whole of his school career Canning remained a strong Whig, and it is remarkable from how early an age his thoughts turned in the direction of the House of Commons. In the autumn of 1787, after leaving Eton and before going up to Oxford, he wrote to a friend, " I need not tell you, my dear Sir, that the law is my road; and that I look forward to it with all eagerness and expectation; and perhaps at some future day, to the House of Commons, a field, open indeed, not so much for *solid pudding* as empty praise." [3] On June 27th of this same year he was admitted to Lincoln's Inn while he was still at Eton. As for politics, another extract from the letter already quoted shows clearly where his interests lay, " Mr. Sheridan has proved himself, both to the family and to myself in particular, a most kind friend. His advice

---

[1] *Diary*, November 28th, 1786.
[2] Roberts, W.: *Memoirs of the Life and Correspondence of Hannah More*, vol. II, p. 46.
[3] *Some Letters of George Canning*, by the Rev. J. Raven in the *Anglo-Saxon Review*, vol. III, December, 1899, pp. 51–52.

and assistance will, doubtless, be to me of every advantage, and
will be always open to me."

During Canning's last term at school his uncle, Stratford, died,
and in his place there were appointed as guardians Barrowes, the
dead man's partner, and his uncle by marriage, the Rev. William
Leigh. Leigh had married the elder George Canning's sister,
and was at that time living at Norwich. Later he rented Ash-
bourne Hall in Derbyshire, and was subsequently Dean of Here-
ford. Leigh was a man of means and some influence, and Canning
spent a good deal of time in his house during his undergraduate
days; indeed, the Leighs began to play the part in his life which
Stratford and his family had done in earlier years. A few months
before, on the death of his paternal grandmother, he had come
into £400 a year. " With this ", he wrote, " I shall, thank God,
be amply enabled to prosecute my studies, both academical and
professional, as a gentleman; and, in short, to answer every wish,
except one, that of providing for my poor mother; but even this
will, I trust, be in my power some years hence. Meanwhile, to
lift her some little way above actual want and to alleviate in some
measure the hardships of her situation, I obtained the consent of
my uncle, and since his death, of my guardian, to allow fifty
pounds a year." [1]

The autumn of 1787 found Canning a freshman at Christ
Church, where he passed four happy and contented years.
While there he came much under the influence of the then Dean,
Dr. Cyril Jackson, who, at a time when Heads of Houses were not
remarkable for the interest they took in those committed to their
charge, was at great pains to get on friendly terms with his under-
graduates. Canning's habits were studious, as a contemporary
has left on record, " Enter his rooms in Peckwater when you
would, you were almost sure to find him occupied with a pen or a
book. Superior to all idle amusements, improvement was his
continual object. He did not even keep a horse, and I have no
recollection that he ever hired one." [2] Such application brought
its reward. Canning became a good classical scholar, and in due
course he won the Chancellor's medal for a set of verses entitled
Iter ad Meccam: he took his Bachelor's degree in the normal way
in 1791, and his M.A. three years later.

[1] *Some Letters of George Canning*, by the Rev. J. Raven in the *Anglo-
Saxon Review*, vol. III, December, 1899, p. 52.
[2] Newton, J. F.: *Early Days of the Right Hon. George Canning*, pp. 5–6.

All the same, he was very far from being the prig which these facts might lead one to suppose, and he was by no means above taking part in the rags so dear to the undergraduate of all generations. It was not unpleasing, he informed the Leighs, " to watch the setting off of a stage coach, and to observe the ostler bringing out his lanthorn to light the passengers in—which he had no sooner done than he places his lanthorn on the ground. One end of a packthread may then be very conveniently passed through the ring at the top of the lanthorn, the other end having been previously fastened to a wheel of the coach—the coach drives on—and the lanthorn, to the great surprise of its owner, manifests a very strong inclination to follow it—and unless rescued in very good time, hop after it down the street, with remarkable celerity and perseverance." Another rag may also be described in his own words, " Some good also hath been found to result from sending some person unobserved into a room on the ground floor at the Bear Inn, where a table was laid for supper, and the party not yet come in—which person ties a string to one of the candlesticks, or both if time serves, and conducts the string along the floor, and out of the window (left open at this time of the year for air) into the street. You may then walk about at your leisure till you imagine the Gentlefolks quietly seated at their meal—and the next time you pass, seizing the loop, which you have left dangling out at window, you may with one twitch remove the candlestick from the table to the ground, with more quickness and dexterity than fifty waiters could have shewn in taking them away." [1]

As at school, so at the university, Canning formed a number of friendships which were to play an important part in his later life. One of the most notable was that with Robert Banks Jenkinson, in whose Cabinet he served for many years. Jenkinson's father had been created Lord Hawkesbury in 1786, and he used that title himself after his father had been elevated to the earldom of Liverpool ten years later. Jenkinson was an exact contemporary of Canning, having been born in the same year; he was also at Christ Church, but had been to Charterhouse, not Eton. In manner Hawkesbury was serious, almost pompous, and he was keenly interested in public questions; unlike Canning, however, he was a strong Tory. Another Oxford friend of Canning was Lord Granville Leveson Gower, the youngest son of the Marquess of Stafford, who was eventually created Earl Granville. He was

---

[1] Marshall, D., *op. cit.*, p. 21.

Canning's junior by three years, and he brought his friend into a new circle of influential people.

Canning had not been long at Oxford before he and Jenkinson were instrumental in founding a debating society at Christ Church. It consisted of six members, and met every Thursday evening in the rooms of one of them. It was typical of many such another institution both before and since. " Sometimes we appeared at the dinner in the hall dressed in our uniform, which was a brown coat, of rather an uncommon shade, with velvet cuffs and collar. The buttons bore the initials of Demosthenes, Cicero, Pitt, and Fox. Thus habited, and much the object of notice to every passing observer, we pleased ourselves with the excessive curiosity which our dress excited. As secret were we as the grave on all that concerned our oratorical institution, and it would be difficult to give an idea of the anxiety evinced by our fellow collegians to discover the meaning of this brown coat and velvet cuffs." [1] Canning's connection with the club was not, however, of long duration, for the Dean advised him that it was unwise for one who, unlike Hawkesbury, had his way to make in the world to parade his desire for Parliamentary honours. Canning, accordingly, resigned, and an extract from a letter written to a fellow-member in September, 1788, reflects his attitude at that time: " I do not think you can blame my conduct, when you recollect that the imputation of Parliamentary prospects, already too much fixed on me, is what, of all others, a person in my situation ought to avoid. I am already, God knows, too much inclined, both by my own sanguine wishes and the connections with whom I am most intimate, and whom I above all others revere, to aim at the House of Commons, as the only path to the only desirable thing in the world, the gratification of ambition; while at the same time every tie of common sense, of fortune, and of duty, draws me to the study of a profession." [2]

An attractive and witty young man rarely lacks invitations, and such was the case with Canning. Indeed, at this early period of his life he made friends as easily as he was later to make enemies. After the death of his uncle, Stratford, he paid fewer visits to that branch of the family, for his aunt was by no means easy to get on with, and she was inclined to forget that he was no longer a schoolboy. A good part of the vacations during Canning's

[1] Newton, J. F.: *op. cit.*, pp. 6–8.
[2] Newton, *op. cit.*, pp. 24–25.

Oxford career were spent with the Leighs, or with new friends such as the great Whig hostess, Mrs. Crewe. This lady was the wife of John Crewe, who sat in the House of Commons without a break from 1765 to 1802, and who was given a peerage by Fox in 1806. Mrs. Crewe was in the early thirties when Canning first made her acquaintance, and it is easy to account for her attraction for the young undergraduate. Fox preferred her " to all women living ", but she " never lost an atom of character, I mean, female honour; she loved high play and dissipation, but was no sensualist ". In her honour the Prince of Wales gave the toast of " True Blue and Mrs. Crewe " at a banquet to celebrate the re-election of Fox for Westminster in 1784. Charles Arbuthnot, who was a well-known figure in politics and society, wrote of her about 1790, " She, I think, is a charming person, and I find her particularly pleasant. . . . Instead of a fine lady she is a comfortable kind of creature that has read a great deal and is amazingly well informed." [1] To her looks Fanny Burney has borne high testimony: " She looked still in a full blaze of beauty. . . . The form of her face is so exquisitely perfect that my eye never met it without fresh admiration. She is certainly, in my eyes, the most completely a beauty of any woman I ever saw. I know not, even now, any female in her first youth who could bear the comparison. She uglifies everything near her." [2]

The Crewes had a house at Hampstead and another in the Lake District, and at both Canning was a frequent visitor. It must be confessed, however, that he was no lover of scenery, and he admitted that a countryside had to be " well-tenanted " to earn his approval. Another house at which he stayed was Trentham in Staffordshire, the home of his friend, Leveson Gower. In such pleasant circumstances did Canning pass his Oxford career, not worrying unduly about the future, and making the most of the present, like a sensible young man. Meanwhile, both at home and abroad events were taking place which were to affect him profoundly.

When Canning came down from Oxford in 1791 the political situation was still under the influence of Pitt's victory over the coalition of Fox and North seven years before, and a General Election which had taken place in 1790 had resulted in a further

---

[1] Cockayne, G. E., and Gibbs, the Hon. V.: *The Complete Peerage*, vol. III, p. 535.
[2] *Diary*, June 18th, 1792.

increase in the Prime Minister's majority. The power of the Whigs was gradually being undermined by the growing popularity of the young Premier in the country, and also by the deliberate policy of the King and Pitt in continually adding to the numbers of the House of Lords, which had been a Whig stronghold ever since the Revolution. Furthermore, the support of the commercial classes had been won for the Government by Pitt's financial policy, for at the end of the War of American Independence in 1783 the country had been to all intents and purposes bankrupt. Abroad, the administration had repaired the national prestige, which had suffered so severely by the Treaty of Versailles. In 1788 Pitt had supported Prussia against France during the Dutch troubles, and had thereby not only checked French ambitions in the Netherlands, but had also brought to an end the isolation of Great Britain in Europe, while two years later he gained a resounding diplomatic victory over Spain in the dispute with regard to Nootka Sound. On the other hand, the ministry was by no means as strong at Westminster as in the country. The King had been mad from November, 1788, to March, 1789, and might become so again at any moment; and the regency of the Prince of Wales would mean the return of the Whigs to office. Then, again, there was an important resignation from the Cabinet soon after the General Election of 1790, namely that of the Foreign Secretary, while owing to lack of support at home the Government had been compelled to give way to Russia in the matter of Ochakoff. Thus, in spite of Pitt's recent victory at the polls, the future of his administration was, in the summer of 1791, none too secure.

The interest in domestic politics, however, soon began to give place first to concern, then to alarm, and finally to panic, at the progress of events across the Channel, and this in its turn had a very great effect upon the development of the political situation at home. So far as Canning himself was concerned, the French Revolution was by far the most important event of his life, and it is certainly not too much to say that his whole career was passed in its shadow. At the moment that he entered the House of Commons the country was in serious danger of revolution, and at the date of his death that peril had by no means passed away, while in the interval the existing insecurity had for some years been gravely accentuated by the threat of foreign invasion. In these circumstances it is hardly surprising that there should have been a modification of political allegiances, and that old loyalties should have been weakened.

At the same time it would be a mistake to suppose that the French Revolution inspired horror even in Tory circles in England from the moment of its outbreak; indeed, the very reverse was the case. The British public is always slow to view Continental movements in their proper perspective, and its first impressions are by no means always its final ones. This was certainly the case with the French Revolution. When Louis XVI began to get into difficulties there was, for a variety of reasons, considerable satisfaction in Great Britain. In the first place, the part played by France in the War of American Independence was far from being either forgiven or forgotten, and there was a natural tendency to rejoice over her troubles. Then the Bourbons had always been the enemies of England, so that their misfortunes were hardly calculated to bring tears to the eyes of the ordinary Englishman. Lastly, it appeared at first as if all that was happening in France was the substitution of a limited for an absolute monarchy, and this naturally made a strong appeal to that section of the British people which believed it had done the same thing a century before. Fox, whose heart always ran away with his head, thought that the French Revolution was the counterpart of the English, and when he heard of the fall of the Bastille, of which event Hawkesbury was an eye-witness, he wrote to a friend who was going to Paris, " How much the greatest event it is that ever happened in the world! and how much the best! If you go without my seeing you, pray say something civil for me to the Duke of Orleans, whose conduct seems to have been perfect: and tell him and Lauzun, that all my prepossessions against French connections for this country will be at an end, and indeed most part of my European system of politics will be altered, if this revolution has the consequences that I expect." [1]

One of the reasons why even Tory opinion in Great Britain was slow to appreciate what was really at issue in France was that the drama there unfolded itself comparatively slowly. The storming of the Bastille took place on July 14th, 1789, but it was not until June, 1791, that the French Royal Family attempted to escape, and another year elapsed before Louis XVI was suspended from the exercise of his functions. On more than one occasion during these years it appeared highly probable that the Revolution would

[1] Hobhouse, C.: *Fox*, p. 223.

be crushed (as it certainly would have been had Louis shown the
firmness displayed by George III during the Gordon Riots), or
that France would settle down under a constitutional monarchy.
That the infection might spread to his own country never at this
stage occurred to the ordinary Englishman. Furthermore, as we
have seen, there had been a crisis in the Near East, another in the
Pacific, and a General Election, so that there was plenty of excuse
for not taking French politics too seriously.

   That this attitude did not remain unchanged was due, in the
first instance, not so much to the passage of events as to the
activities of Edmund Burke, whom Canning had often met at his
uncle's house at Putney. It is not easy to account for Burke's
influence over the British public, which was very considerable
indeed during the last years of his life. He had held office for
only a brief period and he had not been a success, while he generally
emptied the House of Commons when he rose to speak. His
manner and appearance, too, were against him, for he had a
very strong brogue; and Wilkes said of him that just as the Venus
of Apelles suggested milk and honey, so Burke's oratory was
reminiscent of whiskey and potatoes. The dandies of Brooks's
and White's laughed at his large spectacles, ill-fitting brown coat,
and bob-wig. But when Burke got a pen in his hand it was
another matter, as was shown in 1790, the year in which he
published his *Reflections on the French Revolution*, calling attention
to the real significance of the progress of events in France. It was
one of those books that come just at the moment when the
ordinary reader is not unready to think along the lines they
indicate, and its success was instantaneous. Although it was
published at five shillings, no fewer than seven thousand copies
were sold in six days. The King was delighted, and told everyone,
" Read it; it will do you good; it is a book which every gentleman ought to read." [1] As a result of the publication of this book
a large section of public opinion began to move ahead of the
Government with regard to the attitude to be adopted towards
the French Revolution.

   In support of Burke's theories were the growing disorder and
numerous atrocities in France. Society at that time was far more
cosmopolitan than it was later to become, and when heads which
had bowed in London drawing-rooms appeared on pikes in Paris
streets a reaction set in against the French Revolution and all

[1] Newman, B.: *Edmund Burke*, p. 228.

its works. In 1791 Burke followed up his earlier work by an *Appeal from the New to the Old Whigs*, and the effect was considerable. Fox and his immediate supporters might continue to acclaim the progress of events in Paris, but many a Whig, among them Mrs. Crewe, began to entertain doubts whether this was really the right course to pursue.

Such was the political scene when Canning came down from Christ Church in the summer of 1791. He was still an avowed Whig, and in this capacity he had been presented at Sheridan's house to the Prince of Wales. Of this meeting he wrote to Bessy, " I was charmed beyond measure, and far beyond my expectation, with the elegance of his address and the gentlemanliness of his manners. He did me the honour of a good deal of conversation." With Fox he was on the old friendly footing, and during his last term at Oxford he told his cousin that more than once he met " Mr. Fox and his lady [1] at places on the road betwixt here and London, and have paddled about with them and Lord Holland [2] and other folks on the water, and dined by the side of clear streams at Clifden, on cold viands of the most exquisite flavour." [3] Before, however, settling down to read for the Bar, Canning decided to take a holiday abroad, and during the course of it he hoped to improve his French. His companions were Charles Moore, the second son of the then Archbishop of Canterbury, and Hugh Elliott, the British minister at Copenhagen. Canning spent two months in the United Provinces and in the Austrian Netherlands, where he saw something of the disintegrating influence of the French Revolution upon neighbouring countries. He returned to London towards the end of September, 1791, and after a short visit to Wanstead and to Crewe Hall settled down to his legal studies at his chambers in Paper Buildings.

For nine months Canning worked hard, but politics were never wholly absent from his mind, and he joined a debating society, of which Charles Moore was also a member : it met once a month at the Clifford Street coffee-house, at the corner of Old Bond Street. The meetings were of a somewhat informal nature, and it was customary for pots of porter to be consumed during the debates. One night, it is recorded, the topic was the leaders of revolutionary France, and Canning, whose views were already beginning to be

---

[1] Mrs. Armistead, whom he subsequently married.
[2] A contemporary at Christ Church.
[3] Marshall, D., *op. cit.*, pp. 27–28.

influenced by Burke, was declaiming against the memory of Mirabeau, who had died a few months earlier. " Sir," he declared, " much has been said about the gigantic powers of Mirabeau. Let us not be carried away by the false jargon of his philosophy, or imagine that deep political wisdom resides in trained and decorated diction. To the steady eye of a sagacious criticism, the eloquence of Mirabeau will appear to be as empty and as vapid as his patriotism. It is like the beverage that stands so invitingly before you—foam and froth at the top, heavy and muddy within." [1]

Although Canning was only twenty-two, the year 1792 was to be one of the most important in his life, for it was then that he adopted the political standpoint which he never subsequently abandoned. The progress of the French Revolution disgusted him, and shook his confidence in those who, like Fox, applauded what was happening on the other side of the Channel. Canning never hesitated to declare that the French had every right to conduct their own affairs in their own way, but that was a very different matter to approving of the way they conducted them, and still less to desiring a revolution in the British Isles on the French model. Towards the end of the year he wrote to his friend the Rev. John Sneyd, " As to this country—though I am not so enthusiastically attached to the beauties of its Constitution, and still less so determinedly blind to its defects, as to believe it unimprovable—yet I do think it by much the best practical government that the world has ever seen." [2] As the late Professor Temperley put it in his introduction to Miss Marshall's admirable study of Canning's earlier years, " In the political sense he had already been converted by Burke from the doctrines of Fox, and his rally to the side of Pitt was simply the practical illustration of his desire to serve a cause he had already adopted. He had already framed the creed from which he never varied, a preference for monarchy as against republics; for representative governments as against democracies; for classes as against masses; for authority as against license; for moderation as against excess; and for practical advantage as against theoretical perfection."

Yet Canning would have been less than human had he not been influenced by people as well as by events, although he would have been the last to admit that such was really the case. His older

[1] Timbs, J.: *Anecdote Lives of the Later Wits and Humorists*, vol. I, p. 5.
[2] Bagot, J., *op. cit.*, vol. I, p. 37.

friends—Fox, Sheridan, and his aunt—might be Whigs, but Jenkinson, Frere, and Leveson Gower were followers of Pitt. Above all, there was Mrs. Crewe, who was inclining towards the views of Burke; she, too, was a close friend of the Duchess of Portland, whose husband was the leader of that section of the Whigs which was shortly to give its support to the Prime Minister. Like many a young man who is unattracted by girls of his own age, Canning liked the society of a pretty woman in the thirties who talked well, and although it would be untrue to say that Mrs. Crewe was responsible for the change in his political views at this time, she certainly did nothing to discourage it.

What is remarkable was the rancour displayed by the Whigs against Canning, and perhaps this must be regarded as evidence of their appreciation of the worth of the recruit they were losing. After all, the French Revolution was one of those upheavals that inevitably produce a fresh orientation of parties in every country they affect, and to accuse Canning of inconsistency because it did not leave him unmoved is absurd. All the same, he was lampooned by Fox's friend Colonel Fitzpatrick in the well-known verses :

> The turning of coats so common is grown
> That no one would wish to attack it,
> But no case until now was so flagrantly known
> Of a schoolboy turning his jacket.

Having made up his mind, Canning hastened to place his services at Pitt's disposal, and wrote to the Prime Minister, who of course knew all about him, to ask for an interview. This took place at Downing Street on August 15th, 1792, when, to quote Canning's own words in a letter to his Oxford friend Sturges Bourne, the young man " was ushered into that study in which so many great statesmen and great scoundrels have at different times planned their country's ruin and the advancement of their own fortunes ". From the beginning Pitt's attitude towards Canning resembled that of an elder to a younger brother rather than that of a great statesman towards a young aspirant for political honours. At the same time, it would be quite untrue to say that Pitt charmed his visitor into becoming one of his followers, for Canning had made up his mind on that point before he crossed the threshold of 10 Downing Street.

The next step was to find a seat, and an inexpensive one at that. Pitt promised the first suitable vacancy, but there was nothing

available at the moment, and Canning had to wait. In the meantime he made some cautious enquiries with regard to Newcastle-
under-Lyme, a borough where the Sneyd family had an interest,
but he soon appears to have decided that it would be better to see
what Pitt could do, for when, early in the spring of 1793, Mrs.
Crewe persuaded the Duke of Portland to bring Canning into
Parliament for one of his boroughs, the young man refused, saying,
" I will go over in no man's train. If I join Pitt, I will go by
myself." [1] Soon afterwards his patience was rewarded, and a
vacancy was created at Newtown [2] in the Isle of Wight, and
Canning was duly returned unopposed in July, 1793.

In the following month he wrote to Bootle Wilbraham:

> The time and mode in which the offer of a seat was made to
> me, the manner and conditions on which it was accepted by
> me, I reserve for one of the many long conversations which I
> propose having with you after your return to England. This
> much only I will tell you as to the former topick—you were
> never more out in your life, than when you conjectured that
> Jenky had anything to do with the matter, and as to the second
> —the seat does not cost me one farthing nor put me under
> the smallest obligation to any one man, woman or child, Mr.
> Pitt only excepted. My constituents are a select, but not
> unrespectable set of people, who live on the sea-coast in the
> Isle of Wight at a small but convenient town called Newtown,
> and amuse themselves with catching fish, and when Sir
> Richard Worsley vacates a seat, as he does now and then,
> upon a promise or receipt of some snug employment from
> Government—with electing in his room a worthy and
> independent member of Parliament. [3]

[1] Festing, G., *op. cit.*, p. 28.
[2] Not Newport, as often stated; but *cf.* Beaven, Rev. A. B.: *Canning's
First Constituency*.
[3] Bagot, J., *op. cit.*, vol. I, p. 44. Bootle Wilbraham was a year younger
than Canning, and in 1828 he was created Baron Skelmersdale. He died
in 1853.

CHAPTER II

POLITICAL APPRENTICESHIP

WHEN Canning was returned to the House of Commons in the summer of 1793 that assembly was dominated by two men, Pitt and Fox. Lesser luminaries there were, such as Sheridan, Windham, and Burke, who in any other age would have been in the first flight, but they had to yield precedence to those two. The golden age of the House of Commons was beginning, and it was to last for the rest of Canning's life; indeed, it is at least an arguable proposition that with his death it came to an end.

The Prime Minister was thirty-four, having been born in the *annus mirabilis* of 1759 which witnessed his father's most spectacular triumphs, when Canada was won for Britain and Hawke destroyed the French fleet in Quiberon Bay. Yet in many ways Chatham's son resembled his mother's family, the Grenvilles, rather than the Pitts. Save to children, and to his intimates, among whom Canning was soon to be numbered, Pitt was reserved to an extent unknown in his father, and this aloofness was a definite handicap, for it cut him off from that knowledge of public opinion which a more genial man would easily have acquired by intercourse with his followers in Parliament. In looks, too, he recalled the Grenvilles, not least in the nose (so dear to the cartoonists), from which he was said to suspend the House of Commons. He had been Prime Minister for close on ten years, but, as we have seen, his position was by no means secure, and it was very far removed from that of the Premiers of more recent times. The rigid party machinery of a later age did not exist, and Ministers had to rely upon cajolery rather than threats to ensure a majority. The Whig oligarchy was a thing of the past, and the caucus was still in the future. Even as late as 1788 Pitt's own personal supporters were said not to number more than fifty-two, though there voted with him some 185 other members who could be relied upon to follow any minister who was favourably regarded by the King. Fox had about 150 votes in the Commons at his regular command until the outbreak of war with revolutionary France, but the rest of the members were independent both of the Opposition and of the Government, though many of them had to take their orders from the borough-owners.

During the decade before Canning entered the House of Commons the Prime Minister had been defeated three times upon major issues, and such reverses would to-day entail either the resignation of the Government or an appeal to the country. How, it will be asked, was he able to remain in office after these defeats? The answer lies in the difference between Parliamentary custom then and later. In those days every important vote was not made one of confidence, and measures were introduced by private members which would now emanate from the Treasury Bench alone. Members of the same Cabinet often took opposite sides on issues upon which agreement would to-day be considered essential. Catholic Emancipation, for example, was almost to the end regarded as an " open " question, and, as we shall see, Canning and Eldon could be respectively Foreign Secretary and Lord Chancellor although they voted on opposite sides in their respective Houses in any division on the subject. The executive was dependent upon the legislative in fact as well as in theory, and a Prime Minister had to rely more on himself, and less on his office, to control the House than has since become the case. In these circumstances Pitt's defeats were neither meant nor interpreted as efforts to overthrow him; they constituted a warning not to go too fast, and so he regarded them.

In marked contrast to the Prime Minister on almost every score was his old rival, Charles James Fox. Ten years older than Pitt, the Opposition leader had inherited many both of the virtues and the failings of his great-great-grandfather, Charles II. His character and upbringing were very different from those of Chatham's younger son, for Lord Holland " brought up his children without the least regard to morality ", and while Pitt was immersed in the classics, Fox was allowed to go to Spa, where he was given five guineas a night to initiate him as a gamester.[1] The lesson was not lost upon him, but he was always an unlucky gambler. " Fox had three passions: women, play, and politics. Yet he never formed a creditable connection with a woman; he squandered all his means at the gaming-table; and, except for eleven months, he was invariably in opposition." [2] He was perpetually being dunned by bailiffs and money-lenders, and he was sold up; he supported causes of which the vast majority of his fellow-countrymen vehemently disapproved; and yet his personal

[1] Russell, Earl: *Life and Times of Charles James Fox*, vol. I, p. 4.
[2] Quoted by Hobhouse, C.: *op. cit.*, pp. 185–186.

charm was such that he never lost his hold upon the affections of the House of Commons. The Abbé de Lageard once expressed his surprise to Pitt that a country where there was such a parade of virtue as in England should tolerate a statesman of the private life of Fox. " Ah! ", was the reply, " you have not been under the wand of the magician." [1]

That Fox achieved so little in the field of politics was almost entirely his own fault. Burke advised him, " Lay your foundations deep in public opinion ", but that was precisely what Fox was incapable of doing. He was always prepared to sacrifice strategy to tactics, with the result that for a fleeting victory in the House of Commons he would risk his position in the country. The classic instance was when he coalesced with North, whom he had attacked most vehemently over a period of years; this disregard for the ordinary conventions of party warfare was too much for the electorate, and Fox was, save for a few months, out of office for the rest of his life. Although Pitt was a decade younger, he was always the senior in political wisdom. Fox never looked beyond the walls of the House of Commons or the Subscription Room at Brooks's, demagogue though he was on occasion. He was essentially a House of Commons man: that was at once his weakness and his strength.

Canning was certainly not without acquaintances in Parliament, for, apart from Pitt and Fox, Sheridan and Burke, his circle of friends there included, or was soon to include, his Eton and Oxford contemporaries. Frere, it is true, was not elected for West Looe until 1796, but Jenkinson already sat for Appleby, that Lowther borough which had first sent Pitt himself to Westminster, and Charles Ellis for Heytesbury, while Granville Leveson Gower very soon joined them. About the same time there was also returned another young man who was to play an important part in Canning's life, namely Lord Castlereagh. The golden age of the House of Commons was also the opportunity of youth.

If the Lower House contained men of great brilliance, and was less regimented than in more recent times, it was not particularly well-behaved. Members were in the habit of cracking nuts, eating oranges, lying on the benches, and going up into the galleries for a doze. On one occasion North, when Prime Minister, was taxed by a particularly dull speaker with being asleep, and replied that he wished to heaven he was. Once when

[1] *Life of William Wilberforce* (by his sons), vol. I, p. 38.

Burke rose to speak with a packet of papers in his hand, a member exclaimed, " I do hope the honourable gentleman does not mean to read that large bundle of papers, and bore us with a long speech into the bargain." [1] Possibly owing to the amount of liquor consumed, emotions were more easily roused then than now, and the ordinary member was not ashamed to weep in the House; indeed, the shedding of tears in public continued until a much later date. [2] Anger, as well as tears, went unrestrained, and in 1778 no less a statesman than Burke flung a volume of estimates at the Treasury Bench. [3] The dramatic, too, was by no means eschewed. When Burke was endeavouring to rouse the House against the French Revolution he took with him to Westminster a dagger as a sample of an order which France was alleged to have placed in Birmingham. At what he judged to be the psychological moment in the speech he was making on the registration of aliens he produced it from under his coat and threw it on the floor. This, however, was considered to be going a little too far.

Such was the House of Commons at the beginning of the last decade of the eighteenth century.

It was not until six months after his election that Canning took his seat, for there was no autumn session, and in consequence Parliament did not meet until January, 1794. He has himself left on record his feelings on that occasion, so important in the career of all young politicians.

> I got up with I know not how many odd feelings about me, and could not sit still for a moment till it was time to go down to the House. About three I went—and took my station under the gallery (till I had been sworn in I had no right in the body of the House)—then attended the Speaker to the House of Lords to hear the King's Speech—then returned to the House of Commons and took the oaths and my seat. I cannot describe you with what emotions I felt myself walking about the floor which I had so often contemplated in my youth from the gallery, and wondered when I should have a right to tread upon it—I sat down too upon the Treasury Bench, just to see how it felt—and from that situation met the grinning countenance of half my acquaintance who were in the gallery—I was all in a flutter for some

[1] A. A. B. : *Burke, The Founder of Conservatism*, pp. 14–15.
[2] Sickel, W. : *Life of Sheridan*, vol. I, p. 132.
[3] Newman, B., *op. cit.*, p. 75.

C

minutes—but however I bowed to the chair, and shook
hands with the Speaker,[1] and went through all the ceremonies
down to that of paying my fees with the utmost decorum and
propriety—at 4 o'clock the debate began and lasted, as you
will have seen by the papers, for thirteen hours, that is till
5 in the morning. It was to me one of the highest entertain-
ments that can be conceived. I had no notion that there had
been such a difference, as I find there is, in the interest, with
which one hears a debate, when merely a spectator in the
gallery, and that which one feels, as a member, with the
consciousness of having a right to join in it, if one pleases,
and to give one's vote upon the decision.[2]

Canning lost no time in making his maiden speech, which was
delivered on the last day of January. He spoke on the proposal
to grant a subsidy to the King of Sardinia, and it is not without
interest to note that he took the line that the partition of Poland
and opposition to France were questions of expediency rather than
of sentiment. It was held by so great an authority as Joseph
Chamberlain that too good a maiden speech is a handicap to a
new member, for he thereby sets himself a standard which he may
not be able to maintain on future occasions. Canning did not
make this mistake, for his speech rather disappointed some of his
friends, in view of his reputation at Eton and Oxford, though it
seems to have won the approval of his old friend Fanny Burney,
who wrote of his effort, " What an excellent opening Mr. Canning
has made at last ".[3] If, however, Canning's maiden speech did
not create the uproar which greeted that of Disraeli, there can be
no doubt that the speaker himself was quite as obnoxious to the
Opposition, and it was several years before the Whigs forgave
what they considered to be the apostasy of the favourite disciple
of Fox and Sheridan. Canning himself, it may be added, was
quite satisfied with his effort, and the rancour of the Opposition
he found " no great drawback " to his satisfaction.

On the other hand, he was by no means blind to faults of
manner which called for correction. " I find I was about three
quarters of an hour upon my legs—and my faults are—that I
speak too rapidly, so much so as to run myself entirely out of

[1] His future opponent, Addington, elected Speaker in 1789 at the age of
thirty-two.
[2] Marshall, D., *op. cit.*, p. 50.
[3] Letter to Dr. Burney, February 8th, 1794.

breath—and louder than is necessary for filling the House—of which however I could not judge the first time—and that I use too violent and theatrical action, insomuch that people about me are apprehensive of some mischief from me. Lord Bayham I did once hit a plaguey hard blow on the shoulder—Pitt, who was beneath me, sidled a little out of the way, and Dundas was obliged to bob to save his wig from confusion." When the ordeal was over, and " as soon as it was decent to go down the House " he went off to celebrate the occasion with Jenkinson, Charles Ellis, and other friends when " the bumpers of port wine that I swallowed —and the mutton chops that I devoured—and the sensations that I felt are not to be described ".[1]

Whatever degree of success may, or may not, have attended Canning's first speech in the House of Commons, he soon gave promise of those oratorical gifts which were to render him an outstanding speaker in an age of speakers of the first rank, and in January, 1795, he was chosen to second the Address to the Throne. One great advantage the young member enjoyed, and that was the close friendship of Pitt. Hardly had Canning taken his seat than he was writing to Sneyd, " He and I, that is Pitt and I, are upon very comfortable terms. I go to him when I like, and ask questions and get notions and take advice, and he does not seem bored." [2] In the House the Prime Minister was constantly advising Canning when to speak and suggesting the most telling points to make, while there were few parties at Downing Street at which the member for Newtown was not present. In this way Canning very soon became acquainted with the leading ministers, and this was an enormous asset to him so early in his Parliamentary career. A singularly attractive young man he must have been, to judge by a description of him written in later years by his cousin, Stratford: " At the time when Canning first takes up a place in my memory, I was a laughing riotous brat. He was then about twenty-five years old. His features, alternately expressive of deep thought and lively wit, his mild yet penetrating eyes, his full but rather scornful lip, the handsome contour of his thin and slightly freckled face, are still before me. His dark, well-shorn chin bore witness to the colour of his hair, which before he wore powder a raven might have envied." [3]

---

[1] Marshall, D., *op. cit.*, p. 59.
[2] Bagot, J., *op. cit.*, vol. I, p. 47.
[3] Lane-Poole, S., *op. cit.*, vol. I, p. 14,

Canning's first years in the House of Commons witnessed a substantial modification in the political situation. Burke's appeal, combined with the progress of events in France, had divided the Whigs from top to bottom, and in 1794 the Duke of Portland and some of his followers joined the administration, thereby reducing Fox's following to a purely personal one. " There are but forty of them," said Thurlow, " but every man of them would be hanged for Fox." His charm and company seemed preferable to office and honours, and finally, it must be confessed, to the national interest itself. In spite, however, of this accession of strength, the war against France, which had been forced on the country at the beginning of 1793, was carried on by a Government which was in reality a triumvirate of Pitt, Grenville, and Dundas. The Prime Minister retained the Chancellorship of the Exchequer in his own hands, so that he was brought into closer contact with the various Departments than would otherwise have been the case. His cousin, Lord Grenville, was at the Foreign Office, but although he enjoyed the respect of his contemporaries, his cold and repellent personality was liable to freeze supporters and hearten opponents. Both by temperament and energy he was not ill-fitted to face the storms of the Revolutionary and Napoleonic era; and " his defects lay in his coldness, his secrecy, and his reserve ".[1]

Very different was the third triumvir, Henry Dundas, Secretary of State for War, who was moved from the Home Office in 1794 to make way for a Whig. In addition, he was First Commissioner for India and Treasurer of the Navy. Dundas was a jovial personage, and he took greater care of the nation's Imperial interests than his critics are always ready to allow. He knew, however, nothing whatever of military matters, and in those days there was no General Staff. In effect, the conduct of the war rested in the hands of the triumvirate, subject to the by no means infrequent interference of the King. This was in marked contrast to the concentration of power on the other side of the Channel in the hands of that organizing genius, Carnot. Above all, there was the persistent optimism of the Prime Minister to be taken into account, " It will be a short war," he said, " and certainly ended in one to two campaigns ".

Such was the Government which Canning joined as Under-Secretary for Foreign Affairs in January, 1796. This was rapid

[1] Algernon Cecil in *The Cambridge History of British Foreign Policy, 1783–1919*, vol. III, p. 545.

promotion for a young man of twenty-five who was without powerful relations to assist him, and it was a striking tribute to the position which he had won for himself during the two years that he had been in the House of Commons. Canning had as his colleague in office George Hammond, who was the first British minister to the United States,[1] which post he had lately vacated in order to become Joint Under-Secretary at the Foreign Office. Hammond was seven years older than Canning, with whom, as well as with Hookham Frere, he soon stood on terms of the closest friendship. He was not in Parliament, and as the Foreign Secretary was in the House of Lords, it fell to Canning's lot to represent the Foreign Office in the Commons, though this task was not as onerous as may at first sight appear, for the Prime Minister himself frequently spoke for the Government in debates on foreign affairs.

On the other hand, the office work was considerable, and after he had been only a few days in his new post Canning wrote to Leveson Gower:

> I cannot give you a better idea of the sort of employment, which they have continually found for me—than by relating what happened to me on Monday . . . for after labouring the whole morning at the contents of two mails which had arrived, and having got through them by about six o'clock, with no small exertion and fatigue—no sooner had I returned to Park Place with a view of resting myself, and spending a quiet evening, than, before I had well done dinner, came an Austrian courier, with a mountain of papers, which he had been three months collecting throughout the whole ter- raqueous globe—or rather unluckily not throughout the whole, for then Hammond would have divided the trouble with me,—but in every part of the Southern Hemisphere, which is under my immediate protection. It took me till two o'clock in the morning to get through this unwieldy accumulation of papers. I had not had my due refreshment in sleep, before my eyes were opened to another messenger, with another pacquet, not quite so large as the former indeed —but containing work enough for many industrious hours— and he was followed by three mails the same day: the con- tents of which I have but just got through my hands; and I

---

[1] He was twenty-eight at the time of his appointment.

am now sitting here in expectation of another mail, which has become due, while I was working at the others.[1]

With his chief Canning got on well, and he attributed to shyness a good deal of Grenville's haughtiness and reserve. Unlike most young men in similar positions, Canning was, thanks to his intimacy with Pitt, no stranger to his departmental superior, whom he had often met in the friendly atmosphere of the Prime Minister's house; however this may be, he told Leveson Gower that the Foreign Secretary " seems to be a person who improves as you come nearer to him ". Others, perhaps, would say that Canning's attitude towards Grenville was but an example of his *trait*, on which Jenkinson used to chaff him, " of taking mightily to unpleasant people ".

Canning's first months in the department which was to be for ever associated with his name were critical ones. After a brief interval during which the Allies had a few successes, the war had gone extremely badly both for Great Britain and for Austria, Prussia, and Spain, whom she was financing. Not only did it prove impossible to keep the French out of the Low Countries, but the very Dutch, for whose sake Britain had nominally gone to war, overthrew the House of Orange, and welcomed the invaders. The whole left bank of the Rhine was lost, for the dash and enthusiasm of the French armies carried all before them. In the Mediterranean the situation was no better, for Toulon, which had been occupied in the name of Louis XVII, had to be abandoned, and the enemy succeeded in establishing himself in Spain and Piedmont. The only compensation was Lord Howe's victory at sea on June 1st, 1794, which freed England from any immediate danger of invasion. Meanwhile, the Reign of Terror had taken place in France, and in four weeks in the summer of 1794 no fewer than 1,400 people were upon one pretext or another sent to the guillotine in Paris alone. This regime of butchery, however, came to an end with the execution of Robespierre himself, and in November of the next year (1795) the Directory was installed in office. One of its first acts was to appoint Napoleon Bonaparte to the command of the French army in Italy.

The whole position of the war had thus changed very much to Britain's disadvantage. In Northern Europe the cause for which she had gone to war, namely the independence of the Dutch, was

[1] Quoted by Marshall, D., *op. cit.*, pp. 159–160.

irretrievably lost, for she did not possess the land armaments necessary to eject the French from the Low Countries. In the Mediterranean the situation had for a time appeared more hopeful, but, when Napoleon began to over-run Italy, it, too, was altered for the worse. All Britain's allies, save Austria, made their peace with France, and the Austrian armies were going down to disaster before Napoleon on the Italian battle-fields. Worse still, it was clear that very many Italians preferred the French to their own rulers. Great Britain had no possessions of her own in the Mediterranean with the exception of Gibraltar, though from 1794 to 1796 she exercised a precarious hold upon Corsica. When the Italian mainland fell into French hands the British position became untenable, and the Mediterranean had to be abandoned altogether.

Such were the circumstances in which Pitt, much against the wishes both of the King and of several of his colleagues, decided to make an effort to bring the war to an end by negotiation. He felt that at last some form of stable government had been established in France which might be willing to make peace on reasonable terms. His earlier optimism had gone, and the cost of the struggle was frightening him; he was informed that the anti-war party on the other side of the Channel was strong enough to carry the day; and he feared that at any moment Austria might make a separate peace, thus leaving Britain to carry on the conflict alone. The British Prime Minister little knew the men with whom he was dealing. To an overture in the early spring of 1796, suggesting peace on the basis of the restoration of the Low Countries, the Directory haughtily replied that no proposition for the surrender of any of the countries declared by France to be " re-united " to herself would be entertained.

Nevertheless Pitt persevered in his efforts: he may still have believed in the possibility of an accommodation, but he was certainly also influenced by a desire to prove to the Opposition that peace with France was out of the question on any other terms than complete surrender. In September, 1796, therefore, the British Government requested the Danish ambassador in Paris to ask for a passport for an English plenipotentiary, but the Directory rejected the mediation of Denmark, and would only receive an envoy at the direct request of London. Great Britain, in effect, was to sue for peace; but even to this Pitt agreed, and Lord Malmesbury was sent over to Paris to negotiate for a settlement on the basis of the evacuation of the Low Countries by the French in return for the restitution of all conquests made by British arms. Unfortunately, in the middle of the negotiations, Catherine II of Russia, who was distinctly Gallophobe, died, and her successor, Paul, adopted a policy of neutrality. This news emboldened the French to refuse Pitt's terms, and Malmesbury was unceremoniously bundled out of Paris at twenty-four hours' notice. With these negotiations Canning had little to do, but he had ample opportunity of knowing what was taking place, for, apart altogether from his own official position at the Foreign Office, George Ellis,[1] a cousin of his friend Charles, accompanied the mission, and Leveson Gower was also attached to it: thus the incident was an excellent introduction for the young Under-Secretary to the world of diplomacy and foreign affairs.

The following year, 1797, was, with the exception of the naval victory off Cape St. Vincent, one of unrelieved gloom. The closing weeks of its predecessor had witnessed Napoleon's defeat of the Austrians at Arcola, and the French attempt to invade Ireland under the leadership of Hoche, while in January came another French victory, this time at Rivoli, and by April the Emperor was so far reduced that he was compelled to sign the preliminaries of peace at Leoben, of which one of the most onerous terms was the cession of Belgium. At home, the mutinies in the fleet at Spithead and the Nore, and the suspension of cash payments, were sufficient indications of the seriousness of the situation. In spite, however, of these reverses Pitt decided to approach the French Government again, and negotiations were resumed in June, 1797, this time at Lille, with Malmesbury once more as the chief British delegate. On this occasion Canning played a much more prominent part, and in exceptionally difficult circumstances.

He was a close friend of Malmesbury, known to contemporaries as " The Lion " from his fine eyes and mass of white hair, whose wife, nine years older than Canning, had been one of the latter's hostesses when he came down from Oxford. More recently, however, the Under-Secretary had found Lady Malmesbury a trifle overpowering, and he had come to prefer the company of her husband, who was at this time Britain's leading diplomatist. Malmesbury's instructions were a mirror of the French successes

---

[1] 1753–1815. Friend of Wordsworth, Southey, and Scott. Through him Scott made the acquaintance of Canning.

of the previous six months, for he was empowered to recognize the sovereignty of France over Belgium, Luxembourg, Savoy, and Nice, and to promise that Great Britain would return all her conquests save Trinidad and the Cape of Good Hope, while in the case of Ceylon that island was to be exchanged if possible. These terms were, from the French point of view, a marked advance upon those suggested in the previous year, but they provided the only possible basis for an understanding between the two countries in view of Napoleon's victories in Italy. Moreover, in France itself there appeared a distinct possibility of a Bourbon restoration, and it was hoped that the adoption of a conciliatory attitude would encourage the moderates in Paris.

In this resumption of negotiations Pitt received the warm support of Canning, who, in spite of the influence of Burke, was still of the opinion that the policy to be pursued towards France was a question of expediency rather than of principle. " If peace is to be had, we must have it; I firmly believe we must, and it is a belief that strengthens every day ": such was his view, though he confessed that it went against the grain " to continue modes of concession, instead of enforcing the justice of demands ".[1] On the other hand, the Prime Minister was opposed by the King and several members of the Cabinet, including Grenville, who was on the worst possible terms with Malmesbury. In view of the Foreign Secretary's attitude, Canning's position was an extremely delicate one, and he acted as an intermediary between Malmesbury and Pitt, for Grenville was by no means always informed of what was taking place. In effect, Malmesbury wrote three types of reports, namely those that were for Pitt, those that were for Pitt and Grenville, and those that could safely be communicated to the whole Cabinet, and for all these despatches Canning was the clearing-house.

In September came Napoleon's *coup d'état* of the 18th Fructidor, and the hopes of the French Royalists were frustrated for another seventeen years. The influence of events in Paris was soon felt at Lille, and Malmesbury was informed that the French Government would only treat on the basis of a restitution by Great Britain of all conquests made by her from France and her allies. This was too much even for Pitt, and Malmesbury was recalled to London. On October 17th, 1797, the Treaty of Campo Formio,

[1] *Diaries and Correspondence of James Harris, First Earl of Malmesbury,* vol. III, p. 397.

between France and the Emperor, was signed, and the isolation of
Great Britain was complete. These abortive negotiations, relatively unimportant as they are in the history of the Revolutionary
and Napoleonic Wars, had a very considerable effect both upon
the reputation and character of Canning, and also upon his
political views.

The singularity of his position in respect of the three chief actors,
that is to say Pitt, Grenville, and Malmesbury, undoubtedly
developed a taste for intrigue which must always have been latent
in his nature. Certainly it contributed not a little to the growth
of the legend, which did him so much harm, both in later life and
with posterity, that he was always intriguing against his colleagues
in the Government, a legend that became a conviction after the
unhappy duel with Castlereagh. It may be argued that a man of
finer feelings would have resigned rather than act in such a
capacity, but to take this view is to ignore the fact that Canning
acted at Pitt's request, and it was to Pitt that he owed both his
seat and his official position, quite apart from the ties of personal
friendship that bound the two men together. In times of crisis,
when even members of the same Cabinet are wont to differ, it is
not always easy to be equally loyal to all colleagues. Judged by
any absolute standard of ethics, Canning's behaviour towards
Grenville was no doubt reprehensible in the extreme, but in the
circumstances of the time, and taking into account normal
political morality, it is difficult to condemn it. From Canning's
own point of view the tragedy was that it developed his taste,
and gave him a reputation, for backstairs intrigue which stood him
in ill stead in later years.

It was these fruitless negotiations, too, that by impressing upon
him the impossibility of coming to terms with France, converted
Canning from a passive into an active opponent of the French
Revolution and everything for which it stood. In the summer of
1797 he had upheld Pitt in his determination to seek the basis of an
agreement, but in the following year there took place the Irish
rebellion, and this event was by no means without its influence on
Canning. By December, 1798, he had become a strong opponent
of any further attempt to treat with the French, and in reply to a
motion by Tierney calling for a resumption of negotiations he
made his own attitude perfectly plain in a speech which the
Prime Minister termed " one of the best ever heard on any
occasion " :

I do not envy that man's feelings, who can behold the sufferings of Switzerland, and who derives from that sight no idea of what is meant by the deliverance of Europe. I do not envy the feelings of that man, who can look without emotion at Italy—plundered, insulted, trampled upon, exhausted, covered with ridicule, and horror and devastation; who can look on at all this, and be at a loss to guess what is meant by the deliverance of Europe? As little do I envy the feelings of that man, who can view the people of the Netherlands driven into insurrection, and struggling for their freedom against the heavy hand of a merciless tyranny, without entertaining any suspicion of what may be the sense of the word deliverance. Does such a man contemplate Holland groaning under arbitrary oppressors and exactions? Does he turn his eyes to Spain trembling at the nod of a foreign master? And does the word deliverance still sound unintelligibly in his ear? Has he heard of the rescue and salvation of Naples by the appearance and triumphs of the British fleet? Does he know that the monarchy of Naples maintains its existence at the sword's point? And is his understanding, and is his heart, still impenetrable to the sense and meaning of the deliverance of Europe?

Sir, that we shall succeed in effecting this general deliverance, I do not pretend to affirm. That in no possible case we should lay down our arms and conclude a peace before it is fully effected, I do not mean to argue. But that this is the object which we ought to have in view, even if we look to our own safety only—that of this we ought to accomplish as much as our means, our power, our exertions, our opportunities will allow—I do most anxiously contend. If circumstances should unhappily arise to make the attainment of the object hopeless, it will be time enough when they do arise, to give up the hopes of attaining it: but do not let us run before misfortune, do not let us presume disappointment, and anticipate the necessity of disgrace.[1]

In short, it was the French Revolution that determined Canning's political creed. Its earlier excesses had caused him to desert Fox for Pitt, and now the arrogance of the French statesmen

[1] Therry, R.: *The Speeches of the Right Hon. George Canning*, vol. I, pp. 74–76.

compelled his conversion, with the result that the erstwhile Whig became the founder of *The Anti-Jacobin*.

" Canning, I think," said Wellington, " was readier at writing than even at speaking; I never in my life knew so great a master of his pen," [1] and in this new venture he was to bring to maturity the youthful promise shown at Eton in *The Microcosm*. There can be little doubt but that the appearance of this famous publication, of which the first number was dated November 20th, 1797, was the direct result, not only of Canning's changed attitude towards France, but also of the death of Burke, which had taken place at the beginning of July. The importance that Canning attached to this latter event can be judged by the words he used in announcing it in a letter, " There is only one piece of news, but that is news for the world. Burke is dead." It was Burke who had first shaken his allegiance to the Whigs, and now that Burke was gone Canning felt that it was for him to expose to his fellow-countrymen the danger that threatened them from France.

The *Anti-Jacobin* was intended to make its appearance every Monday morning while Parliament was sitting, and it did in fact last from November, 1797, to July, 1798. Its editor was William Gifford, who was fourteen years older than Canning; his career had been varied, for before going to Exeter College, Oxford, he had been a cabin-boy and a shoemaker's apprentice. Among the chief contributors were Canning and Hookham Frere. The policy of the paper was to implicate the whole of the Opposition in the doctrines of its extremists, and in this it was highly successful. Its biting satire has become almost proverbial, and for this Canning was largely responsible. At the same time the literary side of the revolutionary movement was by no means neglected, and, in particular, Kotzebue, Schiller, and Goethe were hotly attacked for the advanced views which they then held. Above all, the paper possessed in Gillray the greatest cartoonist of the day, and the effect which his pencil produced upon contemporaries was very considerable.

He had been born in 1757, and was the son of a Scotsman, who, having been wounded at Fontenoy, subsequently became sexton to the Moravian cemetery at Chelsea. Gillray had a somewhat chequered early career, and was for a time an actor before becoming a student at the Royal Academy. He was also a great admirer

[1] Stanhope, Earl: *Notes of Conversations with the Duke of Wellington, 1831–1851*, p. 297.

of Hogarth. At the age of twelve he had already given proof of his skill as a caricaturist, and from then he displayed marked aptitude for drawing. At that time James Sayer had a considerable reputation as a political cartoonist, and his work was imitated by Gillray, who was, it must be confessed, by no means averse to allowing his earliest attempts to be attributed to Sayer, whose initials he did not, on occasion, scruple to adopt. Soon, however, he became the rival of the older man, whom ere long he far surpassed. When he joined the staff of *The Anti-Jacobin* he was at the height of his fame, and the pavement was daily blocked by the crowd outside 29 St. James's Street, where his prints were displayed. In later years his health declined, owing to his intemperate habits, and he had already sunk into a state of comparative imbecility when he died in 1815.

The articles and poems in *The Anti-Jacobin* were for the most part composite work, but Pitt wrote on finance from time to time, and Canning was the author of several metrical satires. Of these perhaps the best known is that entitled *The Friend of Humanity and the Knife-Grinder*, which gives a very fair idea, not only of Canning's satirical powers, but also of the general tone of the paper.

The Friend of Humanity and the Knife-Grinder.

FRIEND OF HUMANITY:

Needy Knife-Grinder! whither are you going?
Rough is the road, your wheel is out of order—
Bleak blows the blast; your hat has got a hole in't,
    So have your breeches!

Weary Knife-Grinder! little think the proud ones
Who in their coaches roll along the Turnpike-
Road, what hard work 'tis crying all day, " Knives and
    Scissors to grind, O! ".

Tell me Knife-Grinder how came you to grind knives?
Did some great man tyrannically use you?
Was it the squire? or parson of the parish?
    Or the attorney?

Was it the squire, for killing of his game? or
Covetous parson, for his tithes distraining?
Or roguish lawyer, made you lose your little
    All in a lawsuit?

(Have you not read the Rights of Man, by Tom Paine?)
Drops of compassion tremble on my eyelids
Ready to fall, as soon as you had told your
    Pitiful story.

KNIFE-GRINDER :

> Story! God bless you! I have none to tell, Sir,
> Only last night a-drinking at the Chequers,
> This poor old hat and breeches, as you see, were
>   Torn in a scuffle.

> Constables came up for to take me into
> Custody; they took me before the justice;
> Justice Oldmixon set me in the parish-
>   Stocks for a vagrant.

> I should be glad to drink your Honour's health in
> A pot of beer, if you will give me sixpence;
> But for my part I never loves to meddle
>   With politics, Sir.

FRIEND OF HUMANITY :

> I give thee sixpence! I would see thee damned first—
> Wretch! whom no sense of wrongs can rouse to vengeance—
> Sordid, unfeeling, reprobate, degraded,
>   Spiritless outcast!

(Kicks the Knife-Grinder, overturns his wheel, and exit in a transport of Republican enthusiasm and universal philanthropy.[1])

Canning also wrote *The Song of Rogero*, while the first two parts of *The Progress of Man* were by him. In *The New Morality* occur the verses :

> Give me the avowed, the erect, the manly foe!
> Bold I can meet, perhaps may turn, the blow;

> But of all plagues, good Heaven, Thy wrath can send,
> Save, save, O save me, from the candid friend!

It was Peel's unlucky quotation of these lines in the House of Commons that gave Disraeli, who claimed them as Canning's, the opportunity to make one of his most effective retorts nearly half-a-century later.

Parody was another weapon in Canning's armoury, and its application to some lines of Southey was particularly happy. That poet had written the following sonnet " For the Apartment in Chepstow Castle where Henry Marten the Regicide was imprisoned for thirty years " :

> For thirty years secluded from mankind
> Here Marten linger'd. Often have these walls
> Echoed his footsteps, as with even tread
> He pac'd around his prison; not to him

---

[1] Of this poem Frere wrote to Sneyd that it " is a capital thing, though I say it that should not, for Canning and I absolutely performed it in half an hour ".

Did Nature's fair varieties exist;
He never saw the sun's delightful beams;
Save when through yon high bars he pour'd a sad
And broken splendour. Dost thou ask his crime?
He had rebelled against a King and sat
In judgment on him: for his ardent mind
Shap'd goodliest plans of happiness on earth,
And peace and liberty. Wild dreams! but such
As Plato lov'd; such as with holy zeal
Our Milton worshipp'd. Blessed hopes! a while
From man with-held, even to the latter days
When Christ shall come, and all things be fulfilled.

Canning replied with some lines " For the Door of the Cell in Newgate, where Mrs. Brownrigg, the Prentice-cide, was confined previous to her Execution ":

For one long Term, or e'er her trial came,
Here Brownrigg linger'd. Often have these cells
Echoed her blasphemies, as with shrill voice
She screamed for fresh Geneva. Not to her
Did the blithe fields of Tothill, or thy street,
St. Giles, its fair varieties expand;
Till at the last in slow-drawn cart she went
To execution. Dost thou ask her crime?
She whipp'd two female 'prentices to death,
And hid them in the coal-hole. For her mind
Shap'd strictest plans of discipline. Sage schemes!
Such as Lycurgus taught, when at the shrine
Of the Orthyan Goddess he bade flog
The little Spartans; such as erst chastised
Our Milton, when at College. For this act
Did Brownrigg swing. Harsh laws! But time shall come
When France shall reign, and laws be all repealed!

One number of *The Anti-Jacobin* contained an onslaught on Coleridge, Southey, Lloyd, and Lamb:

See! faithful to their mighty dam,[1]
C.....dge, S..th.y, L...d, and L..b:
In splay-foot madrigals of love,
Soft moaning like the widow'd dove,
Pair, side by side, their sympathetic notes;
　　Of equal rights, and civic feasts,
　　Of tyrant kings, and knavish priests,
Swift through the land the tuneful music floats.
And now to softer strains they struck the lyre,
　　They sung the beetle, or the mole,
　　The dying kid, or ass's foal,
By cruel man permitted to expire.

Lamb at any rate did not forget his satirists, and some years later he retaliated on Canning and Frere with the verses:

[1] *I.e*, anarchy.

At Eton School brought up with dull boys,
We shone like men among the school-boys;
But since we in the world have been,
We are but school-boys among men.[1]

The influence of *The Anti-Jacobin* was considerable, and it was by no means without its effect in swinging public opinion to the side of the Government at a critical phase of the struggle against Revolutionary France. Unfortunately, this incursion into the field of journalism gave Canning a taste for displaying his satirical powers, and this weakness was to prove a very serious handicap. It was one thing to ridicule the French and their Whig friends, but it was quite another to aim one's shafts at actual or potential colleagues. In these circumstances, it is not too much to say that if from one point of view *The Anti-Jacobin* enhanced Canning's reputation, from another its ultimate effect was to do him a great deal of harm.

In March, 1799, Canning resigned his Under-Secretaryship, in which he was succeeded by Frere, and was appointed a Commissioner of the Board of Control, a body which had been set up by Pitt's India Act of 1784, and was the forerunner of the India Office. He wrote of his new post to his cousin, Bessy, as " one of less emolument but more ease and dignity ", and he told her that he would " go frisking and flourishing about, so happy in my new liberty, after three years of such slavery as never was slaved ".[2] In the following year he became a member of the Privy Council, and was also appointed Joint Paymaster-General to the Forces as well as Receiver-General of the Alienation Office, the latter being a post that brought him an annual salary. He was only thirty, and had been in the House of Commons for a mere seven years, so that he had no cause for dissatisfaction with the progress he had made. At the moment, however, Canning was not thinking primarily of politics, for since August, 1799, he had been very desperately in love.

[1] Lucas, E. V.: *The Life of Charles Lamb*, ch. XII.
[2] Marshall, D., *op. cit.*, p. 191.

CHAPTER III

IN AND OUT OF OFFICE

It has been said that Canning had no private life, and if by the statement it is meant that his relations with the opposite sex were without scandal, then the assertion is true. He lived in a society where any laxity in sexual morals was not only condoned, but taken for granted, yet his name has never been coupled with that of any woman save her who was to be his wife. When he was a young man he was, as we have seen, attracted by the company of women in their thirties such as Mrs. Crewe, but there is nothing unusual in this, and such an attitude rarely characterizes the real devotee of the sex. In short, promiscuity was contrary to Canning's nature, and when he fell in love it was with one to whom he remained devoted for the rest of his life. Many charges have been preferred against Canning, but it has never been suggested that he was even a philanderer, let alone a libertine.

The lady in question was Joan Scott, who was a few years junior to himself, and was the youngest daughter of General John Scott, of Balcomie, Fife, while her mother had been Lady Mary Hay, daughter of the thirteenth Earl of Erroll. Of her sisters, the eldest had married Lord Titchfield, the heir to the third Duke of Portland, in whose ministry Canning was one day to be Foreign Secretary, while the second was the wife of Lord Doune, afterwards tenth Earl of Moray, but she had recently died. Pitt was then Lord Warden of the Cinque Ports, and it was at Walmer Castle that Canning first met his future bride, though whether the Prime Minister had asked his young friend to stay with him for the purpose of becoming acquainted with Miss Scott must remain the subject of conjecture. The rising statesman certainly had no idea of what was in store for him, for he wrote to his friend Leveson Gower, " Never was any human being less bent upon falling in love than I was when I arrived at Walmer. You will have seen from two letters which I wrote to you during my stay there how very little conscious I was, even at a very late period of it, of any sentiments of the sort." [1]

Canning's feelings were reciprocated by Miss Scott, and the

[1] Granville, Costalia, Countess: *The Private Correspondence of Granville Leveson Gower, First Earl Granville, 1781–1821*, vol. I, p. 250.

young couple enjoyed the powerful support of the Prime Minister.
" He regarded the marriage ", wrote Frere, " as the one thing
needed to give Canning the position necessary to lead a party,
and this was the cause of his anxiety about it, which I would not
have believed had I not witnessed it, though I knew how warm
was the regard he had for Canning. Had Canning been Pitt's
own son, I do not think he could have been more interested in all
that related to this marriage." [1] The day of the fashionable
wedding had not yet arrived, and Canning and Joan Scott were
married on July 8th, 1800, by special licence in Brook Street at
an hour variously stated as half-past seven and half-past eight in
the evening. To quote Frere once more, " I was to be best
man, and Pitt, Canning, and Mr. Leigh, who was to read the
service, dined with me before the marriage, which was to take
place in Brook Street. We had a coach to drive there, and as
we went through that narrow part, near what was then Swallow
Street, a fellow drew up against the wall, to avoid being run over,
and peering into the coach, recognized Pitt, and saw Mr. Leigh
who was in full canonicals sitting opposite to him. The fellow
exclaimed, ' What, Billy Pitt! and with a parson, too! ' I said,
' He thinks you are going to Tyburn, to be hanged privately',
which was rather impudent of me; but Pitt was too much ab-
sorbed, I believe, in thinking of the marriage, to be angry. After
the ceremony, he was so nervous that he could not sign as witness,
and Canning whispered to me to sign without waiting for him." [2]

Mrs. Canning was never a great political hostess, and she was
not widely known to the general public, but she was as devoted
to her husband as he was to her. She copied his letters, listened
to his schemes, sympathized with his grievances, and more than
once attempted to make peace between him and Pitt when the
impatient temper of the one and the calm inflexibility of the other
threatened a rupture. Canning had a high opinion of his wife's
judgment, and that she was far removed from a fool is proved by
the very able defence of her husband's Portuguese policy which
she published after his death. Of one thing, at any rate, there can
be no doubt, and it is that no other woman was ever her rival in
Canning's affections.

As we have seen, Canning had very little money of his own, and
matrimony certainly improved his financial position, for his wife
was generally believed to have brought him a fortune of not less

---

[1] Festing, G., *op. cit.*, p. 31.   [2] *Ibid.*

than £100,000. Like Pitt, however, he had little idea of the value of money at any stage of his career, and in November, 1801, old Frere wrote to his son, " When I was dining at Leigh's the other day, a very fine gentleman called for commands to Mr. Canning's. I learned afterwards that he was going down as cook, at £100 salary. I am afraid our friend will forget his diminution of income by the loss of his place,[1] and miscalculate his expenses, for he has no more notion of the value of money than when he was an Eton school-boy." [2] At the time of his death, it may be added, his effects, sworn under £20,000, amounted to about £5,000 or £6,000.

The Cannings had three sons and a daughter : George Charles, who died in 1820 at the age of nineteen, and to whom the Princess of Wales had stood god-mother; William Pitt, a lieutenant in the Navy, who was drowned at Madeira in the year following the death of his father; Charles John, later Earl Canning, the great Governor-General who saved India in the Mutiny, and was the first to govern that country under the Crown; and Harriet, who married the first Marquess of Clanricarde. Soon after his marriage Canning bought South Hill, near Bracknell, " in every respect the most comfortable house you can imagine " according to Sneyd; he lived there until 1808, when he sold it, and purchased an estate at Hinckley, in Lincolnshire. Meanwhile, events were taking place both at home and abroad which were to bring Pitt's long tenure of office to an end, and to usher in for Canning a new period in his life.

The Irish rebellion of 1798 had convinced Pitt of the necessity of Union, and when this had been effected on August 1st, 1800, the Prime Minister turned his attention to Catholic Emancipation, which in his opinion was the corollary of the measure that had just reached the statute-book. The laws against Roman Catholics, which prevented them from taking any part in the public life of the country, dated from the sixteenth and seventeenth centuries, when the religious question was the most important issue of the day. More recently, a spirit of greater toleration had begun to make its appearance, but it was a long while before Catholics commenced to benefit by it. Almost to a man they were Jacobites, and the Whigs not unnaturally failed to see the necessity of going out of their way to ameliorate the lot of those who were plotting

[1] This letter was written after the formation of the Addington administration. [2] Festing, G., *op. cit.*, p. 57.

their destruction. With the decay of Jacobitism this argument
ceased to operate, but it was soon to be apparent that old pre-
judices die hard. So late as 1767 a priest was condemned to
imprisonment for life, and was actually incarcerated for four
years, for exercising his office. Eleven years later an Act was
passed which enabled Catholics who abjured the temporal juris-
diction of the Pope to purchase and inherit land, and freed priests
from liability to imprisonment. Even this relief, however, was
not effected without occasioning the Gordon Riots. In 1791
a further step was taken. Though still precluded from sitting in
Parliament and holding public offices, Catholics were given complete freedom of worship and education, admission to the legal
profession, and exemption from vexatious liabilities, provided that
they took an oath of an unobjectionable character. Pitt approved
of this measure, which was a private member's Bill, and Fox
supported it, though the latter expressed the wish that it had gone
farther, and declared his dislike of all tests.

In 1793 the Irish Catholics were admitted to the franchise. The
first breach had been made in the ramparts of Protestant ascendancy, and it was a mere question of time when it would be widened.
Yet, if Catholics were allowed to sit in the Irish Parliament, they
would dominate it by sheer weight of numbers, and there would
be civil war, probably accompanied by a French invasion. Pitt
saw that the only way out lay in an Imperial Parliament, when
Catholics could be placed on the same footing as the rest of the
King's subjects, and the most nervous Protestants could sleep
safely in their beds. In this way, too, Ireland could enjoy those
economic advantages which had been denied her in the past. In
these circumstances the Union was effected, and the story of it
belongs rather to the life of Castlereagh, who was Chief Secretary,
than to that of Canning. At the same time, it may not be out of
place to remark that Pitt was far from corrupting the virgin
innocence of the Irish Parliament, as is occasionally stated. One
might as well talk of a negro becoming sunburnt by the English
sun as of the Legislature of Ireland being corrupted by Pitt. All
he did was to apply on a more extensive scale the immemorial
methods of obtaining a majority.

As soon as the Union was an accomplished fact, a meeting of
the Cabinet was called, in September, 1800, to consider the
question of Catholic Emancipation, but Pitt said nothing to the
King of his intentions. This was probably a mistake, but the

Prime Minister doubtless acted in the belief that if he could first of all persuade his colleagues to agree upon a definite line of policy it would be easier to bring the Sovereign round to his way of thinking. Unfortunately, when the notices of the meeting of the Cabinet were sent out, Lord Loughborough, the Lord Chancellor, was in attendance on the King at Weymouth, and he could not resist the temptation to ingratiate himself with his master, even at the expense of his loyalty to his colleagues. Accordingly, he showed the Prime Minister's letter to George, and the anti-Catholic opposition to Pitt's proposals began to gain ground. For the moment Pitt did not press the matter, but he brought it up again in January, 1801, when he found that not only Loughborough, but also Portland and Westmorland, were against him. By this time, too, the views of the King were generally known, and at a *levée* he said for all to hear, " I shall reckon any man my personal enemy who proposes any such measure. The most Jacobinical thing I ever heard of."

In these circumstances it was clear that the crisis could not long be delayed. At the King's request, Addington, the Speaker, sounded Pitt as to his intentions, and in reply the Prime Minister sent the Sovereign a statement of his views, which were, briefly, that he proposed the substitution of a political oath for the existing sacramental test, and also some provision for the Roman Catholic clergy. He added that if the King withheld his consent he would feel himself compelled to resign. George replied to the effect that he was bound by his coronation oath to refuse, and suggested that the matter should not be mentioned again : to this Pitt declined to agree, and placed his resignation in the King's hands.

At first George hoped to retain the existing ministers with Addington at their head instead of Pitt, but several members of the Cabinet proved unwilling to serve under the proposed new Prime Minister. This was the line Canning took, and on February 14th, 1801, he wrote to Sneyd from the Pay Office :

> My story is a very short one—Pitt resigns, no matter for what reason, and I feel it right to follow him out of office. Most people feel it right to stay in, and form the new adminis- tration. He is of their opinion—which is rather hard upon me you will say, and so it is perhaps. But I am of my own, and that is enough. It is not at all good fun going out of

office, I can tell you, and out of the best house in London,
and to have to look about at this time of year for a little street
house, three windows in front, instead of it, and to have a
Mr. Wollup or Lord Glenbubby come into all my comforts,
instead of me. I never liked anything less, but I think I
should have liked myself less, if I could have allowed myself
to be prevailed upon by Pitt's arguments or entreaties to let
him transfer me to his successor Mr. Addington.

Now I hope you will be glad that I transported Frere last
autumn,[1] to be out of the way of all the storm. If you will
own this I will reward you by sending you his last letter to
read. Here—see in what good spirits he writes, and how
little he apprehends any danger, and how little he looks to
have the next dispatch from the foreign Office to him signed
by Hawkinson.[2]

Do not let these changes prevent your coming to Town;
we shall still be able to give you a bit of dinner at our house
in Whitehorse Lane or Sweeting's Alley.[3]

It soon became clear that a new ministry, on a definitely anti-
Catholic basis, would have to be constituted. At this point in the
negotiations the King went out of his mind, and there was a
further delay of about three weeks until he recovered his sanity.
As soon as he was better he proceeded to lay the blame for his
illness upon Pitt, who thereupon took the rather extraordinary
course, in view of his previous attitude, of sending an assurance to
the monarch through his doctor that he would not raise the
subject of Catholic Emancipation again during the King's lifetime.

Different explanations have been given of this somewhat inex-
plicable action of Pitt, but the most probable is that he desired at
all costs to avoid driving the monarch permanently out of his
senses. If the regency of the Prince of Wales and the Premiership
of Fox would have been dangerous in 1789, they would have
been nothing short of a disaster in 1801, when the figure of
Napoleon was beginning to cast its shadow over all Europe. In
any event, Pitt drew no personal advantage from the line he had
taken. There now appeared to be no valid reason why he should
be replaced by Addington at all, and Canning, who put Pitt's

[1] Frere had gone to Lisbon as Envoy Extraordinary and Minister Plenipotentiary.
[2] Robert Jenkinson, now Lord Hawkesbury, the new Foreign Secretary.
[3] Bagot, J., op. cit., vol. I, pp. 180–181.

retention of office even before Catholic Emancipation, used all his power to induce him to change his mind. It was in vain. Addington had received his appointment, and showed no disposition to relinquish it; while Pitt, as Canning complained, would not make any " forward movement towards the King ", and promised to give Addington his support. On March 14th, 1801, he finally resigned, after having been continuously in office for over seventeen years. It is some satisfaction to note that the Judas of the crisis, the Lord Chancellor, was not retained in the new administration. When he died four years later the King observed, " He has not left a greater knave behind him in my dominions ". When this was repeated to Thurlow, himself no mean judge of such matters, he remarked, " Then I presume that His Majesty is quite sane at present ".

There can, however, be little doubt but that there was also another motive behind Pitt's resignation, and that was the conviction that the time had come to make another effort to secure peace with France. He felt that he personally was too unpopular with the French, and too disliked by the First Consul, to initiate negotiations with any hope of success. However this may be, he resigned office, as he had accepted it, from the loftiest motives; and he left Whitehall to face relative poverty.

In these events Canning had played a by no means unimportant part, and the change of government was to prove inimical to his fortunes in more ways than one. In the first place, it involved a temporary estrangement from Pitt, against whom Canning's feelings were for a brief space fairly strong, as may be gathered from a letter to Frere dated July 12th, 1801. After alluding to the loss of an earlier communication Canning wrote:

> Was it in that, or in any previous or subsequent letter, for instance, that I told you that I considered my intercourse with P. as closed for ever? I did so consider it for some time. His conduct towards me was neither what I had a right to expect from him nor what any one man would have had a right to expect from another under similar circumstances. Confidence, just enough to mislead, and not enough to guide; enough, and more than enough, to make one feel one's self a party to all that he did, and bound therefore in common honour to share in all the consequence of it, but stopping short of the point at which one might have begun to see that

he had an intention of separating himself from those who ought naturally to be his followers; complete and unreserved sacrifice of me to A.[1]

What Canning was inclined to forget was that if a political leader has duties towards his followers, they likewise have duties towards him. There are bound to be occasions when he cannot take his subordinates into his confidence, but must require them to trust him, and to follow him without question; now, in spite of his devotion to Pitt, this was exactly what Canning was not prepared to do, and the result was this brief coldness between the two men. A reconciliation was, however, effected before the end of the year.

More serious were the differences which developed in consequence of Pitt's resignation between Canning and some of the members of the new Government, which he refused to join partly out of pique and partly because of his views upon Catholic Emancipation. Like many men of great intellectual power, Canning had a contempt, which at this stage of his career he took no great pains to hide, for those who were less gifted than himself, and their promotion over his head roused in him the most lively feelings of resentment. " The truth was that Canning had one great fault during the early part of his career, though, seeing how it had marred both his usefulness to his country and his personal advancement, he afterwards had the good sense to cure himself of it. The fault was an extreme restlessness. Conscious of the possession of great powers, he was inclined to deny the credit of any ability to those who came into competition with him, to disapprove of everything which he had no share in doing." [2] So far he had been the spoilt child of fortune, and he had much to learn in the school of adversity.

Extracts from two letters to Frere well illustrate Canning's attitude both towards the new administration and Pitt's support of it. The first letter was dated September 30th, 1801:

> I remember writing to you once, while I was endeavouring to make up my mind to comply with P.'s wishes, and had actually got so far as to bring myself to believe that I could not bear being out of office much longer. This was a false

---

[1] Festing, G., *op. cit.*, pp. 47–48.
[2] Yonge, C. D.: *The Life and Administration of Robert Banks, Second Earl of Liverpool, K.G.*, vol. I, p. 156.

fictitious feeling, which P.'s representations, and my own interest and anxious meditations upon them had generated— but which upon sober reflection, passed away again, and left me in a condition to determine, as the enclosed letter will show you. . . . I would rather be let alone—for a time at least—than have any offer made me. I could not now take any office with comfort—nor I think with credit—anything but responsible office neither now nor ever.

You will easily conceive how much I must have wanted you, during the struggle that I have had with myself and with others upon this occasion. Your letter came, not opportunely—with its recommendation of poor P. to forgiveness and reconcilement. I do love him, and reverence him as I should a Father—but a father should not sacrifice me, with my good will. Most heartily I forgive him. But he has to answer to himself, and to the country for much mischief that he has done, and much that is still to do. I cannot help this— but I can help having a hand in it, and I will. . . .

Leveson is the person with whom I have consulted most upon this business. He is strenuous in approving my determination. Next to him I have talked with Scroggs,[1] who is entitled to be consulted with by me on such points, by having refused to take the Under Secry. in the Home Office, when it was offered him at the time of the change, against my remonstrance—but almost solely, I believe, on my account.[2]

Canning wrote again on November 7th:

I need not say to you that the idea of the possibility of being entirely separated from P.—of taking part on a different side from him in the H. of C. is very painful to me. But surely the situation in which he places me is cruelly unfair. Determined, he assures me, never again to take a leading part in public life himself, and devoting himself to the support of a man, of whom I know he must, and does think as I do, that he is utterly unfit to fill the station in which he is placed—has he a right (indeed he does not pretend to it) or am I, in the most refined construction of what I owe to him, bound—to consider my allegiance as bound up in his, and necessarily transferable with it?—to consider myself as obliged to give my support to measures, not his, not in all cases which he

[1] *I.e.*, Sturges Bourne.　　　　[2] Festing, G., *op. cit.*, pp. 57-58.

approves, but which, even disapproving, he thinks it right to support the man who proposes them—because he has said he would—because the man relied on 'his promise—and because he is magnanimously resolved to keep his word, cost him what it may in character and consistency. Am I bound to this though he may chuse to think himself so—even after the pretext on which A.'s government, feeble and foolish though it is, was represented originally as entitled to the support of all right-thinkers and well-disposed—the keeping out Opposition—is not only done away—but done away by A.'s own act—and those very men whom he was put in to exclude, and whose exclusion was the ground on which support was claimed for him, are taken to his bosom—when peace has been already made in their spirit—and when they (as may probably be soon the case) and not he, are the most efficient and ostensible Members of Govt. in the House of Commons? . . .

I will not become factious if I can help it—I really have no inclination to it—and I do believe I shall be able to guard myself against any seductions, either of ill company, or of tempting opportunity: but I believe too, at least I very much hope, that a temperate and mitigated Opposition in Parliament, in which one should judge and act fairly upon measures as they arose, contending, however, uniformly all the while and upon every occasion that the Man was utterly the fool he is, and that it is mischief and madness to trust the Country in his hands—might do a great deal of good, and presents a highly respectable line of Conduct, not to say a very amusing one—for the opposition to a fool *quaetenus* fool, would be a new, and hitherto unexhausted ground.[1]

In these letters Canning opened his heart to his friend in faraway Lisbon, and the comment of Frere's biographer is very much to the point: " So, in mere gaiety of heart, and thinking that it would be ' very amusing '—as he had thought, no doubt, of schoolboy pranks at Eton, of boyish escapades at Christ Church, and of the wildest vagaries of *The Anti-Jacobin*, did Canning prepare to sow the crop that he was to reap throughout his life in the estrangement of old friends, the undying rancour of enemies, and the surly distrust of the general public. ' The character for

[1] Festing, G., *op. cit.*, pp. 61–62.

honesty and well-meaningness and so forth ', which by Canning's own admission no one denied to Addington, was, after all, a more valuable possession than all his own brilliant talents. It appealed to the mass of dull respectability which constitutes the majority of Englishmen, as Canning's impassioned eloquence and dazzling wit could never succeed in doing." [1]

With the resignation of Pitt's administration there certainly began a period in Canning's life which cannot by any stretch of imagination be described as glorious, or even as moderately successful, for in spite of his good resolutions he displayed a factiousness which reflected little credit upon him. Granted that he was sincere, as there can be no doubt that he was, in his belief that peace could be made only by the sacrifice of British interests, it was surely his duty as a follower, let alone as a personal friend, of Pitt not to proceed to active opposition when it was clear that the ex-Premier wished to give Addington an opportunity to show what he could do. Pitt's attitude during the early days of the new Government was one of benevolent neutrality, an attitude in many ways similar to that of Austen Chamberlain, Birkenhead, and those associated with them, towards Bonar Law's administration; but from the very first Canning lashed the Treasury Bench with the scorpions of his wit. He neglected no opportunity of attempting to embroil Pitt with the ministers, but in the end he failed, for it was circumstances rather than Canning that finally brought Addington to the ground. In fact, by the virulence of his attack Canning did more harm to himself than to those he ridiculed, and the measure of his failure can be judged by the fact that when Pitt took office again he was unable, or unwilling, to give Canning any more important post than that of Treasurer to the Navy.

One of Frere's favourite stories was that of a peer, " a fine specimen of a thorough-going old country Tory ", who came to call on his father with the news that Pitt was out of office and that Addington had taken his place. He ran over the names of all the members of the new Cabinet, and, rubbing his hands with satisfaction, observed, " Well, thank God, we have at last got a ministry without one of those confounded men of genius in it ". Canning neglected no opportunity of driving this fact home, and the violence of his attacks upon Addington have rarely been equalled, and never surpassed, in British politics. The Prime

[1] Festing, G., *op. cit.*, pp. 62–63.

Minister was ridiculed alike in prose and verse, in the House of
Commons and on the printed page. Some of these satires were
good enough fooling, as, for instance, the famous lines:

> Pitt is to Addington,
> As London is to Paddington.

When a proposal was made to defend the Thames estuary by
means of block-houses, Canning wrote:

> If blocks can the nation deliver,
> Two places are safe from the French;
> The first is the mouth of the river,
> The second the Treasury Bench.

Addington had appointed his brother, Hiley, as Secretary at
War, and his brother-in-law, Bragge Bathurst, to be Treasurer of
the Navy, and this spurred Canning to the following lampoon:

> How blest, how firm the Statesman stands
> (Him no low intrigue can move)
> Circled by faithful kindred bonds,
> And propped by fond fraternal love,
> When his speeches hobble vilely,
> What " Hear him's " burst from brother Hiley;
> When his faltering periods lag,
> Hark to the cheers of Brother Bragge.
>
> . . . . .
>
> Each a gentleman at large
> Lodged and fed at public charge,
> Paying (with a grace to charm ye)
> This the Fleet, and that the Army.

If Canning had stopped at this, he would still have gone a little
too far, but he threw all discretion to the winds, and in execrably
bad taste proceeded to sneer at Addington on the score of his
birth, which he of all people was not entitled to do:

> My name's the Doctor. On the Berkshire hills
> My father purged his patients—a wise man,
> Whose constant care was to increase his store,
> And keep his eldest son—myself—at home.
> But I had heard of politics, and longed
> To sit within the Commons' House and get
> A place; and luck gave what my sire denied.

The first important move of the new Government was to come
to terms with France, and in March, 1802, the Treaty of Amiens
was signed. Great Britain agreed to restore to the French all
her naval conquests, namely Martinique, St. Lucia, Tobago, and
other sugar islands, as well as all their posts and factories in India,
and Goree in West Africa. To the Dutch she returned the Cape

of Good Hope, Demerara, Essequibo, and Surinam, besides Curaçoa and several other small islands, retaining only the Dutch posts in Ceylon. Of her conquests from Spain she retained only Trinidad. She further consented to evacuate Egypt, Malta, and Elba, the first reverting to Turkey, and Malta to the Knights of St. John. The Ionian Isles became the Republic of the Seven Islands. By comparison, the sacrifices made by France were slight. She recovered every one of her former colonies, and shifted on to her Spanish and Dutch allies the burden of loss, namely Trinidad and Ceylon. She agreed, it is true, to evacuate South Italy, but she continued to exercise control over the Batavian, Helvetian, Ligurian, and Cisalpine Republics.

The reason for this unequal settlement was that although Great Britain was in a relatively strong position, Addington was not the man to make use of his opportunities. He did not realize that in all bargains the man who is most warmly bent on obtaining the object of discussion is inevitably the weaker, and he made no secret of his desire for peace. Nor, it must be confessed, was the Government helped to take a firm line with Napoleon by the wave of pacifism which was sweeping across the country. When General Lauriston, the A.D.C. to the First Consul, arrived in London for the ratification of the Preliminaries, he was dragged in triumph through the streets by the mob, a proceeding which Canning described as a scene of " disgrace to the country ". Pitt preserved silence on the treaty, while Grenville attacked it on the score that it purchased " a short interval of repose by the sacrifice of those points on which our security in a new contest may principally depend ". Canning had no belief in the duration of such a peace " unless Bonaparte changes his system—which is not very likely, or is overthrown, which would be too provoking a piece of good luck for this wretched, pusillanimous, toadeating administration. . . . I shall for ever thank God that I had no hand or thought, no privity or concurrence, no share whatever, act or part, in a transaction of such eternal disgrace and infamy." [1]

Nevertheless, Addington and his colleagues, by stressing the commercial benefits to be derived from the peace, obtained large majorities in both Houses of Parliament, whose opinion was well expressed by Sheridan when he said it was " a peace which all men are glad of, but no man can be proud of ". They had yet to learn that the mind of the new master of France was set, not on

[1] Festing, G., *op. cit.*, pp. 69–70.

commerce, but on power, and that the very idea of compromise was wholly foreign to his character.

Canning was remarkably active politically during the spring of 1802, and on May 27th he brought forward a motion to control slavery in the recently acquired island of Trinidad. " It seems to me ", he told the House of Commons, " as if Providence has determined to put to the trial our boasts of speculative benevolence and intended humanity, by putting into our power a colony where, if we pursue our old course, it must be purely for its own sake, without the old inducements or the usual apologies. This day is a day of tests : I trust we shall all abide the trial." [1] Canning was supported by the faithful Sturges Bourne, but Addington was not going to allow the Government to be put in a false position when Pitt might divide against them, so the Prime Minister " veered round and pledged himself body and soul " to all that Canning had asked, " and a great deal more ", thus leaving him most reluctantly obliged " to take Pitt's advice and close at once with Addington's pledge as if I believed them ".

During these months Canning had two objects in view, one was to keep the name and fame of Pitt before his fellow-countrymen, and the other was to persuade the ex-Premier to adopt an attitude of open hostility towards the Government. In pursuance of this first aim, he organized a big dinner in the City on Pitt's birthday, May 28th, though neither Pitt nor Addington was present, and he himself composed the famous song, of which the last line very clearly reflected the writer's opinions :

> And, oh! if again the rude whirlwind should rise,
> The dawning of peace should fresh darkness deform,
> The regrets of the good and the fears of the wise
> Shall turn to the Pilot that weathered the Storm.

Canning sent a full description of the dinner to Frere in a letter of seven sheets, begun on June 1st, and finished six days later :

> I am glad you like the song. I suppose it may be good as you say so. But it has been received and applauded here (meaning in London, at Merchant Taylors' Hall) with an enthusiasm so much beyond its possible merits, that I was becoming rather ashamed of it—especially as I myself, not aware of my being detected as the writer, took a very fair share in applauding. But that is no great matter. The effect

[1] Therry, R., *op. cit.*, vol. II, p. 25.

and impression of the dinner altogether was much more than I could have ventured to expect. As your Father and Hammond were both there, and as they were both writing to you the next day, I need not tell you all that passed—Addington not there—Hawkesbury coming—but retiring to dinner into a private room.   Ld. Cornwallis—my Lord of Amiens— retiring at a proper time into a corner of the room that his health might be drunk with the more delicacy, and returning never the better—820 people present, the flower of every rank and description of persons in London—the song taken in its true intent and meaning—repeated, with increased acclamations, and the last verse called for over again—these are, I think, the principal features by which you may judge of the tone and temper of this celebration.

For its effect (beyond exciting ideas and impressions favourable to Pitt's return into power) I will not answer. As to P. himself, that the whole thing goes to his heart, and that he feels with a deep and quick sense, beyond what I should have believed him capable of feeling, the testimonies of public and private attachment, I know.   But that he will stir hand or foot to place himself where he ought to be, I hardly hope.[1]

As Canning surmised, these efforts were in vain so far as they were intended to achieve the detachment of Pitt from Addington. Parliament was dissolved in June, and at the ensuing General Election the Government won a sweeping victory, very largely owing to the support of the ex-Premier.   At this election, it may be noted, Canning was returned for Tralee, in Co. Kerry: at the General Election of 1796 he had left Newtown for Wendover, and had since sat for this latter borough.   All the same, Pitt's own views regarding Addington were not so flattering as his public support of the Government might appear to imply.   He described the Prime Minister as " without exception the vainest man he had ever met with ", and as " a man of little mind, of consummate vanity, and of very slender abilities ".   The thought that such a one was at the head of affairs was not likely to contribute to Pitt's peace of mind.   Yet when Canning went to see the ex-Premier at Walmer in the early autumn his leader said he had promised to support Addington and from this pledge only the latter could

[1] Festing, G., op. cit., pp. 78–79.

release him. Canning thereupon besought him to ask for release, but Pitt said that would savour too much of an intrigue to return to power, and added, " My ambition is character, not office ".

Meanwhile, Napoleon was giving such evidence of his intentions as to make it every day clearer that the Treaty of Amiens was nothing more than a truce. He annexed the Duchy of Parma and the continental possessions of the King of Sardinia. He sent troops into Switzerland to occupy the chief passes of the Alps, and he ordered the Cisalpine and Batavian Republics to put crushing duties on British goods. This was bad enough, but worse was to follow. He requested Addington to expel those members of the French Royal Family who had taken up their residence in Great Britain, and asked for the suppression of certain newspapers which had criticized his methods of government. These demands were of course refused. The First Consul then raised the subject of Malta. The Knights of St. John were not yet ready to return there, but Napoleon insisted that the British troops should nevertheless be withdrawn at once. When this was refused, and the annexation of Piedmont and Parma was raised by the British ambassador, Lord Whitworth, the First Consul publicly upbraided the Englishman at the Tuileries in March, 1803.

The object of this outburst was to work French opinion up in favour of war, and to place the responsibility upon Britain. Such leading Frenchmen as Talleyrand, Fouché, and Joseph Bonaparte were strongly in favour of peace, but their opinions counted for nothing against the determination of the First Consul either to humiliate England or to fight her. In London pacifism was still the order of the day. On April 3rd the French ambassador wrote to Napoleon, " The prayers, the needs, and the wishes of this country are for peace ". The following day he returned to the subject: " Everybody wants peace. By preserving the peace of Europe you will crush this country without appealing to the arbitrament of the mailed fist . . . and you are in a most favourable position to decide the world's destiny for all time." [1] The reasoning was sound, but the advice was rejected. Yet by conceding a few points to Britain and concentrating on his navy Napoleon would soon have had the world at his feet. However, he looked at the problem from the point of view of a soldier, not from that of a statesman, while no advantage meant anything to him unless it had been obtained by force. For the successful

[1] Coquelle, P.: *Napoleon and England*, pp. 53–57.

prosecution of his designs in the East he must secure control of the Mediterranean, and for this he must obtain Malta; therefore he was prepared to fight for Malta.

In these circumstances even Addington began to appreciate the truth of Madame de Stael's observation that, next to the fault of signing the Treaty of Amiens, that of not breaking it would be the greatest; indeed, the situation was such that open war was safer than Napoleon's peace, and in the middle of May, 1803, hostilities began again.

This darkening of the international horizon was a further incentive to Canning to secure the return of Pitt to power, and he was continually going down to Walmer, where as Lord Warden of the Cinque Ports the ex-Premier was occupied with the preparations to resist the threatened French invasion, to urge his leader to attack the Government, and to these months belong some of the most violent of his lampoons upon Addington. For a time, however, Pitt, although dissatisfied with the lack of vigour shown by ministers in the prosecution of the war, refused to be implicated, and on one occasion when Canning and his friends brought forward a vote of censure on the Government he showed his disapproval by moving the previous question. In the early weeks of 1804 the situation was further complicated by a temporary return of the King's insanity, but by April the ex-Premier had become convinced that his duty to the country required him to act. " He seems in perfectly good heart, indeed," Canning wrote, " but shudders a little at the brink, just as I suppose George [1] does at the edge of the tub of cold water. He must in." A few days later Pitt strongly criticized the whole defence policy of the Government, and, on the resignation of Addington, he was once more called upon to form a ministry.

Although Canning was admittedly one of the best speakers in either House, and his ability was unquestioned in any quarter, Pitt was not able to offer him a place in the Cabinet, and this was eloquent proof of the bitterness which he had roused by his attacks on Addington. Virulence, indeed, rarely pays in British politics. Those who most bitterly attacked Walpole gained little in the end by their vindictive campaign; Disraeli undoubtedly suffered for some years on account of the violence of his onslaughts on Peel; and the position of Baldwin was strengthened rather than weakened by the fierce attacks made upon him by a section of the Press.

[1] Canning's eldest son.

E

Canning should have realized that in going so far as he did in his opposition to Addington he was doing more harm to himself than to " the Doctor ", but the thought apparently never occurred to him. Possibly this was due to the fact that he was an Irishman. By nature, Canning was at all times impulsive, but this impulsiveness when translated into political action often took the form of a violence of phrase which gave him a reputation for vindictiveness and instability. Such being the case, Pitt found himself unable to give Canning any higher appointment than the Treasurership of the Navy, although his contemporaries, Hawkesbury and Castlereagh, became respectively Home Secretary and President of the Board of Control, a fact which was hardly calculated to soothe their colleague's feelings.

The new administration had not been formed without difficulty. In view of the danger from France, the Prime Minister wished to construct it upon the broadest possible basis, and at once opened negotiations with the Whig leaders for their inclusion. This plan was nipped in the bud by the King, who refused to have Fox in the Cabinet, and although the latter readily agreed to his own exclusion, which he had fully expected, and urged his followers to join Pitt, many of them refused to do so. Addington, too, smarting under his defeat, at first hung back, but later came in as Lord President, having gone to the House of Lords as Viscount Sidmouth.[1] This caused much ill-feeling, and Canning promptly tendered his resignation, but was induced to withdraw it. In short, save for the addition of Pitt himself and Canning, the ministry differed but little from that which it had succeeded, though there had been a general reshuffle of offices.

Canning's second experience of office was not a particularly happy one, for he was in uncongenial company and he rated low the ability of more than one of his colleagues. He had not long been at the Admiralty before a quarrel took place between Hawkesbury and himself. The dispute originated in the statement of a third party that he owed his advancement to his friendship with the new Home Secretary, and, on hearing this, Canning, who seems to have assumed that his old friend was himself responsible for the story, at once declared he would resign. The long-suffering Pitt acted as mediator, and peace was soon made. " The transaction redounds to the credit of both, of Canning as well as

---

[1] One of the few instances in which an ex-Premier, on being raised to the peerage, has not been created an earl.

of Lord Hawkesbury. For it is only with men of really fine and
generous dispositions that a reconciliation, after a dispute of so
serious a kind, can be so complete as to leave no soreness behind
it. But it was such in this instance. They at once returned to
their former habits of cordial intimacy: which was never again
interrupted." [1] All the same, the incident was regarded by
contemporaries as further proof of the contention that Canning
was a thoroughly intractable colleague.

Not long after this a crisis arose respecting his own department.
The First Lord of the Admiralty was Dundas, now Viscount
Melville, a relative of Mrs. Canning, and during the first weeks of
the year 1805 he was charged on the report of a commission with
having misapplied public money while Treasurer of the Navy in
Pitt's previous administration. The Opposition at once took the
matter up, and the attack upon Melville was led by Samuel
Whitbread, the brewer, who even suggested Impeachment; this
led Canning to compose the following verses while sitting on the
Treasury Bench:

> I am like Archimedes for science and skill,
> I am like the young prince who went straight up the hill;
> And, to interest the hearts of the fair, be it said,
> I am like a young lady just bringing to bed:
> If you ask why the eleventh of June I remember
> So much better than April, or March, or December.
> 'Tis because on that day, and with pride I asure ye,
> My sainted progenitor took to his brewery.
> On that day in the month he began making beer,
> On that night he commenced his connubial career;
> On that day he died, when he had finished his summing,
> And the angels all cried, "Here's old Whitbread a-coming!"
> So the day I still hail with a smile and a sigh,
> For his beer with an *e*, and his bier with an *i*;
> And one day every year, in the hottest of weather,
> The whole Whitbread family dine altogether.
> My lords, while the beams of the hall shall support
> The roof which o'ershades this respectable court
> (Where Hastings was tried for oppressing the Hindoos);
> While the rays of the sun shall shine in these windows,
> My name shall shine bright as my ancestor's shines,
> Emblazoned on journals, as his upon signs.

What had happened was that Melville had been negligent in
the extreme, in that he had not prevented the Paymaster from
engaging in private speculation with the naval balances. He had
not himself touched a penny, but as head of the department
affected he was responsible. Pitt was determined to do what he

[1] Yonge, C. D., *op. cit.*, vol. I, p. 160.

could for an old friend and colleague, and Canning advised him to
defy the Opposition: the other ministers, however, considered
that the sense of the House was against such a course, and it was
decided to move for the appointment of a Select Committee to
make further investigations.

The debate, which began on April 8th, 1805, and lasted well on
into the morning of the following day, was one of the most notable
and dramatic in Parliamentary annals.   Canning, as well as Pitt
and Castlereagh, spoke strongly in defence of the accused minister,
and at 4.0 A.M. Wilberforce rose.   The Prime Minister is said to
have leant eagerly forward to hear what his oldest friend would
have to say, but when that most upright of men supported the
prosecution he sank back in obvious misery.   The division showed
an equality of votes; and there was absolute silence while the
Speaker, white as a sheet, made up his mind how he should give
his casting vote.   Finally, he decided against the Government,
and there ensued a scene which testified at once to the enthusiasm
and the bad manners of the Whigs.   One member gave the " view
halloa ", and many crowded to the exit to see " how Billy Pitt
looked after it ".   A few of the Prime Minister's supporters
formed a phalanx round him, and he was helped out of the House
in a state bordering upon collapse.   In due course, it may be
added, Melville was impeached, but was acquitted on every count.
When the news of Trafalgar arrived, Pitt wrote to him in his
retirement that his energy at the Admiralty had largely contributed
to the victory.

Melville was succeeded at the Admiralty by Lord Barham, an
appointment which so irritated Sidmouth that he left the Government in July, 1805.   Canning thus announced the fact to Frere:

> The Doctor is out again,
> So things may come about again.

Canning played little part in general politics for the remainder
of the year, but his relations with Pitt were as cordial as they had
been a decade earlier, and during the autumn the Prime Minister
promised him a seat in the Cabinet within the course of a few
weeks.   Meanwhile Pitt's health was rapidly declining, ruined as
it was by the weight of the responsibility which he carried, and by
the irregular hours which he kept.   He went to Bath in December,
1805, and there Canning joined him.   The two friends spent a
pleasant week together, and Canning amused himself with com-
posing a poem on Ulm and Trafalgar.   At the beginning of 1806

the Prime Minister returned to Putney, and on January 23rd he died. Canning was with him the night before his death, and the younger man's grief may be gauged from some lines which he wrote to his wife after the funeral in Westminster Abbey: " It is all over, dearest Love, I have seen poor Pitt laid in his grave, and I feel somehow a feeling of loneliness and dismay which I have never felt half so strongly before. I wish I had been able to get into my chaise and go down to shelter myself with my own dear Love at South Hill. But that may not be. How dreary, nevertheless, all society and all politics appear at this moment." [1]

Six years later, in a speech at Liverpool to his constituents, Canning explained how the death of Pitt had affected his political outlook :

> Gentlemen, you see that I speak to you as freely of the conduct and policy of the Government, as of the conduct of those to whom I am politically opposed. To one man, while he lived, I was devoted with all my heart and with all my soul. Since the death of Mr. Pitt, I acknowledge no leader. My political allegiance lies buried in his grave—but I have, though not his immediate counsels to follow, his memory to cherish and revere. So far as I knew his opinions on subjects which were in his time, as well as now, of great public interest, I have adhered, and shall adhere, to those opinions as the guides of my public conduct. Where I can only reason from analogy on new questions, whatever they may be, the principles which I imbibed and inherit from him; principles which, I well know, have alone recommended me to your choice this day. [2]

These words well represented the facts. For the rest of his life Canning had many friends and followers, but none of them ever stood to him in the same relation that Pitt had done. In the future, apart from his wife, Canning faced the world alone.

The immediate effect of Pitt's death was the dissolution of the administration over which he had presided. The King first of all asked Hawkesbury to form a ministry, but he declared his inability to do so, and strongly advised George to have recourse to the Opposition. The monarch made up his mind " to swallow a bitter pill ", to quote Hawkesbury, but he felt that he could hardly, without loss of dignity, turn to Fox, so he sent for Grenville, who

[1] Marshall, D., *op. cit.*, p. 298.   [2] Therry, R., *op. cit.*, vol. I, p. 35.

had for some years separated himself from his former party.   In
this way the ministry of " All the Talents " came into being with
Fox [1] at the Foreign Office; Canning refused to join, and in his
absence its designation was a misnomer.   He went even further,
and during the Government's twelve months' tenure of office he
was one of its leading opponents in the House of Commons.
Indeed, this short spell of Opposition showed his contemporaries
what a formidable Parliamentary figure he had become.

The new Cabinet was predominantly Whig, but it included the
Lord Chief Justice of the King's Bench, Lord Ellenborough, and
such a departure from constitutional practice as this appointment
was excused by the Government on no more substantial ground
than the desirability of making Ellenborough's talents available
for the defence of the administration.   Canning severely criticized
the inclusion of the Lord Chief Justice in the ministry, and said
that he thought the administration of justice a matter of such
infinite importance that he would not purchase all Ellenborough's
ability for an hour's suspicion of his character as a judge.   Canning also attacked the Government's defence measures, and so
strong was his disapproval of Grenville and his colleagues that
he even voted against Fox's bill for the suppression of the slave
trade, in spite of his own motion with regard to Trinidad only four
years before.   Canning never questioned the maxim that it was
the duty of an Opposition to oppose everything.

Although the life of the existing Parliament had another three
years to run, and there was no particular need for an appeal to the
country, Grenville forced a General Election in November, 1806.
Canning took advantage of the dissolution to return to his old
constituency of Newtown, Isle of Wight, though he forsook it
again the following year for Hastings.   The Government won a
victory at the polls, but in spite of that its days were numbered.
In February, 1807, it introduced a Bill which had the effect of
granting commissions in the Navy and Army to Roman Catholics.
The King declared that he had been misinformed as to the scope
of the measure, and not only demanded its withdrawal, but also
a promise that the subject should not be raised again.   The
Government refused to give such a pledge, and resigned.   The
Duke of Portland, who had already been Prime Minister in 1783,
was then summoned to form a ministry, and in the new administration Canning at last attained Cabinet rank as Foreign Secretary.

[1] He died in the following September.

CHAPTER IV

THE FOREIGN OFFICE

THE new administration was a good deal stronger in both Houses than its immediate predecessor had been, and it might well have laid a better claim to be a ministry of " All the Talents ". In the Lords it was represented by the Prime Minister himself, as well as by Camden, Eldon, Chatham, Westmorland, Mulgrave, Hawkesbury (who had been raised to the peerage during the lifetime of his father), and Bathurst, while in the Commons were Canning, Castlereagh, and Perceval. In this Government, too, Sir Arthur Wellesley, the future Duke of Wellington, held office outside the Cabinet as Chief Secretary for Ireland. The real leader, however, was not the Prime Minister, who was close on seventy, but the Chancellor of the Exchequer, Spencer Perceval.

Born in 1762, a younger son of the second Earl of Egmont, he had been educated at Harrow and Trinity College, Cambridge, and was one of the outstanding barristers of the day. In his last year as a stuff-gownsman his income was £1,012, and ultimately his private practice brought him four to five thousand a year. Perceval was first returned to Parliament in 1796 for Northampton, and, although sound rather than brilliant, he soon began to acquire a reputation in the House of Commons. He was a favourite of Pitt, who had made him Attorney-General in his second administration, and now he was Chancellor of the Exchequer at the age of forty-five. " He spoke ", said a contemporary, " without the disagreeable cant of the Bar, was never tedious, was particularly distinct in matters of business, and explained his financial measures with clearness and ability. His style was singularly acute, bold, sarcastic, and personal." Perceval was, it may be added, a devout, if somewhat narrow, Christian, and he was peculiarly acceptable to the King owing to his determined opposition to Roman Catholic claims. He led the House of Commons.

The one real weakness of the ministry was the Premier himself. It was not yet the custom to select as Prime Minister a man who was an outstanding political figure, and on several occasions since the Revolution a nonentity had been chosen solely because he was the only man under whom others would serve. For this reason recourse was had to Portland in 1807, but he soon proved to be too feeble to play the part cast for him. He deputed Hawkesbury to lead in the Upper House, which he never addressed during the two-and-a-half years that he was Prime Minister, and which there is no evidence of him even having attended during this period. In the end it was to be his incompetence, combined with bad health, that brought about the fall of the Government.

The formation of the Portland administration in 1807 marked the last occasion on which a British monarch forced the resignation of a ministry that had a majority in the House of Commons and replaced it by one more in accordance with his own views on one of the most important questions of the day, in this case Catholic Emancipation. It is true that William IV acted in a somewhat similar fashion in 1834, but he had the excuse that a leading member of the Government had left the Lower House, whereas his father's behaviour towards Grenville was a definite step in that policy of personal rule which he had pursued ever since he ascended the throne. In these circumstances it is by no means surprising that the Opposition declared the change of ministers to be unconstitutional, and there was a heated debate on the subject, in which Canning played a prominent part. The Government obtained a majority of only thirty-two, so Parliament was dissolved on April 27th, 1807, and the King's Speech was little more than a personal plea for a majority for the new administration. Once again it was proved that George III was a better judge of the temper of the country than was the House of Commons, and the ministers were returned with a working majority. Home affairs were, however, rapidly receding into the background, for, in spite of the victory at Trafalgar eighteen months before, the power of Napoleon had so increased that it hung like a cloud over every nation in Europe.

Canning fully realized the strain to which his department was going to be subjected in view of the seriousness of the international situation, and he was determined to have an efficient Under-Secretary, knowing, as he did, from personal experience the amount of work to be done by whoever held that office. He offered the appointment to a young friend, Charles Bagot, whom he had originally met through Sneyd, and who had just been returned to the House of Commons at the age of twenty-five for the borough of Castle Rising.

(Private)   *Foreign Office,*
                                   August 8, 1807, 6 P.M.

DEAR BAGOT,
    I have intended for two days to write you a much
longer letter than I have now time to write to-day. But I
have stated the substance of what I had to say to Mr. Pole,[1]
who has undertaken to convey it to you.
    I intreat you not to decide without weighing well all the
chances of inconvenience and uncomfortableness; and possibly of final disappointment, if you should engage hastily and
unadvisedly, and without a thorough knowledge of your own
strength, and confidence in your own determination.
    French is essentially indispensable—and far more of it than
The Morning Chronicle allows me to possess. But that I
suppose you have.
    The labour is very hard; and it is daily and constant. It
requires entire devotion to it. I think Parliament is wholly
incompatible with the due discharge of the duty. I am sure
Fitz-Harris [2] has felt it almost impossible to support the
fatigues of both. But I should not wish you absolutely to
decide on relinquishing Parliament at present. It would be
well to have the next four or five months' trial whether the
office suits you so far as to be worth that sacrifice. And, if
unluckily it should not suit you upon trial, I can not promise
that like Fitz-Harris (and Sancho) you shall retire to the
Government of an Island.[3]
    I am sure you will feel that I deal most fairly by you in
putting the unpleasant and disheartening parts of my proposal
forward, and calling upon you to take them fully into your
consideration.
    When you have made up your mind you will let me know.
And I am afraid I must add that you must be prepared to
follow your determination (if affirmative) to London, in ten
days or a fortnight.
                                   Yours very sincerely,
                                   GEO. CANNING.

[1] William Wellesley Pole, brother of the future Duke of Wellington.
He took the additional name of Pole on inheriting some property in Ireland.
He was Bagot's father-in-law.
    [2] Then Under-Secretary: afterwards second Earl of Malmesbury.
    [3] Fitz-Harris had been appointed Vice-Admiral of the Isle of Wight.

P.S.—Taking snuff is in your favour.   I think there is only
the Swede that smokes, except indeed the Turk, but he is in
Mr. Hammond's department.

The reference to *The Morning Chronicle* requires explanation.
Canning's opponents were always charging him with his ignorance
of the French language, and that newspaper published a story
which seemed to give point to the accusation.   When Canning
was Under-Secretary at the Foreign Office it alleged that the
Russian ambassador, who spoke every tongue but English, had an
interview with him.   They were getting on slowly when the
ambassador had an inspiration : he repeated emphatically words
which sounded like " Oroom, oroom ", and at the same time
slapped his breeches' pocket.   Canning's classical education,
combined with his quickness of brain, stood him in good stead ;
the word was not pronounced that way either at Eton or Christ
Church, but what was meant was clearly *aurum*—gold.   The two
men understood one another at last, and in due course a Russian
subsidy was proposed to Parliament.   The legend grew, and when
Canning became Foreign Secretary in 1807 he was advised to

> Brush up your very best jokes, I pray ;
> And though you can't speak any French, they say,
> Why, as for that matter,
> Fitz-Harris can chatter.
> And you can keep out of the way.

In spite of the fact that less than six months in office had been
too much for Fitz-Harris, and also of Canning's warnings, Bagot
accepted the appointment, though he was a little distrustful of his
French.   " I cannot write it," he confessed, " and am utterly
incapable of conversing in it, but have been in the constant habit
of reading it for my own amusement."   Nevertheless he received
the following note from his father-in-law :

MY DEAR CHARLES,
          I have only time to tell you that Canning does not
write to you—expects you in town, accepts you as his Secretary, and has named you to Nobbs,[1] who highly approves.
                                                        W. W. P.

The international situation had gone from bad to worse since
the death of Pitt, and Canning found himself confronted by a

[1] The King.

state of affairs which might well have daunted a far more experienced Foreign Secretary. The overthrow of Austria at Austerlitz in 1805 had been followed by that of Prussia in the following year: at Jena and Auerstadt the system of the great Frederick collapsed like a house of cards, and Berlin itself was occupied by the French. While these events were taking place Grenville and his colleagues had neglected nothing that was calculated to encourage the enemy and to depress their fellow-countrymen. They refused to support a vote of thanks to the Volunteers for their services when invasion threatened, and they abolished all their pay and allowances; they repealed the Additional Force Act; and they suspended the ballot for the Militia. Abroad their policy was equally futile. Fox had attempted direct negotiation with Talleyrand, in which the Englishman tried, as he put it, to act on the assumption that the two countries would treat as Great Powers, but he soon discovered that this was not at all Napoleon's idea. The Emperor's diplomacy constantly assumed the same form, that is to say, separate treaties with different countries, combined with the hurried continuance of aggression while negotiations were taking place, so as to compel the other party either to accept the aggression or to fight in unfavourable circumstances.

No advantage had been taken by the Grenville Cabinet of the reappearance of Prussia in the field after ten years' neutrality, and, even after the drawn battle between the French and Russians at Eylau in February, 1807, had raised the hopes of every enemy of France, nothing was done. It is true that the policy pursued by Prussia ever since the outbreak of the French Revolution had not been such as to render her either an attractive or a reliable ally, but adversity makes strange bedfellows, and she was too useful a source of support against Napoleon to be neglected by a British Government. Moreover, the situation at the beginning of 1807 was by no means hopeless. In spite of the disasters which had overtaken them, there were still considerable bodies of Prussian troops in the field, the Russians had checked Napoleon at Eylau; and the Swedish armaments were as yet untouched. Nevertheless, Grenville allowed the precious weeks to slip past, and by the time Canning took office it was too late. He and Castlereagh at once assembled such troops as they could collect, but only to find that the previous ministry had dispersed the transports that Pitt had always kept ready for such an emergency. Eventually, a force was sent to the island of Rügen, which belonged to Sweden, but the time had passed when it could usefully have co-operated with the Northern allies, for Dantzig had surrendered to the French in May, thus bringing to an end the resistance of Prussia, and on June 14th Napoleon overthrew the Russians at Friedland.

Nor was this all, for if Grenville and his colleagues had neglected the main theatre of war, they had by no means refrained from dissipating British strength in quite useless expeditions all over the world. Unfortunately for Canning, these chickens came home to roost after he had assumed control of the Foreign Office, and exceedingly ill-omened fowl most of them turned out to be. Two expeditions had been sent to the Near East in the hope of coercing the Sultan into a rupture with France, and both failed dismally. Admiral Duckworth succeeded in getting his fleet through the Dardanelles, but was unsuccessful in persuading the Turks to do what was required of them, and he only managed to re-pass the Narrows after considerable loss. A force that was sent to Egypt surprised Alexandria, but was repulsed before Rosetta; and the sole result of these attempts to gain cheap laurels in the Near East was to throw the Porte into the arms of Napoleon. In the West, an incompetent general was ordered to take Buenos Aires, which he not only failed to do, but also lost Monte Video, which had been conquered earlier in the year, and British prestige was hardly repaired by the court-martial that dismissed him from the service. The solitary success that the Grenville administration could claim to its credit was a victory at Maida, in Calabria, but as the troops engaged had to be at once withdrawn for the defence of Sicily, it served no useful purpose save to demonstrate the superiority of the British line over the French column, and the very scene of the engagement would soon have been forgotten had it not given its name to a London suburb.

The summer of 1807 thus saw Napoleon at the height of his power, for hardly had Friedland been fought than the Tsar proceeded to come to terms with his enemy at the expense of his friends. Russian diplomacy has always enjoyed an unenviable reputation for duplicity, but it has rarely betrayed such complete perfidy as during the ten days which elapsed between the battle of Friedland and the meeting of Napoleon and Alexander I at Tilsit. There is, however, just this to be said in favour of the Tsar and his counsellors: the Russian armies had been beaten in the field, Prussia was crushed, Gustavus IV of Sweden was proving himself impossible both as an ally and as a monarch, and, most important of all, the British Government had done nothing to assist in the struggle against the common enemy. These were certainly reasons for peace, but not for a peace which had as its basis an alliance with France directed against Russia's former friends. When, in later years, Canning came face to face with the Holy Alliance, it is not surprising that he should have seen in the idealistic Tsar a perfidious autocrat who came to terms with Napoleon on the famous raft in the middle of the Niemen.

The two Emperors had their first meeting on June 25th, and on the 7th of the following month the Treaty of Tilsit was signed. The public articles provided for the reduction of Prussia to the rank of a second-class Power, but the secret ones affected Great Britain far more closely. By these the two Emperors agreed that if the British Government did not mitigate the severity of the Orders in Council, which had forbidden trade with France and her allies, and restore all maritime conquests made since 1805, they would summon Portugal, Denmark, and Sweden to close their ports against British shipping, while any of these Powers which refused to comply with the order was to be treated as an enemy.

Great Britain was thus exposed to the gravest danger, for she was threatened both on her own shores and in her commerce. When Napoleon marched away from the Channel in the late summer of 1805 it was clear that the invasion of England would not become a practicable proposition again until Europe was at his feet: that condition was fulfilled at Tilsit. It is true that France had lost the bulk of her fleet at Trafalgar two years before, but if she could obtain possession of the fleets of Portugal, Denmark and Sweden she would more than repair her losses, and thus be in a position once again to form plans for the invasion of the British Isles.[1] Napoleon has himself left his intentions clearly upon record:

> After Russia had joined my alliance, Prussia, as a matter of course, followed her example; Portugal, Sweden, and the Pope alone remained to be gained over, for we were well aware that Denmark would hasten to throw herself into our arms. If England refused the proffered mediation of Russia, the whole maritime forces of the Continent were to be employed against her, and they could muster 180 sail of the line.

[1] Rose, J. H.: *Napoleonic Studies*, pp. 133–165.

In a few years this force could be raised to 250. With the aid of such a fleet, and my immense flotilla, it was by no means impossible to lead a European army to London. One hundred ships of the line employed against her colonies in the two hemispheres, would have sufficed to draw off a large portion of the British navy; while eighty more, assembled in the Channel, would have sufficed to assure the passage of the flotilla and avenge the outraged rights of nations. Such was at bottom my plan.

The Franco-Russian agreement had hardly been concluded before Canning knew of it, including the secret provisions regarding Great Britain. The source of his information is one of the mysteries of diplomacy, and for many years credence was given to the story that when Napoleon and Alexander met there was an agent of the Foreign Office behind a curtain listening to their conversation. Unfortunately for those who would like to believe this romantic legend, the accounts of the expenditure of Secret Service money for the year in question give it no support, and the probability is that Canning received the news from some official of the Tsar's household, where Anglophil sympathies were strong and the most important secrets were rarely kept. Granville Leveson Gower was British ambassador at St. Petersburg, and he had already warned his old friend that a French attack on Denmark was by no means impossible: by June 26th he had already sent off news of the Franco-Russian *rapprochement*, and this reached the Foreign Office on July 16th. In any event, it is clear that what arrived in London was merely a report of the preliminary conversation between the two Emperors on June 25th, and not a copy of the secret clauses of the actual treaty, for Canning believed that every moment was of the most vital importance if the Franco-Russian plans were to be forestalled, whereas had he been acquainted with the terms of the treaty itself he would have realized that he had until December to take the necessary precautions.

" A dull and unimaginative man would probably have decided to await further developments before making even preliminary preparations. But Canning's was an imaginative mind, keenly patriotic and fired with intense hatred of Napoleon." [1] In the light of the knowledge available the danger seemed to the British Government to be imminent, and of the three directions from

---

[1] *The Cambridge History of British Foreign Policy*, vol. I, p. 362.

which it threatened, the Danish was the most menacing, for Sweden was still at war with France, while before Napoleon could lay hands on the Portuguese fleet he would have to come to terms with Spain. Under the influence of Canning the Cabinet then acted with rare promptitude.

Before the end of July a naval squadron under Admiral Gambier, and a military force commanded by Sir Arthur Wellesley, had left for Copenhagen, and with them went one Jackson, lately the British minister in Berlin, whom Canning sent to negotiate an offensive and defensive alliance with the Danish Crown Prince, afterwards Frederick VI, who was at the time regent for his father, the mad King Christian VII. Jackson was far from being the luckiest or the most skilful of diplomats, as his later behaviour in Washington amply attests, but on this occasion he had little latitude in his instructions. He had to insist, as a preliminary to the conclusion of the alliance, upon the surrender of the Danish fleet, which the British Government pledged itself to return intact at the end of the war. In any case the negotiation would have been a difficult one, for Great Britain had been unpopular in Denmark ever since the attack on Copenhagen six years before, but Jackson did not improve matters by very obviously offering the alliance at the cannon's mouth. The Crown Prince refused to negotiate, and Jackson called on Gambier and Wellesley to enforce the British terms. Wellesley defeated the Danes at Roskilde, and Copenhagen was bombarded by land and sea. On September 8th, 1807, the Crown Prince made an unconditional surrender, and the Danish fleet was incorporated in Gambier's squadron. The British land and sea forces then proceeded to Sweden, where they received a warm welcome from Great Britain's last remaining ally on the mainland of Europe.

Canning was well satisfied with what had been done, and he wrote that the Copenhagen expedition had prevented " a Northern confederacy, an invasion of Ireland, and the shutting of Russian ports ".[1] Others did not share his satisfaction, and such prompt and spirited action on the part of Great Britain took the world by surprise. Napoleon, whose hands were still wet with the blood of the murdered Duc d'Enghien, professed the utmost horror at so flagrant a violation of the rights of small nations, of which he declared himself to be the protector; and he set the tone for all who drew their inspiration from him when he declared that

[1] *Paget Papers*, vol. II, p. 363.

" blood and fire had made the English masters of Copenhagen ",
although he was at that very moment meditating the adoption of
exactly the same policy with regard to Portugal. The Tsar was
profoundly shocked by conduct for which there were many
precedents in the history of his own country, and held up his
hands in horror at such a violation of international law. The
neutral states, much as they all feared the power and ambition of
Napoleon, were alarmed at the treatment meted out to one of
their number, and for a time the whole Continent echoed with
denunciations of the British Foreign Secretary. Soon, however,
the French Emperor was himself to be guilty of such acts of
aggression as to throw the bombardment of Copenhagen completely into the shade.

At home there was a considerable difference of opinion, for
the doctrine that the end justifies the means has never recom-
mended itself to the British public in its entirety, and not even the
importance of the victory that had been achieved could reconcile
a large body of people to the methods by which it had been gained.
Tom Moore was thus only expressing the views of very many of
his fellow-countrymen when he wrote :

> If Grotius be thy guide, shut, shut, the book,
> In force alone for law of nations look.
> While Cobbett's pirate code alone appears
> Sound moral sense to England and Algiers.

There was no autumn session in 1807, but when Parliament re-
assembled in February of the following year the Opposition hotly
attacked the Government in both Houses, and some acrimonious
debates ensued. Canning made a spirited reply in the Commons
to the speeches of Ponsonby and Sheridan, though his defence was
undoubtedly weakened by his inability, for obvious reasons, to
cite the information he had received concerning the Tilsit negotiations. In the end, however, his conduct was approved by 253 to
108 votes in the Commons, and by 105 to 48 in the Lords, where
the case for the Government was put by Hawkesbury.

There can be little doubt but that by the strict letter of the
international law of the time, *pace* Tom Moore, Canning was
justified. On the eve of the bombardment of Copenhagen the
British commanders issued the following summons :

> To convince the Danish Government and the whole world
> of the reluctance with which His Majesty has recourse to

arms, we, the undersigned, at the moment when our troops are before your gates, and our batteries ready to open, renew to you the offer of the same advantageous terms which we formerly proposed : viz., if you will consent to deliver up the Danish fleet, and to our carrying it away, it shall be held in deposit merely, and restored in as good a state as received, with all its equipments, as soon as the provisions of a general peace shall have removed the necessity which occasioned this demand. But if this offer is now rejected it cannot be repeated.

The intention of the British Government was thus not to take permanent possession of the Danish fleet, but merely to intern it for the duration of the war, and on this point Grotius is quite clear :

I may, without considering whether it is merited or not, take possession of that which belongs to another, if I have reason to fear any evil from his holding it; but I cannot make myself master or proprietor of it, the property having nothing to do with the end which I propose. I can only keep possession of the thing seized till my safety is sufficiently provided for.

As this was precisely what Great Britain proposed to Denmark, there was obviously no breach of international law.

Unfortunately, in this imperfect world law and justice are by no means always synonymous, and it is possible to be legally right and yet morally wrong; in these circumstances the ethics of Canning's action remain to be considered. It is true that the seizure was made in time of peace, but it was a peace of a very relative nature, for Great Britain was at war with France, of whom Denmark had been the ally only a few years before, as Canning did not fail to remind his critics, and into whose arms she was about to throw herself again. Moreover, as we have seen, the Danish armament would have gone a long way towards repairing the French losses at Trafalgar, and the use to which Napoleon proposed to put it has already been indicated. Such being the case, it is impossible to resist the conclusion that in view of all the evidence, Canning had every justification for what he did, and a modern authority has gone so far as to say that " certainly no

F

action was ever better justified ".[1] In spite, too, of the protests
which it aroused, there can be no doubt that in the long run
Canning's drastic act raised British prestige all over Europe, for it
showed that Great Britain once more had an administration that
was determined to face Napoleon.

Hardly had the captured Danish fleet been brought safely back
to British ports than Canning took another step which was
probably just as distasteful to the French Emperor, although for
more personal reasons. One of the consequences of the Treaty
of Tilsit was that poor Louis XVIII, who had been living at Mittau,
had to set out on his travels again, and, after a short sojourn in
Sweden, he landed at Yarmouth at the end of October, 1807.
Canning and Hawkesbury would have preferred Louis to take
up his residence in Scotland, and the Foreign Secretary wrote to
Bagot: " If we could have obliged him to go to Edinburgh, well—
but having once consented to his landing, we ought not to let
him land like a Scrub; and leave him without protection or
attention. Somebody ought to have been sent to greet him at
landing. . . . The mischief is not yet irreparable, and it strikes
me very forcibly that you are the fittest person to repair it. I
would therefore have you set out as soon as you can (I know you
will hate me for this, but I cannot help it) on the road to Yarmouth." [2] Nor was this all, for Canning induced the Government to grant Louis a pension of £6,000 a year. The French
Empire might or might not be permanent, but there were definite
advantages in having the alternative master of France a guest on
British soil.

Meanwhile, there were the Swedish and Portuguese fleets to
be considered, and Canning showed the same promptitude where
they were concerned. In respect of Sweden, it soon became
obvious that Gustavus IV was impossible. Sir John Moore was,
indeed, sent with a force to co-operate with the Swedes, but he
was then withdrawn, and in any case the Swedish fleet was too
small to affect the balance of naval power in Europe. With
Portugal the case was very different, for not only was she Britain's
oldest ally, but events were moving so fast that the slightest delay
was fraught with the gravest danger. That country was governed
by a Prince Regent, afterwards John VI, on behalf of the mad

---

[1] Richmond, Admiral Sir Herbert: *British Strategy, Military and Economic,*
p. 104.
[2] Bagot, J., *op. cit.*, vol. I, p. 250.

Queen Maria I, and Canning lost no time in coming to terms with him. The Prince Regent agreed to surrender the Portuguese fleet, and to retire to Brazil, but he was dilatory in carrying out his promises. In the meantime Napoleon had not been idle. In October he concluded the Treaty of Fontainebleau with Spain, by which he secured permission to march French troops across Spanish territory in return for a promise to partition Portugal, and he then sent Junot to occupy Lisbon. It was not until the French were in the very suburbs of the Portuguese capital that the Prince Regent handed his ships over to the British and set sail for Rio de Janeiro. Canning had won the race with Napoleon by a very short head indeed, but he had won; and the Portuguese fleet, like the Danish, was under the White Ensign, not the tricolour. He also signed a Convention with Portugal authorizing a temporary British occupation of Madeira.

The year 1807 thus closed more favourably from the British point of view than had seemed possible only a few months before, and for this the praise is due to Canning, who had imparted to his country's foreign policy a direction and a vigour which it had not recently known. It had been hard work, and at the end of October he wrote to Bootle Wilbraham, " I have been watching an opportunity for the last month of getting out of Town for a few days at least to Hinckley. I have not seen my children since May, nor Mrs. C. since the end of July." Some share of the credit, too, must be awarded to Mulgrave and Castlereagh, at the Admiralty and the War Office respectively, for the way in which they seconded Canning's vigorous foreign policy by providing the necessary armaments at very short notice. Henceforth the invasion of the British Isles was out of the question. The ambitious schemes concocted by Napoleon and Alexander at Tilsit had come crashing down like a house of cards. The Danish and Portuguese fleets were in British, not French, ports, and the Corsican's triumphal entry into London was as far off as ever. It is true that, owing to the intractability of the Swedish King, the Tsar was in a fair way to obtain possession of Finland, but that mattered not at all to Great Britain. On the other hand, Britain had neither an ally nor a soldier on the mainland of Europe. Napoleon was the undisputed master of the Continent.

If the war was not to end in a stalemate, both Powers must adopt new tactics, and this they proceeded to do. Britain intensified her blockade of the countries under the control of France, and

Napoleon retaliated by endeavouring to strike at the most vulnerable part of his adversary, namely her commerce. " The battle between the sea and the land was to be fought out on commerce. . . . The Imperial soldiers were turned into coastguardsmen to shut out Great Britain from her markets; the British ships became revenue cutters to prohibit the trade of France. The neutral carrier, pocketing his pride, offered his services to either for pay, and the other then regarded him as taking part in hostilities." [1]

In such a war Napoleon clearly enjoyed many advantages. He controlled nearly the whole coast from Hamburg to Leghorn; the rulers of Austria, Prussia, and Russia were at his bidding; and the Spaniards, Dutch, West Germans, and Italians were his vassals. In these circumstances the French Emperor may well have felt justified when, at Berlin in November, 1806, he had decreed that the British Isles were henceforth in a state of blockade and isolation, had forbidden on the part of all his dependent countries any commerce with them, and had declared every subject of King George III found in a country occupied by French troops to be a prisoner of war.

The British Government retaliated by a series of Orders in Council which were issued at intervals throughout the year 1807. Of these regulations Canning was the author, and he defended them as a " justifiable measure of retaliation on France ". By the first of these orders vessels were forbidden to trade between any ports in the possession of France, or of her allies if under her control. By the second, issued after the extension of Napoleon's Continental System to the Mediterranean, general reprisals were granted against the goods, ships, and inhabitants of Tuscany, Naples, Dalmatia, and the Ionian Islands. By the third, all ports from which the British flag was excluded were declared in blockade, all trade in their produce unlawful, and their ships a prize, while all vessels carrying certificates of origin, a measure upon which Napoleon had insisted to prevent evasion of his system, were declared liable to capture. By the fourth, the sale of ships by a belligerent to a neutral was pronounced illegal, because the French had managed to preserve much of their commerce by fictitious sales, which enabled them to trade under neutral flags.

Napoleon heard of the last of these Orders in Council when he was in Italy in November, 1807, and in reply he issued the Milan

---

[1] Mahan, A. T.: *Influence of Sea-Power on the French Revolution and Empire*, vol. II, p. 289.

Decrees. In these he declared every neutral ship which submitted to the Orders to be denationalized and good prize of war; and the same judgment was passed upon every vessel sailing to or from any port in the United Kingdom or its colonies or possessions. In short, each combatant had now instituted a total blockade of the other, and it remained to be seen which was in the better position to effect its purpose.

The countries under the domination of France were not long in feeling the consequences of this extension of the war into the economic sphere. They were cut off from all those tropical products which the progress of civilization had rendered necessary for the modern world, especially sugar and coffee, together with most of the silk, cotton, and dyes needed for textile manufacture. Not unnaturally, the ports of Germany and the Netherlands were considerable sufferers from the blockade, and it had not long taken effect before a citizen of Hamburg was writing, " There is no longer any trade as it existed formerly . . . more than 300 vessels are laid up." [1] In consequence there was a growing discontent with French rule, and a considerable increase in smuggling; this was repressed by Napoleon with increasing severity, and he became the more unpopular as a result. In France itself the general run of prices was higher by one-third than it had been before the Revolution. As for Great Britain, what principally enabled her to defeat Napoleon's attempt at strangulation was the wealth of the West Indies, though the French Emperor's decrees were by no means without effect, for a widespread depression began to make itself felt in consequence of the closing of the Continental market for manufactured articles. The glamour of Wellington's victories in the Peninsula cannot disguise the fact that there was very real distress in many quarters at home while they were being won.

One unfortunate result of the Orders in Council was a progressive deterioration in British relations with the United States, and three years after Canning had left the Foreign Office this led to war. The two grievances which were specially resented by the Americans were the constant search of their ships for deserters, and the refusal of the British authorities to recognize their custom-house arrangements. As the law then stood a British subject could not get rid of his nationality, but the United States was full of English and Irish emigrants, as well as of deserters from British ships, and

[1] Perthes, F.: *Memoirs*, vol. I, pp. 148 and 162.

these facts caused many complications.   American warships were continually being stopped and searched, and more often than not some of the crew were detained.   The most notable case was that of the *Chesapeake* in February, 1807, which was forcibly boarded by the *Leopard*, and from which three citizens of the United States were removed.

The purely economic issue was somewhat complicated.   It was a breach of international law for neutrals to trade between the colony of a belligerent and the mother country, but they might do so, for their own supply, with the colony.   Furthermore, if they imported from the colony or colonies more than they wanted, they might re-export it even to the mother country, and the proof of a *bona-fide* interrupted voyage was the payment of the custom-house dues in the ports of the neutral.   In the United States, however, these dues were not paid in money, but in bonds, which were cancelled when the goods were re-exported.   The payment was thus fictitious, and the British officials refused to recognize the arrangement.   In 1807, the President of the United States, Jefferson, secured the passage of Acts of Non-Intercourse and Embargo, of which the object was to induce Great Britain and France to modify their policy towards American trade.   Nominally these measures applied equally to both belligerents, but in practice they only affected Great Britain, for her rival was debarred from direct trade with the United States by the British command of the sea.

Such was the situation with which Canning was called upon to deal.   At no stage of his career could he have been described as an admirer of the United States, its institutions, or its policy, and his description of the American navy in 1812 as " half-a-dozen fir frigates, with bits of bunting flying at their heads ",[1] excited great indignation on the other side of the Atlantic.   On the present occasion, however, whatever may have been his private feelings, he fully realized the disadvantages of having a hostile United States in view of the state of affairs existing in Europe.   His presence at the Foreign Office, too, was not without its effect upon Washington.   " The altered tone of respect and deference, from one of arrogant and haughty superiority, in the Government of America, produced by the policy of Mr. Canning, and the closing an apprehended breach between the two countries, which the indiscretion of our British minister had widened, are not the least of the many proofs which he has given of his peculiar fitness for

---

[1] Timbs, J., *op. cit.*, vol. I, p. 33.

presiding over the foreign policy of England." [1] Such was the eulogistic language of his contemporaries.

However this may be, Canning certainly endeavoured to reach an agreement with the United States both with regard to the *Chesapeake* case and the Orders in Council, and he put forward a set of definite proposals with this end in view. Where he was handicapped, however, was in not being able to find the right man for the legation at Washington, always a difficult post to fill. David Erskine, who was then minister, exceeded his instructions, and had to be recalled, and his successor, F. J. Jackson, of Copenhagen fame, offended the Americans by his attitude towards them. Consequently Canning's efforts failed, though war did not break out until 1812. It is to be noted in this connection that although the Government received many petitions from Lancashire and Yorkshire to cancel the Orders in Council, it maintained them, " doubtless nerved thereto by the masterful will of Canning ".[2]

The early months of the year 1808 witnessed the beginning of what can only be described as the next round in the contest between the French Emperor and his British foe. The plans made at Tilsit had miscarried, and the attempt to put a stop to Britain's commerce with the mainland of Europe was proving none too successful, so Napoleon, fertile as ever in alternative schemes, decided to attack his rival in another quarter. If he could gain possession of Spain, and, better still, of Spanish America, not only would he be able to deal a severe blow at British commerce in the Atlantic, but he would also be in a position to threaten the route to the East round the Cape of Good Hope. To carry out such a project he was admirably situated, for the Treaty of Fontainebleau had, from a military point of view, left Spain at the mercy of the French, while the extraordinary situation existing at Madrid provided an excellent opportunity for interference in Spanish domestic affairs.

The third generation of the House of Bourbon in the Peninsula had succeeded in making the Spanish monarchy ridiculous, a fact which even in their last days the Habsburgs had never accomplished. The King, Charles IV, was as uxorious as his grandfather, Philip V, and was entirely governed by his wife, who, in her turn, was completely in the hands of her lover, Godoy, who had been created Principe de la Paz. The Prince of Asturias, later

---

[1] Therry, R., *op. cit.*, vol. I, pp. 44–45.
[2] *The Cambridge History of British Foreign Policy*, vol. I, p. 367.

Ferdinand VII, was in violent revolt against his parents, but his own reputation was none too good. In due course the King applied to Napoleon to arbitrate upon his differences with his son. The French Emperor summoned both men to Bayonne, where they were forced to resign their rights to the Spanish throne, and then imprisoned in France. Thereupon he presented the Spaniards with a new sovereign in the person of his own brother, Joseph, hitherto King of Naples—soon to be known to his unwilling subjects as *Pepe Botellas*, from his alleged partiality for the bottle.

Canning was neither slow to realize himself, nor to impress upon his colleagues, the threat to the national interests which was involved in the establishment of a Bonaparte at Madrid, but for the moment there was nothing to be done. Britain might be mistress of the seas, but her fleet could not sail across the Pyrenees, and Napoleon was incontestably master of the Continent. Nevertheless, Canning was determined that if the French obtained Spain it should at any rate be Spain without the Indies. Great Britain, without an ally on the mainland of Europe, could not stop the passage of French armies across the Continent, but she could stop the passage of French fleets across the Atlantic; and with the Danish and Portuguese navies in his pocket Canning was in a position to take full advantage of the growing discontent with Spanish rule which was beginning to manifest itself in the Americas. The area of the war was being extended with every year that passed, and the French invasion of the Peninsula was destined to have the most far-reaching consequences both in the Old World and in the New.

The idea was not novel, and it had been familiar to Canning ever since the days of his Under-Secretaryship. Eighteen years before, in 1790, when Great Britain appeared to be on the eve of war with Spain over the question of Nootka Sound, Pitt had got into touch with that very remarkable man, Francisco de Miranda, the *Precursor* as he is known in Latin-American history. Miranda was very far from being the conventional revolutionary of popular imagination, who alternately starves in a garret and postures on a barricade. He was a familiar figure in the clubs of St. James's; he went racing at Newmarket; and he visited Oxford. Nor did he confine his attention to London and the upper classes: he went everywhere and he saw everything, from the interiors of ducal mansions to those of common prisons. No detail of English life was too minute to escape his notice, and he touched it at many points. Miranda was essentially a man of the world, and it was of no small value to the cause of the Spanish colonists that the first of their number to be known in London should have been one of such striking personality. Pitt and Miranda saw a good deal of one another, and had not the progress of the French Revolution prevented Louis XVI from coming to the aid of Spain it is more than likely that the first risings in Spanish America would have been made with British support. In 1804 the two men were again in communication.

British prestige in the Americas was none too high at the beginning of 1808 in view of the recent failure to take Buenos Aires and the enforced surrender of Monte Video. This circumstance, together with the advice of Miranda, induced Canning to favour Venezuela as the spot where the most telling blow might be struck against the supremacy of Spain in America. It was within easy reach of Jamaica and Trinidad, and there was considerable discontent at the course of events in the Peninsula. Canning saw Miranda on January 3rd, and for the next few months both men, together with Castlereagh, were busy with preparations for an expedition of which it was finally decided that Sir Arthur Wellesley should take command.[1] That stout Tory, it may be remarked, did not altogether relish the idea of co-operating with rebels: " I always had a horror ", he admitted afterwards, " of revolutionizing any country for a political object. I always said, if they rise of themselves, well and good, but do not stir them up : it is a fearful responsibility." [2] The progress of events in Spain, however, soon caused the abandonment of these plans. The efforts of Canning to foster the revolutionary movement in Spanish America could not be continued when Great Britain and Spain were in alliance, but they mark the origin of the policy which he was to pursue when he returned to the Foreign Office in 1822. No British Government, as has been said, could prevent France, whether it were the France of Napoleon or of Louis XVIII, from conquering Spain, but it could prevent the inclusion of Spanish America in the French sphere of operations, which was what Canning was preparing to do in 1808, and what he actually did fourteen years later.

The events in the Peninsula which deranged the Foreign Secretary's plans were nothing less than the uprising of the Spanish

[1] Robertson, W. S.: *The Life of Miranda*, vol. II, pp. 4–27.
[2] Stanhope, Earl, *op. cit.*, p. 69.

people against the invader, and for Napoleon it was the writing on the wall. Hitherto popular sentiment throughout Europe had generally favoured the French, but the rigours of the Continental System, combined with the increasing harshness of Napoleon's despotic rule, had produced a reaction, and of this the proud and independent Spaniards were the protagonists. It was in reality the beginning of the end, though the end itself was to be postponed for another six years.

On May 2nd, 1808, the population of Madrid rose, and there took place in the Puerta del Sol a sanguinary struggle which was to begin a new era in history. The insurrection in the capital was soon put down, though not without considerable bloodshed, for in the field the Spaniards were no match for the victors of Auster-litz, and a victory of Marshal Bessières at Medina del Rio Seco at the beginning of July enabled Joseph to enter the capital before the end of that month. Punitive columns were then sent out in various directions to secure submission to the new monarch, and it was the disaster which overtook one of these that may be said to mark the first step in the downfall of Napoleon. At Bailen, in Andalusia, General Dupont was compelled to lay down his arms with 20,000 men. The news of this surrender, even in those days of imperfect communications, was not long in reaching all parts of Europe, and it encouraged every enemy of Napoleon and of France. In reality the victory had been achieved by the regular Spanish infantry, which had not lost its old hard-fighting qualities, but it was generally believed to have been won by armed peasants, and the news that the French veterans had been defeated by such means roused the greater enthusiasm.

All over Spain men sprang to arms, and in every district a *junta* was formed to organize resistance to the invaders. These bodies owed a more or less nominal allegiance to a *junta central*, which carried on the government in the name of the absent Ferdinand, for even Spanish loyalty could no longer tolerate Charles IV, who for the future was relegated to obscurity, though he did not actually die until eleven years later. Unfortunately, these *juntas* showed little disposition to co-operate, for the absence of the monarch had given full vent to those centrifugal tendencies which are always so strong in Spain, and the task of negotiating with them was one that the Foreign Office was to find by no means easy.

Almost the first thought of the Spanish patriots was to turn to Great Britain for help, and in June the representatives of the *junta* of Asturias arrived in London. Canning and his colleagues in the Cabinet at once realized the importance of what had happened, and, as the Foreign Secretary told the House of Commons, from the beginning there existed " the strongest disposition on the part of the British Government to afford every practicable aid in a contest so magnanimous ". He went on to declare : " We shall proceed upon the principle, that any nation of Europe that starts up with a determination to oppose a Power which, whether professing insidious peace or declaring open war, is the common enemy of all nations, whatever may be the existing political relations of that nation with Great Britain, becomes instantly our essential ally."

Peace was accordingly made with Spain, and Frere was appointed to act as the intermediary between the Foreign Office and the *junta central*. Frere had experienced several changes of post since he had been appointed to Lisbon in 1800. Two years after that he had been transferred to Madrid, but in August, 1804, he was recalled " in consequence of circumstances having occurred that made it impossible for him any longer to communicate personally with the Prince of Peace ", though he received an annual pension of £1,700, and was made a Privy Councillor. In June, 1807, Canning was about to send his old friend to Berlin, but owing to the Treaty of Tilsit the project had to be abandoned. One of Frere's first exploits in his new post was to secure the return to the Peninsula of the Spanish division which Napoleon had sent to Denmark. They knew nothing of what was happening in their own country, and it was due to Frere's ingenuity that contact was made with them.

Their commander, the Marqués de la Romana, was well known to Frere, and a priest called Robertson was found willing to risk his life by taking a message through the French lines. The difficulty was to convince the Spanish general of the credentials of Robertson, and this was got over in an extremely original manner. When reading the poem of *El Cid* together Frere had once suggested to Romana that the line " *Aun vea el hora que vos merezca dos tanto* " should read " *Aun vea el hora que vos merezcades tanto* ", and Robertson was instructed to recite this amended line, known only to Romana and Frere, as proof that he could be trusted. After many hairbreadth escapes, the priest, disguised as a German schoolmaster, reached the Spanish commander, and repeated the line that was his passport. Unfortunately Romana

knew no English and Robertson was equally unacquainted with
Spanish, so the two were forced to converse in Latin. However,
the priest made himself understood, and with the aid of the British
fleet by far the greater part of the Spanish troops was returned to
the Peninsula to take part in the struggle against Napoleon.

In view of the changed situation the British Government decided
to send to the Peninsula the armament which had been prepared
for America, and in the second week of August, 1808, Sir Arthur
Wellesley landed in Portugal, which was almost wholly in the
possession of the French, with a force of some 12,000 men, and
with the rather vague instructions to afford " the Spanish and
Portuguese nations every possible aid in throwing off the yoke of
France ". Subsequent events were to prove how sound was the
appointment of Wellesley, which was to no small extent due to the
advocacy of Canning, but instead of leaving him in supreme
command the War Office proceeded to appoint three more
generals with varying degrees of authority. Sir John Moore, who
was recalled with his army from Sweden, was sent out a little later
than Wellesley with instructions to co-operate with him, while both
of them were directed to place themselves under the orders, not
only of Sir Hew Dalrymple, the Governor of Gibralter, as Com-
mander-in Chief, but of Sir Harry Burrard, when he should arrive,
as second in command. This fatal division of responsibility
reflects adversely upon the competence of Castlereagh at the
War Office.

Wellesley landed at the mouth of the River Mondego, and proceeded to march from there along the coast to Lisbon, where Junot
was feverishly concentrating his forces. He routed a small
French detachment at Roliça, and then found his path blocked by
the enemy at Vimeiro. The tactical offensive was taken by the
French, but the battle resulted in a British victory, and had it been
pressed home the French would in all probability have been cut
off from Lisbon. Unfortunately, however, Burrard had arrived
by this time, and he refused to sanction a vigorous pursuit. On
the following day he was, in his turn, superseded by Dalrymple,
who was of a similar opinion, and it was decided to await the
arrival of Moore before undertaking any further operations. In
the meantime, however, overtures for an armistice had been
received from Junot, and as a result the Convention of Cintra was
signed. By this agreement the French army was to surrender
Lisbon and the other Portuguese fortresses intact, but was to be

allowed to return to France with its arms and baggage at the expense of Great Britain. Wellesley, it may be noted, disapproved of negotiating with Junot instead of compelling him to capitulate, and he disagreed with certain terms of the armistice, but he was a party to it as a whole. In any event, the court of enquiry which followed the recall of the three generals concerned found nothing in their conduct deserving of censure, though the attitude of the nation as a whole can best be judged by the popular song of the day:

> Sir Arthur and Sir Harry, Sir Harry and Sir Hew,
> Doodle, doodle, doodle, cock a doodle doo!
> Sir Arthur was a gallant knight, but for the other two,
> Doodle, doodle, doodle, cock a doodle doo!

Canning was having a short holiday at Hinckley when the Convention of Cintra was concluded, and he was absent from the meeting of the Cabinet at which it was approved, but he shared to the full the popular resentment against it. He wrote to Perceval:

> . . . The mischief to result from it appears from every point of view, and from every quarter of the world.
> Portugal must hate us for the article giving up their plunder. Instead of hailing us as deliverers, they must consider us as having interfered only to sanction and secure French robbery. By no other probable combination of circumstances could the French not only have kept what they had stolen, but have carried it out of the country unmolested. . . . Could the malice of all our enemies combined suggest a more shameful and ridiculous exhibition, a more degrading caricature of our maritime power than to see it employed in the transport of seventeen or eighteen thousand enemies—half to fight against Spain, and half to fight against the King of Sweden? [1]

Canning's annoyance is easily explicable, for upon him and his department fell the task of dealing with the remonstrances of the Portuguese and other allies. Indeed, the whole transaction brings out very clearly the difficulties that confront a British Foreign Secretary in time of war. He is responsible for the smooth working of the arrangements with his country's allies, and yet military decisions are continually being taken upon which he

[1] Walpole, Sir Spencer: *The Life of the Right Hon. Spencer Perceval*, vol. I, pp. 295–296.

is often not consulted, with the result that he is left to explain away as best he can a *fait accompli* to indignant allied diplomats. On the other hand, there was much to be said for the Convention of Cintra, which, incidentally was condemned by the French Emperor as roundly as by Canning, though with considerably more justification. In compelling the French to evacuate Portugal it struck a very severe blow at the whole Napoleonic system, for it opened the Portuguese ports to British shipping, and it rendered more remote than ever the hope of striking effectively at British maritime supremacy.

Meanwhile, a joint overture had been received from Napoleon and the Tsar, made with the intention of placing upon Great Britain the responsibility for the continuance of the war. Napoleon and Alexander had another meeting, their last in this world, at Erfurt at the end of September, 1808, and outwardly the French Emperor had never seemed so powerful. " To all appearance . . . the sun of Austerlitz rode high as ever in the heavens. As Napoleon held high court with Alexander in those early autumn days in the old Hanseatic town, whilst kings and sages bent before him, there seemed no end to his greatness. The Spanish insurrection seemed but as the rumbling of a distant volcano; the *malaise* of Austria no more than a cloud upon the horizon; to the east the sky remained rich with promise, and he tried once more to bewitch Alexander with the magic of the gorgeous vision." [1] All the princes and statesmen of Europe were there in token of submission to their conqueror. The scene was magnificently staged, but there was one notable absentee, namely Britain, and in the end her absence was to mean more than the presence of all the other Powers.

In spite of Napoleon's efforts to dazzle the Tsar it soon became clear that Alexander was not in so complacent a mood as he had been at Tilsit. The Russian monarch refused to be a party to any threats to Austria, and the French Emperor retaliated by insisting upon the postponement of the partition of the Ottoman Empire, which had been adumbrated at their earlier meeting. Outwardly, however, the alliance between France and Russia was preserved, and a secret convention was drawn up which assigned Finland and the Danubian Principalities to Russia in return for the Tsar's recognition of Joseph Bonaparte as King of Spain and a promise of help to France in case she was attacked by Austria. The last

[1] Cecil, A.: *Metternich*, p. 48.

act of the two monarchs was to send a note to George III summoning him to make peace, with the object, as already mentioned, of holding Great Britain responsible for the prolongation of the war.

To this message Canning replied expressing the Government's desire to open negotiations, provided that all parties were included, but that Great Britain would not treat unless her Spanish allies were admitted to the conference. Napoleon retorted that the Spaniards were rebels, and he could not recognize them. In these circumstances it was clear that no settlement was possible, and Canning wrote to the Tsar, expressing his master's regret that Alexander should have sanctioned

> an usurpation unparalleled in the history of the world. . . . If these be the principles to which the Emperor of Russia has inviolably attached himself . . . deeply does His Majesty lament a determination by which the sufferings of Europe must be aggravated and prolonged. But not to His Majesty is to be attributed the continuance of the calamities of war, by the disappointment of all hope of such a peace as would be compatible with justice and honour.

This despatch was dictated to his young cousin, Stratford, who was now launched on his official career, and who wrote of the occasion years afterwards, " I cannot easily forget the first diplomatic dinner at which I was present under his auspices, and still less the composition, which I took down as he uttered it, of his once celebrated reply to the Emperor Alexander's offer of mediation for peace between England and France." [1]

While this exchange of notes was taking place the Spanish revolt was spreading, and it was having unfortunate repercussions in England. The outcry which followed the conclusion of the Convention of Cintra had resulted in the appointment of Moore to the supreme command of the British forces. He seems to have owed his promotion to the King, and with the exception of Sir Arthur Wellesley was the best general the country possessed, though his innate pessimism hardly suited him for the task by which he was now faced. Castlereagh, although not very enthusiastic with regard to Moore's appointment, supported him with commendable loyalty; for when he was taking his leave of that nobleman, almost his last words were, " Remember, my Lord, I protest against the expedition, and foretell its failure." When this

---

[1] Lane-Poole, S., *op. cit.*, vol. I, p. 30.

observation was repeated by Castlereagh to his colleagues in the Cabinet, the Foreign Secretary exclaimed, " Good God; and do you really mean to say that you allowed a man entertaining such feelings with regard to the expedition to go out and command it? " [1] The appointment of Moore, and the circumstances attaching to it, were among the more important causes of the quarrel between Canning and Castlereagh.

The position was further complicated by the mistrust which soon made itself felt between Moore and Frere. The diplomat was as much inclined to excessive optimism as the soldier was the reverse, and he firmly believed, as Moore did not, that in co-operation with the Spaniards lay the one hope of success. Canning's instructions on this point were precise:

> You will recollect, that the army which has been appropriated by His Majesty to the defence of Spain and Portugal, is not merely a considerable part of the disposable force of this country, it is, in fact, the British army. The country has no other force disposable. It may, by a great effort, reinforce the army for an adequate purpose; but another army it has not to send. The proposals, therefore, which are made, somewhat too lightly, for appending parts of this force, sometimes to one of the Spanish armies, sometimes to another, and the facility with which its services are called for, wherever the exigency of the moment happens to press, are by no means suited to the nature of the force itself, or consonant to the views with which His Majesty has consented to employ it in Spain. You are already apprised by my former despatch (enclosing a copy of General Moore's instructions) that the British army must be kept together under its own commander, must act as one body for some distinct object, and on some settled plan. . . . The part assigned to the British army in the combined operation must be settled with Sir John Moore, and he will be found not unambitious of that in which he may be opposed most directly to the enemy.

These are hardly the words of a man who, as has been alleged, wished to place the British forces under the control of the Spanish authorities, or who was desirous of tying the hands of Moore, however much he may have disapproved of his original appointment.

[1] Stapleton, A. G.: *George Canning and His Times*, p. 160.

In spite, however, of instructions from home the friction between Frere and Moore increased rather than diminished. Napier pours scorn upon the diplomat as " a person of mere scholastic attainment ", which, of course, was enough to damn him in the eyes of any professional soldier, but in more than one passage the historian of the Peninsular War admits that Spanish enthusiasm was great, so that it is difficult to resist the conclusion that it was Moore's own pessimism that was the main cause of his failure to co-operate with his allies. Like so many regular soldiers, he was discouraged by the absence of all that he had been accustomed to associate with the prosecution of a successful war, while his remark to Castlereagh shows that he had no enthusiasm for his task. Frere is unlikely ever to be accorded full justice, for there is always a tendency for the soldier to receive all the sympathy, and the civilian all the blame, at any rate at the hands of posterity, for what has gone wrong. There were faults on both sides, but it would appear that Frere was more sinned against than sinning.

Actually, the military situation was extremely favourable when Moore assumed command on October 7th, 1808. The Spanish victory at Bailen and the evacuation of Portugal had thrown the French upon the defensive, and Moore's instructions were to co-operate with the Spanish armies that were holding the line of the Ebro. Owing to circumstances, such as the difficulty of securing the necessary transport, for which it is only fair to say that he was in no way to blame, Moore advanced extremely slowly, and by the middle of November he had not got any farther than Salamanca. By that time the whole position had changed for the worse. Napoleon himself had undertaken the conduct of operations in the Peninsula, and French troops were pouring into Spain at an alarming rate. By November 23rd the three main Spanish armies had been beaten, and on the 4th of the following month the French Emperor entered Madrid. Moore spent four whole weeks at Salamanca, where the news of these successive disasters reached him, and he then determined to make an attack upon the French lines of communication. What followed, namely Moore's victory and death at Corunna, is too well known to require recapitulation, but British gallantry in the face of tremendous odds cannot disguise the fact that Britain was too late with her aid. Moore, in short, failed to co-operate with the Spaniards, and for that failure he was blamed by Canning.

Moore's retreat, and the failure of the Spanish resistance, led

G

to Frere's withdrawal into private life, where he placed succeeding generations under a heavy debt by his translations of Aristophanes, but before he left Spain he negotiated, on Canning's instructions, a treaty of alliance with the *junta central* by which both parties agreed never to make peace with Napoleon except by common consent. Frere was succeeded by the Marquess Wellesley, a brother of Sir Arthur, as British representative in Spain, but as some considerable time elapsed before Wellesley arrived at his post the Opposition endeavoured to hold Canning responsible for the delay. In point of fact, it was occasioned by the nobleman's desire to take his mistress with him, a course to which his wife was so strongly opposed that she even communicated with Canning on the subject. The Foreign Secretary could hardly give the real reason from the Treasury Bench, and his silence was interpreted to his disadvantage. Finally, on April 2nd, 1809, Sir Arthur Wellesley was appointed commander-in-chief in the Peninsula ; a choice which had Canning's whole-hearted support, and which events were fully to justify.

As may be imagined, the Opposition was also not slow to take advantage of the French successes to criticize the Government, and on February 24th, 1809, Ponsonby and Tierney had moved " that it is indispensably necessary that this House should inquire into the causes, conduct, and events of the late war in Spain ". In replying, Canning defended both Moore and Frere, and in particular he poured scorn upon the Whig argument that " before assistance had been given to Spain, it ought to have been ascertained whether or not the Spaniards were instigated by the monks ; whether they were encouraged by the higher ranks, or animated by Popery ; whether they were wedded to their ancient institutions, or disposed to shake off the oppression of their former government ; to abjure the errors of a delusive religion, or prepared to forswear the Pope and the Grand Inquisitor ". Canning declared that " these were questions better suited for the employment of a period of learned leisure than for the hours of action ", and continued :

> The policy of His Majesty's Government was different ; they felt that the Spanish nation wanted other and more aids than lectures on municipal institutions ; they were content that a British army should act in Spain, though the Grand Inquisitor might have been at the head of the Spanish armies ;

though the people might have been attached to their ancient monarchy, and with one hand upheld Ferdinand VII, whilst with the other they worshipped the Lady of the Pillar. To assist the patriotic efforts of the Spanish nation was the sole object, and they did not wish to inflict upon that country any change as the price of that assistance. God forbid! that we should ever be so intolerant as to make a conformity to our own opinions the price of an assistance to others in their efforts for national independence; or to carry the sword in one hand, and what we might choose to call the Rights of Man in the other!

Canning's speech was rendered the more memorable in that the latter part of it was frequently interrupted by cries of " Fire ", but Sheridan reassured the Foreign Secretary by whispering across the table that it was not the Houses of Parliament but Drury Lane Theatre, in which he was himself heavily involved, that was on fire. When Canning sat down Windham rose to reply, but Lord Temple suggested the propriety of adjourning the debate " in consequence of the extent of calamity which the event just communicated to the House would bring upon a respectable individual, a member of that House ". Sheridan, however, observed that " whatever might be the extent of the individual calamity to himself he did not consider it of a nature worthy to interrupt their proceedings on so great a national question ". The debate, therefore, continued until three o'clock the following morning, when the House divided, and the Government had a majority of ninety-three.[1]

It was at this time that Canning took the first step in a course of action which has ever since been the occasion of controversy, and which was to place him under a cloud for several years. The growing animosity between Castlereagh and himself has already been noted, and in all probability it had its origin even earlier in Canning's jealousy of his colleague's rapid rise, which his rival ascribed to family influence. Castlereagh was one of the finest products of the Anglo-Irish aristocracy of the eighteenth century; he had proved a useful Chief Secretary at the time of the Union with Ireland; and he was rightly regarded as sound and trustworthy; but, in marked contrast with Canning, he was a very poor speaker. " At his best he was sensible and pedestrian; at his worst he was dull, rambling, and even ridiculous . . . it was

[1] Therry, R., op. cit., vol. II, pp. 363–378.

sometimes Castlereagh's fate in later years, when he particularly wished to impress the House of Commons, to draw from it titters of merriment." [1]   On one occasion he implored honourable members " not to turn their backs on themselves ", while on another he referred to " the Herculean labour of the honourable member, who will find himself quite disappointed when he has at last brought forth his Hercules ".

It was, thus, character and courage that had brought Castlereagh to the fore.   The latter quality he betrayed not only in his earlier days when he tried to separate two fighting mastiffs, but also when he faced assassination in Dublin in 1798.   Yet, at this stage of their political association, Castlereagh and Canning had little in common in spite of their reverence for their dead master, Pitt.

The unfortunate result of Moore's campaign precipitated a crisis, for by the spring of 1809 Canning's very limited stock of patience was at an end, and on March 24th he wrote to the Prime Minister tendering his resignation : he could work with Castlereagh no longer.   Portland showed the letter to the King, and they both agreed that as it was out of the question to allow Canning to resign Castlereagh should himself be transferred to some other office.   To this Canning agreed, and also to the suggestion that nothing more should be said about the matter for the moment in view of the international situation.   Castlereagh, however, was not informed of what was intended, for Earl Camden, who had originally been deputed to approach him, had also been asked by the Prime Minister to postpone the disclosure, though this fact was unknown to Canning.   Why Portland could not have spoken to Castlereagh himself is by no means clear, and as Head of the Government it was certainly his duty to have done so, but he seems to have shrunk from what was undoubtedly an invidious task, and his timidity was to have very serious consequences a few months later.

The event which provided Portland with a reason, or at any rate an excuse, for not immediately reconstituting his Cabinet was the appearance of Austria once more in the field as the enemy of Napoleon.   There were several explanations of this action.   The French Emperor had foolishly neglected the advice of Frederick the Great never to " maltreat an enemy by halves ", while the British successes in the Peninsula, combined with the growth of national feeling in Germany, seemed to render the moment

[1] Lockhart, J. G.: *The Peacemakers, 1814-1815*, p. 237.

opportune. Nevertheless, there was little previous negotiation between Vienna and London, and Austria and Britain were nominally at war. When, however, Francis II drew the sword the British Government did all it could to help him. The cost of the war in the Peninsula was a serious drain upon the Exchequer, but Canning managed to send £250,000 in silver bars to Trieste. The King, not unreasonably, insisted that before any actual help was given peace should be formally made, and the ensuing delay prevented any real co-operation. Napoleon, too, was still invincible on the field of battle, and by the beginning of July the resistance of Austria was at an end : Vienna had fallen and Wagram had been fought, so that when, on the 29th of that month, Canning acknowledged the receipt of the Austrian ratification of peace with Great Britain, he received it " accompanied by the afflicting intelligence of the armistice concluded between the Austrian and French armies ".

While Napoleon was beating Austria to her knees the Portland Government was giving proof that it had inherited from its predecessor that partiality for small expeditions which has been the cause of so many disappointments in numerous wars. First of all, 15,000 troops were assembled for a campaign against Naples, and, together with a contingent of Sicilians, they commenced operations early in June. All that was accomplished, however, was the capture of the islands of Ischia and Procida, and the castle of Scylla, after which the expedition was withdrawn. The defeat of Austria, and the abortive attempt against Naples, were to some extent offset by Sir Arthur Wellesley's victory, for which he was created Viscount Wellington, at Talavera at the end of July, but this in its turn was thrown into the shade by the failure of the Walcheren expedition.

The strategy was sound, for it was to capture Antwerp, and had this been effected the consequences for the whole of Europe would have been incalculable. Nor was the expedition prepared on any niggardly scale, for it consisted of thirty-five ships-of-the-line and nearly 40,000 troops, but in all else the fates were against it from the start. It sailed on the very day on which arrived the news of the armistice between France and Austria. There was a complete lack of medical stores and of sanitary precautions against the notoriously unhealthy climate of Walcheren, which was to be its base. Above all, the King had insisted upon the military command being given to Lord Chatham, Pitt's elder brother, while the

fleet was under the orders of Sir Richard Strachan.   What ensued
was well described in a contemporary ballad :

> Great Chatham with his sabre drawn
> Stood waiting for Sir Richard Strachan;
> Sir Richard, longing to be at 'em;
> Stood waiting for the Earl of Chatham.

Chatham had been found wanting in various capacities over a
period of years, and he was one of the most indolent men alive—
the " late " Earl of Chatham he was generally termed.   An officer
on his staff wrote, " We should not have known that there was a
commander-in-chief had we not seen in his garden, twelve miles
away from our front, two turtles sprawling on their backs for his
dinner.   He never came down until two o'clock in the day." [1]
Such a man was peculiarly ill-fitted to conduct a campaign in which
rapidity of action was essential, and so it is not surprising that the
Walcheren expedition was a failure, costly alike both in lives and
in the national reputation.

This catastrophe precipitated the final breach between Castlereagh and Canning.   The Foreign Secretary, more than ever convinced of his colleague's inadequacy at the War Office, now
demanded that the promise made to him in the spring should be
fulfilled.   The Prime Minister once again hesitated to commit
himself, but on September 6th he told Canning not only that his
health necessitated his own resignation, but also that nothing had
been said to Castlereagh of the proposed change in his position.
On learning this Canning at once resigned, and so did Portland,
who was really far from well ; two days later Castlereagh adopted
the same course, and a political crisis of exceptional importance
was clearly at hand : for Canning it was also to have an unfortunate personal aspect.

[1] Quoted by Fletcher, C. R. L.: *An Introductory History of England*, vol.
IV, p. 264.

CHAPTER V

UNDER A CLOUD

THE fall of the Portland administration was almost immediately followed by Castlereagh's enlightenment regarding the negotiations that were afoot, of which he had previously been in complete ignorance: he now heard that Canning, so long ago as the previous March had been complaining of him to the Prime Minister, and he was not unnaturally indignant at what he considered to be an unworthy intrigue against him by a colleague behind his back. He thereupon sent the following letter to Canning:

St. James's Square, Sept. 19.

SIR,

It is unnecessary for me to enter into any detailed statement of the circumstances which preceded the recent resignations. It is enough for me, with a view to the immediate object of this letter, to state, that it appears a proposition had been agitated, without any communication with me, for my removal from the War Department; and that you, towards the close of last session, having urged a decision upon this question, with the alternative of your seceding from the Government, procured a positive promise from the Duke of Portland (the execution of which you afterwards considered yourself entitled to enforce), that such removal should be carried into effect. Notwithstanding this promise, by which I consider you pronounced it unfit that I should remain charged with the conduct of the war, and by which my situation as a minister of the Crown was made dependent upon your will and pleasure, you continued to sit in the same Cabinet with me, and to leave me not only in the persuasion that I possessed your confidence and support as a colleague, but you allowed me, in breach of every possible principle of good faith, both public and private, though thus virtually superseded, to originate and proceed in the execution of a new enterprise of the most arduous and important nature, with your apparent concurrence, and ostensible approbation.

You were fully aware that, if my situation in the Government had been disclosed to me, I could not have submitted to remain one moment in office, without the entire abandonment of my private honour and public duty. You knew I was deceived, and you continued to deceive me.

I am aware it may be said, which I am ready to acknowledge, that when you pressed for a decision for my removal, you also pressed for its disclosure, and that it was resisted by the Duke of Portland, and some members of the Government, supposed to be my friends. But I never can admit that you have a right to make use of such a plea, in justification of an act affecting my honour; nor that the sentiments of others could justify an acquiescence in such a delusion on your part, who had yourself felt and stated its unfairness. Nor can I admit that the head of any administration, or any supposed friends (whatever may be their motives), can authorize or sanction any man in such a course of long and persevering deception. For, were I to admit such a principle, my honour and character would be from that moment in the discretion of persons wholly unauthorized, and known to you to be unauthorized, to act for me in such a case. It was, therefore, your act and your conduct which deceived me; and it is impossible for me to acquiesce in being placed in a situation by you, which no man of honour could knowingly submit to, nor patiently suffer himself to be betrayed into, without forfeiting that character.

I have no right, as a public man, to resent your demanding, upon public grounds, my removal from the particular office I have held, or even from the administration, as a condition of your continuing a member of the Government. But I have a distinct right to expect that a proposition, justifiable in itself, shall not be executed in an unjustifiable manner, and at the expense of my honour and reputation. And I consider that you were bound, at least, to avail yourself of the same alternative, namely your own resignation, to take you out of the predicament of practising such a deceit towards me, which you did exercise in demanding a decision for my removal.

Under these circumstances, I must require that satisfaction from you, to which I feel myself entitled to lay claim.

I have the honour to be, Sir,

Your obedient humble servant,

CASTLEREAGH.

This letter covered three sheets of folio, and when, on opening it, Canning caught sight of the last few lines, he is said to have exclaimed, " I had rather fight than read it, by God ! " He at once sent the following reply:

> *Gloucester Lodge,*
> *September* 20, 1809
> (*half past ten A.M.*).
>
> My Lord,
> The tone and purport of your Lordship's letter, which I have this moment received, of course precludes any other answer, on my part, to the misapprehensions and misrepresentations, with which it abounds, than that I will cheerfully give to your Lordship the satisfaction that you require.
> I have the honour to be, my Lord,
> Your Lordship's most obedient humble servant,
> Geo. Canning.

The duel itself took place near the Telegraph on Putney Heath, within sight of the house where Pitt died—surely a melancholy reflection for both parties—at six o'clock on September 21st, 1809. Castlereagh had Lord Yarmouth [1] as his second, and Canning was attended by Charles Ellis. After taking their ground they fired by signal, but missed. After the first fire the seconds endeavoured to compose the matter, though without success, and they then declared that after a second shot, whatever might be the result, they would not be parties to any further proceedings. At the second fire Canning was slightly wounded in the thigh, and the duel came to an end.

Fuller details were given in a letter which Joseph Planta, at that time *précis* writer at the Foreign Office, sent to Stratford Canning, who was then in Constantinople:

> Your cousin has delayed the mail for these few days, in order to give him and myself time to write you some account of the extraordinary and painful occurrences which have lately taken place. They are briefly as follows. Your cousin finding the greatest difficulty in forming such an administration as he thinks the present state of the country

[1] Afterwards sixth Marquess of Hertford. He was the original of the Marquis of Steyne of *Vanity Fair*, and of the Marquess of Monmouth of *Coningsby*.

requires has offered his resignation. In the meantime, in consequence of transactions which you will see more fully detailed in a paper which I send you, Lord Castlereagh wrote such a letter, and sent such a challenge to your cousin, as it was impossible for him (in his opinion) to decline. A duel has in consequence taken place, in which Charles Ellis was your cousin's second, and Lord Yarmouth second to Lord Castlereagh. The parties fired once without effect, but in the second fire your cousin was wounded in his left thigh. The ball entered about eight inches below the hip, and, taking an outward direction, passed out again on the left side of the hinder part of the thigh. The wound, though a smart one, is, thank God, by no means dangerous; and your cousin is doing as well as he possibly can. The duel took place on Thursday morning, 21 September; it is now ten days since that, and the wound is healing very fast. Howe attends your cousin.

. . . The challenge was received on the Wednesday and . . . the duel took place the next morning. The most profound secrecy was observed on Wednesday on the subject, and neither Hammond nor Bagot was made acquainted with it. Your cousin had first applied to Henry Wellesley [1] to be his second, as he knew Charles Ellis was particularly engaged doing the honours of Claremont to the Queen. As Henry Wellesley could not, however, from some particular reasons, go out with your cousin, he (H. Wy.) went immediately down to Claremont, and as soon as the Queen left him, C. Ellis came up to town. After seeing your cousin he went to Lord Yarmouth, and did everything in his power, as from himself, to explain the matter to Lord Y. so as to prevent the meeting from taking place. Lord Y. seemed very willing to make up matters if possible, but Lord C. was inflexible. At one o'clock in the morning, therefore, Charles Ellis came to your cousin's at Brompton, and found him fast asleep; he waked him and told him that the duel must take place the (same) morning. Your cousin then turned round and went to sleep again till five o'clock, when he got up, and he and Mr. Ellis proceeded to Putney Heath. In what a tranquil and delightful state of mind he must have been to have slept quietly at such a time. I should not enter

[1] Later Lord Cowley.

so much into particulars with anybody but you; but to you every particular I know will be interesting.

Ross [1] and myself were walking quietly down to the office the morning of the 21st when we were struck dumb with the news as related to us in Downing Street by a person belonging to Lord Castlereagh's office. We hastened to Bruton Street, but not finding your cousin there, we immediately proceeded to Brompton (where he has bought a place called Gloucester Lodge), and there we found him stretched on a sofa attended by Charles Ellis. He received us with the same kind smile which is almost always on his countenance, and the whole scene, together with the remembrance of the danger which we had escaped (for Howe says that one inch to the left would have been almost instant death from the fracture of the principal bone of the thigh) affected me so, that I was almost in tears. Ross was immediately sent down to Mrs. Canning, and I remained at Gloucester Lodge to copy the letters and other papers which he thought necessary to send to his friends on the occasion. I have been in attendance every day since, and it is from Gloucester Lodge that I write. Mrs. Canning arrived in town on the Friday night, and has, of course, remained here in constant attendance on her husband ever since. I like her very much. I was never acquainted with her before.

This famous duel has assumed so important a place in English political history that it is not easy to arrive at a final judgment. The King was annoyed with both combatants, and in a letter to Liverpool he said it " had occasioned him not more serious concern than surprise, that two persons holding the situations of Secretaries of State, and still in possession of the seals of office, should have been guilty of so total a dereliction of duty as to violate the laws which they were bound to maintain by the authority vested in them ".[2]

The first reflection which must inevitably occur is that the two antagonists were both Irishmen who preferred to fight first and enter into explanations afterwards. Moreover it is difficult to

[1] Tyrell Ross, private secretary to Canning at the Foreign Office, 1807–1809.
[2] Yonge, C. D., *op. cit.*, vol. I, p. 295.

estimate the effect that would have been produced upon contemporary public opinion by the refusal of either party to fight once the dispute had arisen. Nevertheless, on the major issue Castlereagh was surely in the right. There was, indeed, nothing improper in the earlier behaviour of Canning, or even of Portland, but once the King's consent to the proposed change had been obtained, the Prime Minister should have informed Castlereagh of the course he intended to adopt, even though the transfer of office was not to take place for some months. The real culprit was thus Portland, and his hesitation may well have been due to his growing infirmities, but some blame also belongs to Canning for not making sure that Castlereagh was told of what was intended. Unfortunately, at this period of their lives the two men were far from being on good terms, and, so long as Castlereagh was removed from the War Office, Canning does not seem to have cared a jot what were his feelings in the matter. Indeed, the only really satisfactory aspect of the whole business is the fact that the duel left no lasting ill-feeling between the two statesmen, and was, in reality, the beginning of a reconciliation.[1]

The resignation of Portland was followed by some lively intrigues for the succession. Canning and Perceval both aspired to it, and as neither of them would serve under the other, it was clear that a further crisis was at hand. The surviving members of the Cabinet met on September 18th, and advised the inclusion of Grenville and Grey in the Government, but those noblemen proved unwilling to co-operate. All this time Canning was vehemently pressing his own claims alike upon the King and his colleagues, but he suffered from several considerable handicaps. In the first place he was temporarily incapacitated by his wound; then he was suspect to the King on account of his advocacy of the Roman Catholic claims; while, above all, not a few of the ministers resented his superior attitude and his recent behaviour to Castlereagh. Accordingly, it is hardly surprising that the prize went to Perceval, who was the senior in any case, and one of Canning's first acts on his recovery was to resign the seals of his office as Foreign Secretary.

His own account of the circumstances which led up to his resignation and to the duel is contained in a letter which he wrote to Bootle Wilbraham before the end of the year:

[1] *Cf.* also the Memoir preceding Therry's edition of Canning's speeches, *op. cit.*, vol. I, pp. 59–83.

(Private)   *Hinckley,*
                                        December 19, 1809.

MY DEAR BOOTLE,

    Your letter found me here—escaped at length from
the plagues and turmoils which attended and followed my
retreat from Office. It used to be difficult to get in—at all
times; but I never knew that getting out again was a matter
of so much difficulty before.

    I am very much gratified by the judgment which you pass
upon the late transactions. You conjecture aright, that I
have cause to complain of some of the Members of the
present Government: of Perceval pre-eminently; whose
conduct has been such as appears to my mind, irreconcilable
with any principle of good faith, publick or private.[1] He
well knew that I should resign upon finding that nothing had
been done towards performing the engagement made to me
by the Duke of P. (in the King's name) for a change in the
War Department. The week before that change ought to
have taken place, he led me by repeated letters and by an
effusion of confidence on his part, which at length extorted
a return of confidence on mine—to a disclosure of my opinion
as to the best mode of constituting a Government in the
event, then not immediately in contemplation, of the Duke of
Portland's retirement. Having got these opinions from me
thus in confidence, he asked my leave to communicate them
to three persons, Lord Harrowby, Lord Liverpool, and his
brother Lord Arden—for the purpose (as he said) of con-
sulting with them whether he could not consent to some
arrangement by which he should put himself out of the way.
And, then without any further permission from me, he communicated them generally to all the world:—for the express
purpose of leading all the world to believe that my resignation
was founded, not on the Duke of Portland's breach of
promise, but on the refusal of my Colleagues to adopt my
opinions as to the formation of a Government. To bring this
delusion to bear it was necessary that the D. of P. should
resign at the same moment with me—and accordingly he was
advised so to time his resignation, and I heard of it for the
first time from him at the same moment at which he (the D.

[1] Perceval's side of the case may be found in Sir Spencer Walpole's
biography, vol. I, p. 347 *et seq.*

of Portland) announced to me that the arrangement of the War Department was not to be executed.

The poor D. of P. was not aware till afterwards of the mischief that he was doing—and of the malicious construction to which this coincidence of our resignations would and was intended to give rise. When he became aware of it afterwards he would willingly have retracted his resignation. But then it was too late to remedy the mischief, and besides in his state of health, I would not have precipitated the event of his resignation by a day, and would not ask him to continue in Office by a day beyond the period at which his own mind had been made up to retire.

From the time when my resignation became publick by the duel, the Government newspapers were let loose upon me with charges of ambition, etc., and under cover of these charges P. canvassed every new person whom he invited to take office, and every man in office whom he purported to retain it—by a communication of the substance of our confidential correspondence—and in many instances of the correspondence itself; representing to everybody the question treated—in that correspondence, and not the question of the change in the War Department, as the ground of my resignation. After stating this to you I need hardly add, in answer to your question, that with P. in his present situation my return to office is impossible.

But further and on publick grounds I must see reason to be assured that the Government is more equal to the task which it has to perform—that it is constructed and conducted on principles better calculated to meet the dangers and difficulties of the times, than I found it to be, while I was a member of it; before I can venture again upon the fearful responsibility, which belongs to the conduct of a department in administration. The details on this subject are not to be explained in a letter: but I am confident I can satisfy you that mere Office, on the terms on which it would be to be held without some such improvement in the principle of the Government itself, would neither be desirable for my own credit or interest, nor for any service that I could hope to render to the country.

On the other hand, with such improvement, I feel no obstacle to acting with many, with most, of the present Ministers on some future occasion. But that occasion it is not for me to hasten—nor shall I from any apprehension of retarding it, forbear from taking that part in Parliament which really and *bona fide* I may think right. That my notion of what is right certainly will not lead me to form any junction at present with any party in opposition. So you may be quite at ease as to "the Talents and Lord Sidmouth", though after the offer made by the Government to Lord Grenville and Lord Grey there is nothing of principle or consistency to prevent me from forming a junction with them, if I liked it, but I do not. My intention is to act in the House of Commons independently of any of the existing parties, to support the Government where I think them right, to uphold of course the general system upon which this or any other Government must stand against the Reformers, but to oppose the Government without scruple or hesitation where I think them wrong; not counting the company in which I may find myself on such divisions, but certainly not suffering myself to be deterred by the foolish fear of being seen in such company from giving effect to my opinion by my vote whenever I think it right to do so.

I hope this account will quiet your apprehensions; and I hope it will meet your wishes and opinions. Let me know if it does—or what you would have wished it otherwise.

My wound is entirely healed, and I feel no inconvenience remaining from it.

Remember me to Mrs. W. Bootle and believe me,

Ever very sincerely yours,

G. C.

P.S.—I ought not to omit to tell you that whatever reason I may have to complain of the conduct of some of my Colleagues, I have every reason to be satisfied with the unvarying kindness of the King.[1]

So ended Canning's first period of membership of the Cabinet. The two and a half years during which he had presided over the Foreign Office were among the most critical in the history of Great Britain, and it was in no small measure due to him that they were not among the most disastrous. When he took office Napoleon's star was still in the ascendant; when he gave up the

seals it was, in the eyes of no less experienced an observer than
Talleyrand, beginning to wane.   It was Canning who had snatched
the Danish and Portuguese fleets from under the very guns of the
grande armée, and thus prevented the seat of war from being
transferred to Kent and Surrey; it was Canning who had concluded the alliance with Spain, which made the campaign in that
country the running sore of the French Empire; and it was
Canning who, by his negotiations with Miranda, had ensured
that if France did obtain possession of Spain, it should at any
rate be Spain without the Indies.   He has been acclaimed with
justice as the disciple of Pitt, but during this earlier period at the
Foreign Office he rather displayed the characteristics of Chatham.
There was the same appreciation of the issues at stake, the same
promptitude of action, and, above all, the same refusal to despair
even when the outlook was blackest.   Nor is it any exaggeration
to say that he adopted the line of policy that within five years
transferred Napoleon from the Tuileries to Elba.   The second
period of his reign at the Foreign Office was so remarkable that
it has only too often blinded posterity to the fact that what he
accomplished between 1807 and 1809 would by itself have been
sufficient to give Canning a high place among British Foreign
Secretaries.

Unhappily, there was another side of the picture.   However
great were the services that Canning rendered to his country
during his first tenure of office as Foreign Secretary, there can be
no doubt that the circumstances connected with his resignation
only served to strengthen the suspicion with which he was already
regarded in many quarters.   Indeed, it would probably be true
to say that the autumn of 1809 was the high-water mark of his
unpopularity, and the reason is not far to seek.

The reputation for intrigue which he had already acquired was
enormously enhanced by the circumstances of his duel with
Castlereagh.   It was not so much that the duel itself outraged
public opinion, for that particular method of settling a political
difference was the custom of the time, as the chain of events that
led up to it.   The full facts were known only to a few, and Portland's death within a few weeks of his resignation prevented
Canning and his friends, from motives of common decency, from
placing the blame where it really belonged, namely upon the
shoulders of the dead Prime Minister.   Such being the case, it is
not surprising that in the House of Commons, and in political

circles outside, Canning should have been regarded as a man, brilliant without doubt, but with whom it was impossible to work as a colleague. To Sidmouth and his supporters, who had never forgiven his treatment of them when they were in office, were now added Castlereagh and his following, and together they formed a very large section of the Tory party.

While Canning was only partly to blame for the series of events which led up to the duel, his behaviour during the negotiations that followed Portland's resignation is very much open to criticism. Like Lord Randolph Churchill later in the century, Canning adopted the attitude that no Tory administration could be formed without him, and he found his Goschen, first in Perceval, and then in Liverpool. It was said of him at the time that he never made a speech without making an enemy, and he could not resist a witticism, no matter how much harm it might do him. Malmesbury, although a friend and an admirer, referred to Canning's " dangerous habit of quizzing, which he cannot restrain ". There is, indeed, a certain type of statesman, generally of the greatest genius, who, during the earlier part of his career, takes no heed of the feelings of those whom he sweeps aside in his climb to office, but, when the prize of leadership is almost within his grasp, it is always those upon whom he has trampled who rise up and prevent him seizing it. Such was the fate of Canning, and although he did gain the promised land in the end, he was first of all doomed to spend many years in the wilderness.

In addition to these personal drawbacks, there was also his advocacy of Catholic Emancipation to add to his unpopularity. It is difficult, at this distance of time, to realize the bitterness which the question roused at the beginning of last century. Canning took the line that the existing disabilities upon Roman Catholics had been imposed, not on account of their religion, but of their politics, and now that Jacobitism was dead the time had come to repeal them. The adoption of such a policy brought Canning at once into conflict with the King, who held that he was bound by his coronation oath to refuse his consent to any such reform, and he precipitated, as has been shown, the fall of two administrations on these grounds. George, if short-sighted and stubborn, was at any rate honest, which is probably more than can be said for the attitude of the majority of those who opposed Canning on this question. Prejudice, not principle, though it may masquerade as such, too often sways the rank-and-file of great

H

parties, and so it was on this occasion. All the Tory strongholds held out against any concession to Roman Catholics. The Anglican clergy, the universities, and the country clergy, who had been drinking healths to a Roman Catholic King over the water not so many years before, were solidly anti-Catholic, and their leaders, seeing from what quarter the wind was blowing, were content to follow where they ought to have led. Canning, however, never faltered in his beliefs, though it is clear that in these critical years of his life such an attitude only increased the by no means inconsiderable number of his enemies.

Seven years were to elapse after his resignation of the Foreign Secretaryship before Canning again held office, and eighteen before he attained to that of Prime Minister, for which he had unsuccessfully striven with Perceval in the autumn of 1809. During the period he was passed in the race for promotion, not only by Perceval, but also by Liverpool and Castlereagh. Had Canning consented to serve under Perceval when Portland resigned he would almost certainly have become Prime Minister on Perceval's murder three years later, while had he entered Liverpool's Cabinet as Foreign Secretary in 1812 he, not Castlereagh, would have played the predominant part in the settlement of Europe when Napoleon fell. Pride forbade him to join any administration save on his own terms, with the result that Liverpool, " the Arch-Mediocrity " as Disraeli so unjustly called him, became Prime Minister, and Castlereagh represented Great Britain at the Congress of Vienna; while the irony of the whole situation was that when at last Canning re-entered the Cabinet in 1816 it was in the comparatively subordinate capacity of President of the Board of Control.

Of the circumstances which thus deprived the country of his services for so long Canning was, as we have seen, partly the cause and partly the victim. For his advocacy of Catholic Emancipation in the teeth of the most violent opposition, there can be nothing but praise; his duel with Castlereagh was certainly unfortunate, but the main responsibility for it rested with Portland; while for his scant regard for the feelings of others he was himself to blame. From the point of view of the country as a whole there can be no doubt it was a great misfortune that during seven important years one of the ablest of contemporary statesmen should have been absent from the national counsels.

In spite of his work at the Foreign Office, and of the political crisis in which he played so large a part, it was at this stage of his career that Canning gave further proof of the importance which he attached to the growing influence of the Press. His work in connection with *The Anti-Jacobin* had already earned him the distinction of being one of the first British statesmen to realize what might be accomplished in this direction, and he had more than once impressed upon Pitt the necessity of providing an anti-dote to the virulent attacks of the Whig papers. In 1809 this need was even greater than it had been twelve years before, for in 1802 the first number of *The Edinburgh Review* had made its appearance, and its influence, always hostile to the Tory Government, was very considerable indeed. In these circumstances, John Murray, the publisher, wrote to Canning in September, 1807, pointing out the harm which was being done to the Tory cause by *The Edinburgh Review*, and suggesting that the time had come to found a rival, which he declared himself ready to finance. On this, Canning, through his cousin, Stratford, introduced Murray to Gifford, the late editor of *The Anti-Jacobin*, and the scheme thereupon rapidly took shape.

From the beginning all associated with the project realized the value of Canning's active aid, and long before the first number was published Sir Walter Scott wrote to George Ellis:[1]

> As our start is of such immense consequence, don't you think Mr. Canning, though unquestionably an Atlas, might for a day find a Hercules on whom to devolve the burden of the globe, while he writes for us a review? I know what an audacious request this is, but suppose he should, as great statesmen sometimes do, take a political fit of the gout, and absent himself from a large ministerial dinner which might give it him in good earnest—dine at three on a chicken and pint of wine, and lay the foundation of at least one good article? Let us but once get afloat, and our labour is not worth talking about; but, till then, all hands most work hard.

The first number of *The Quarterly Review*, as the new venture was termed, appeared at the end of February, 1809, and although Canning was not a contributor to this issue he wrote an article for the second, in conjunction with Sharon Turner, the historian, taking as its text the manifesto of the Archduke Charles to the German people; in this he appealed for general support for the

[1] The cousin of Charles Ellis.

Austrian defiance of Napoleon, and expressed the belief that even
" this generation " might witness his overthrow, " the terror of
Europe and the scourge of humanity ". His next contribution,
this time in collaboration with George Ellis, so delighted Gifford
that he wrote to Murray, " In consequence of my importunity,
Mr. Canning has exerted himself, and produced the best article
that ever yet appeared in any Review ". Once relieved of the
burden of office Canning was a frequent contributor until he went
to Portugal, and of the first twelve numbers no fewer than seven
contained articles that were largely inspired and partly written
by him.[1]

Meanwhile, Perceval and his colleagues were under no illusions
as to the weakness of the new administration, and during the
greater part of the year 1810 negotiations were in progress for the
inclusion in the Cabinet of the Tory leaders who remained outside
the Government. Canning had been succeeded at the Foreign
Office by Lord Wellesley, and it was he who principally urged
upon the new Prime Minister the need of strengthening the ministry. Canning had little love for Perceval, and as early as April
he seems to have had doubts whether Wellesley was adopting the
right course to achieve the end he had in view, for in that month
he wrote to Bagot:

> I am induced by something that I have heard to-day, to
> recur to the opinion which I expressed to you three weeks
> ago, that every effort of W's unaccompanied by a tender of
> his resignation will be baffled and despised—baffled by P. and
> despised by the K.[2]

Wellesley's intention was to include Canning, Castlereagh, and
Sidmouth in the ministry, but this plan failed because Sidmouth
refused to sit in the same Cabinet as Canning. He then, in June,
proposed to resign the Foreign Office to Canning, which the latter
willingly agreed to accept provided that Wellesley himself remained
in the Government, and that arrangements were made to suit his
friends. This negotiation, too, broke down, in circumstances
which are best set out in Canning's own words in a letter written
to Wellesley in September:

[1] *The Quarterly Review*, vol. CCXLIX, p. 188.
[2] Bagot, J., *op. cit.*, vol. I, p. 351; *cf.* also Walpole, Sir Spencer, *op. cit.*,
vol. II, p. 79 *et seq.*

I am to understand (from your second letter) that no offer whatever has been made to Ld. C. [Castlereagh]. I am to understand that Perceval communicated with him, as you did with me at Easter, for the purpose of ascertaining his disposition to act with the present Government, and that Perceval was selected by the Cabinet for this communication on the same grounds as you were for the communication with me, not in virtue of his station in the Government.

I understand, however, that the intimation of the intended offer was sufficiently plain to enable Ld. C. distinctly to anticipate it. And I understand that upon his intimation of his intention to decline it, the idea of any attempt at strengthening the Government was for the present laid aside.

Upon all these points I should have nothing to say; I should have nothing to do with them if nothing had been said or done towards me. The Government is unquestionably master of its own policy and conduct.

What more you have written to me, I suppose is only between yourself and me. Upon it I have only to observe that I should be sorry to have to think that you had consented that the question of any proposition to me should depend for its decision on an answer of Ld. C., but that I do not collect from either of your letters whether the question of a separate proposition has been discussed, subsequently to the receipt of Ld. C's answer of whether it was by common understanding and agreement, considered as decided by that answer? [1]

This letter finally put an end to negotiations which had been going on since the beginning of the year.

It must not, however, be imagined that Canning spent the whole of the three years during which Perceval was Prime Minister skulking, like Achilles, in his tent, and awaiting an invitation to enter the Cabinet upon his own terms. No man was more devoted to his wife and family, though his domestic happiness was already being clouded by the continued ill-health of his eldest son: now that he was out of office he was able to spend more time with Mrs. Canning and his children. As has already been mentioned it was at this time that the Cannings moved from South

[1] Bagot, J., *op. cit.*, vol. I, pp. 358–359; *cf.* also Walpole, Sir Spencer, *op. cit.*, vol. II, p. 136 *et seq.*

Hill to Hinckley, and they also changed their London residence. During his bachelor days Canning had lived successively in a " small snug comfortable house " in Charles Street, St. James's Square; in no. 5a, Albany; and at 13 Spring Gardens. While he and his wife were at South Hill their town house was, first, 37 Conduit Street, and then 24 Bruton Street, but in 1809 they acquired Gloucester Lodge, which was situated where Gloucester Road crosses Cromwell Road. It had been built by the Duchess of Gloucester, after whom it received its name, and the house was finally pulled down in 1850. Perhaps it may be added that when Canning became Foreign Secretary in 1822 for the second time he had one of the rooms in the Foreign Office fitted up as a bedroom so that " when the House sits late the Right Honourable Gentleman will be able to retire earlier to rest, and with less fatigue, than in going so far as Gloucester Lodge ".[1]

Somewhat later Canning had a house at Brighton—100 Marine Parade, and from it there was a tunnel, leading under the road to the beach, by means of which the steep descent from the cliff could be avoided. This passage has given rise to many conjectures. One writer, who claims to have seen it, recalls " a subterranean passage leading from his study . . . which was of an octagon form; it was thickly padded and lined with green baize . . . there was one window which looked out on the beach, and at high water the sea came up to the wall: entire privacy was thus secured ". It was here, we are further told, that " after the example of another great orator, he was wont to rehearse his speeches when the sea was at its roughest, trying which voice should out-top the other ". Another authority, not to be outdone, declares that in this octagonal room the Foreign Secretary received visitors whose calls it was not desirable should be generally known, amongst others, George IV, " who often consulted Canning on matters of which he did not wish the public to know ".[2]

Canning, like many another Tory statesman both before and after him, notably St. John and Disraeli, took himself very seriously as a country gentleman, and he displayed great pride in his estate at Hinckley: that he looked to it for profit as well as pleasure is evident from a paragraph in a letter to Bagot:

I buy my land upon the same principle on which Frank North, when he became Lord Guilford, directed his house-

[1] *The Times*, September 25th, 1822.
[2] *Notes and Queries*, vol. CLXXIII, pp. 362–363.

keeper, Mrs. Lovingberry, to buy his candles, a great many to
the pound and not small. 3 per cent! to be sure not. Who
could afford that? I prefer 5. I am not in Norfolk but in
Lincolnshire. Not in marshes but in fens.

Whether he made his farming pay is very much open to question.
There was at one time a suggestion that Canning should visit
the seat of war in the Peninsula, but it came to nothing. In short,
whether he was in or out of office, for him the chief centre of
interest was the House of Commons, and the part which he played
in the debates on the great financial and constitutional problems
that were then agitating the country proved not only his determination that his eclipse should be a very partial one, but also
testified to his interest in other questions than those which came
within his special province of foreign affairs.

In 1797 it had proved necessary to suspend cash payments,
and this had been followed by an enormous increase in the amount
of paper money, so that by the time Perceval succeeded Portland
at the head of the Government the result of this policy of inflation,
combined with the cost of the Peninsular War, had precipitated a
crisis. The cost of living had risen very considerably indeed,
while there was an increasing scarcity of specie, together with a
serious loss in its provision for the service of the army at the seat
of war, where paper money was not negotiable. Furthermore,
the situation was not improved by the violent disagreement
between the rival schools of political economists as to whether or
not it was in reality beneficial to the country, the one maintaining
that it had promoted the expansion of foreign commerce and
internal industry, and the other that the reverse was the case.

In these circumstances a committee was appointed to enquire
into the whole question, and among its members were Canning
and Huskisson, the chairman being Francis Horner, a Whig.
The committee issued its report in September, 1810, and it was of a
highly controversial nature. The conclusion was reached that the
high price of gold was mainly due to the quantity of paper money
in circulation, and not to the quantity of the metal sent to the
Peninsula. This excessive amount of paper money was attributed
to " the want of a sufficient check and control in the issues of
paper from the Bank of England, and originally to the suspension
of cash payments, which removed the natural and true control ".
The committee realized, however, that paper could not suddenly

be rendered convertible into specie without dislocating the entire business of the country, and its recommendation therefore was that Parliament should pass the necessary legislation for terminating the suspension of cash payments at the end of two years.

As Therry remarks in the Memoir which serves as an introduction to his collection of Canning's speeches, " it was unusual with Mr. Canning to make any great effort in this department of Parliamentary subjects ", but he offers an explanation which probably comes very near the truth. " No man could be ambitious of occupying, as a principal minister of the British Crown, any of the highest offices of the state, without desiring to be acquainted with subjects so intimately blended with the most complicated and ramified system of finance, which was ever known in the world ".[1] In short, Canning wished to impress upon the political world that he was not merely a specialist in foreign affairs. In general he agreed with the majority report, which was also signed by Huskisson, and he supported it in a speech which friends and foes alike admitted to be remarkable for its power and lucidity. At the same time he dissented from the proposal that Parliament should fix a definite date for the resumption of cash payments, and he suggested that this should not take place until six months after the conclusion of a general peace.

It only remains to add that in the following year, 1811, the Government, with Castlereagh and Vansittart for its spokesmen, carried several counter-resolutions which affirmed the rise in the price of gold to be due for the most part to the exclusion of British trade from the Continent, and also adopted Canning's opinion on the resumption of cash payments by declaring it to be " highly inexpedient and dangerous to fix a definite period for the removal of the restrictions on cash payments prior to the conclusion of a definite treaty of peace ". The restriction on cash payments was not, in fact, removed until 1819, when an Act to that effect was passed by the Liverpool administration, of which Canning was one of the leading members.

The report of this committee, and the debates to which it gave rise, were remarkable for the scope they afforded to the genius of William Huskisson, who was henceforth to be very closely associated with Canning. The two men had been born in the same year, and Huskisson had entered the House of Commons as the representative of Morpeth in 1798. A strong Midland accent,

[1] *Op. cit.*, vol. I, p. 87.

no great presence, and a certain coldness of manner were definite liabilities, but his worth was soon proved in a minor office, and Pitt, in 1804, appointed him Secretary to the Treasury, where his peculiar talents were well displayed. Huskisson joined Canning in opposition to the ministry of "All the Talents", but returned to his old post in the Portland administration, which he again relinquished when Perceval became Prime Minister. From more than one point of view Huskisson was excellently suited to work with Canning, for if his oratorical ability fell far below that of his friend, he made up for it with a knowledge of facts and figures that has probably never been equalled, save by Gladstone and Bonar Law. Grenville declared that " there is no man in Parliament, or perhaps out of it, so well versed in finance, commerce, trade, and colonial matters ", while Melbourne once told the diarist that in his opinion Huskisson was the greatest practical statesmen he had known, and the one who best united theory with practice. However much the unreformed House of Commons may have delighted in the feast of oratory of which it so often partook it could also appreciate solid worth, and this was Huskisson's claim to distinction. He contributed to Canning's immediate following that balance in which its leader was judged by so many of his contemporaries to be lacking.

Apart from the financial condition of the country the Perceval administration had to face the difficulties occasioned by the illness of the King. The death of his favourite daughter, Princess Amelia, combined with the failure of the Walcheren expedition, precipitated George's final relapse into insanity in November, 1810, and the Prince of Wales was thereupon made Regent under several temporary restrictions. These provoked a protest not only from the Prince, but also from his brothers, and the Whigs seized the opportunity to fish in the troubled waters. For a time it seemed as if the Government must be dismissed, but it soon appeared that age had weakened the Whig principles of the Regent, who also resented the dictatorial tone assumed towards him by Grenville and Grey. Accordingly, the Prince made no effort to displace Perceval, and at the end of twelve months, when it had become clear that the King's recovery was out of the question, the restrictions upon the Regent were removed without any evil consequences to the ministry.

Canning's attitude towards this problem was clearly defined both in his speeches and letters, and is marked by that lucidity of thought which always distinguished his views upon any subject. His first consideration was that his old master, for whom he had a sincere affection, should be surrounded by servants whom he knew, but he was also firm upon the point that the Queen, to whom had been committed the charge of her husband, should have no political patronage whatever. At this time Canning was not very well acquainted with the Regent personally, and as an old friend of the Princess of Wales he was unlikely to be prejudiced in his favour, but he saw at once the danger of having two Courts, which were bound to be in opposition to one another. For the most part Canning's views coincided with those of the Government, with the result that the friction between the Queen and the Regent, although it never actually ceased, caused the minimum of inconvenience to the country.

In the spring of 1812 the Foreign Secretary, Wellesley, who had made more than one fruitless effort to get Canning back into the Cabinet, resigned. He was actuated by two motives, namely, differences of opinion with his colleagues on the Roman Catholic question, and his annoyance at what he considered, somewhat unjustly, to be the lack of vigour they were displaying in the prosecution of the war. This resignation appeared to provide an excellent opportunity for a general reconstruction of the ministry, especially as the Lord President followed the Foreign Secretary into retirement. Canning was once more approached, and on March 18th, 1812, he replied with a letter to Liverpool which gives a clear idea both of his general political attitude at the time, and also of the feelings he entertained towards the old friend of his Christ Church days, who was about to enter upon his fifteen years' Premiership:

> I have communicated to such of my friends as I had an immediate opportunity of consulting the minute taken in your presence of the proposition which you conveyed to me yesterday.
>
> In a case in which I felt that my decision either way might be liable to misapprehension, I was desirous rather to collect the opinions of persons whose judgment I esteemed than to act on the impulse of my own first feeling.
>
> The result of their opinions is, that by entering into the Administration upon the terms proposed to me, I should incur such a loss of personal and publick character as would

disappoint the object which H.R.H. the P.R. has at heart, and must render my accession to his Government a new source of weakness rather than an addition of strength.

To become a part of your Administration with the previous knowledge of your unaltered opinions as to the Policy of resisting all consideration of the state of the laws affecting His Majesty's Catholick subjects would, it is felt, be to lend myself to the defeating of my own declared opinions on that most important question—opinions which are as far as those of any man from being favourable to precipitate an unqualified concession, but which rest on the conviction that it is the duty of the advisers of the Crown, with a view to the peace, tranquillity, and strength of the Empire, to take that whole question into their early and serious consideration and earnestly to endeavour to bring it to a final and satisfactory settlement.

With this result of the opinions of those whom I have consulted, my own entirely concurs; and such being the ground of my decision, it is wholly unnecessary to advert to any topics of inferior importance.

After the expressions, however, with which you were charged on the part of all your Colleagues, I should not be warranted in omitting to declare that no objection of a personal sort should have prevented me from uniting with any or all of them in the publick service, if I could have done so with honour, and if in my judgment a Cabinet so constituted in all its parts could have afforded to the country, under its present great and varied difficulties, an adequately efficient administration.

I cannot deny myself the satisfaction of adding that the manner of your communication with me had entirely corresponded with the habits and sentiments of a friendship of so many years: a friendship which our general concurrence on many great political principles has strengthened, and which our occasional differences have in no degree impaired.[1]

An unsuccessful attempt was also made to include Grenville and Grey in the administration, and the only accession of strength that was finally obtained was provided by the inclusion of Sidmouth and Castlereagh in the ministry.

[1] Bagot, J., op. cit., vol. I, pp. 387–388.

These changes had hardly been accomplished before another crisis was precipitated by the murder of Perceval in the lobby of the House of Commons on May 11th, 1812. His murderer, who gave himself up as soon as he had effected his purpose, was a bankrupt merchant who fancied he had a grievance against the Government of which Perceval was the head, but although the motive which prompted the crime was personal rather than political, it nevertheless had serious repercussions, for it was by no means obvious who was going to succeed the dead man.

At first there was an attempt to reconstitute the existing administration by the inclusion of Canning and Wellesley, but this was unsuccessful: Canning adopted the same attitude as in March, while Wellesley based his refusal on " the imperfect scale on which the efforts in the Peninsula were conducted ", though in point of fact Wellington, his own brother, had already pronounced his complaints on this score to be groundless. Such was the situation on May 21st, when a private member moved in the House of Commons an address to the Regent asking him to take such measures as might be best calculated to form an efficient administration. This was treated by the Government as a vote of no confidence, and when the motion was carried, after an official amendment had been defeated, albeit only by a majority of four in a very thin house, the ministry resigned.[1] The Regent thereupon entrusted Wellesley with the formation of an administration which should have as its programme the release of Catholics from certain disabilities, and the vigorous prosecution of the war in the Peninsula. Wellesley approached Canning, who was quite ready to join a Government formed on such a basis, but he was by no means so successful with other leading statesmen. The Whigs scouted the idea of any coalition with their political opponents, apparently from no other reason than a desire to embarrass the Regent, whom they had not forgiven for his desertion of their party; while Liverpool bluntly declared that he would not serve under Wellesley.

In these circumstances Wellesley was compelled to abandon all hope of forming a ministry, and Liverpool was commissioned to undertake the task. Once more Canning was approached, but he refused to accept office unless, as would apparently have been the case had Wellesley's efforts been successful, the leadership of the

[1] *The Annual Register* for 1812, pp. 79–83.

House of Commons went with it. At this, Castlereagh, whose inclusion in the ministry Liverpool deemed to be essential, declared that although he was quite willing to resign the Foreign Office to Canning, he would not join any administration in which he did not himself lead the House of Commons. The negotiations then fell through, and another Tory ministry was formed from which Canning was excluded.[1]

His attitude on this occasion shows that Canning had learnt nothing during the past three years, and that he still believed he could enter any ministry on his own terms. This time, however, he did not display any of the bitterness towards his old colleagues that had followed the resignation of Portland, and he was the first to acknowledge the magnanimity of Castlereagh in offering to resign the Foreign Office in his favour. Yet there can be no doubt but that his obstinacy was his ruin once again, and so it, combined with his failure to control his impatience, resulted in him having to give place to Castlereagh. The ultimate result, however, was that he now began to learn his lesson, and impulsive as his temperament remained to the end, Canning, like Disraeli, in later life acquired the art of giving an appearance of moderation which stood him in good stead.

The year 1812, however, was not to be without its triumphs, as well as its disappointments, for Canning. It was at this time that he declared himself more openly in favour of Roman Catholic claims than previously, and on June 22nd he actually succeeded in carrying a motion in their favour through the House of Commons by 235 to 106. The question had by now become an open one among the Tories, but in view of the fact that the Regent was coming to hold the same views as his father, although they commanded less respect when held by him, it cannot be said that Canning improved his prospects by taking this line. Such being the case his attitude does him the more credit, and must go a long way to counteract the feeling of irritation caused by his over-weening ambition in the ministerial crises of 1809 and 1812. If impatience was the chief item on the debit side of the account of Canning's character, there can be no doubt that his courage was his greatest asset, and it was never more clearly shown than in his advocacy of Roman Catholic claims at this particular moment. It ever there was a time in his career when circumstances counselled

[1] For particulars of these negotiations, *cf.* Yonge, C. D., *op. cit.*, vol. I, pp. 401 *et seq.*

prudence in regard to an issue upon which his party was divided, it was in 1812; yet he threw discretion to the winds, and in so doing adopted a course of which both the Regent and the Prime Minister disapproved. It may, indeed, have been folly, but it was the type of folly which reflects the highest credit upon those who commit it.

CHAPTER VI

LIVERPOOL AND LISBON

PARLIAMENT was dissolved in the autumn of 1812, and Canning, who had sat for Hastings for the last five years, was invited to stand for Liverpool. His candidature for that city had been mooted earlier, but he had felt that he could not afford " the hazard of any such expense as a contest for Liverpool would probably occasion ". That the invitation should have been repeated when his political fortunes were very low, and the possibility of his return to office was exceedingly remote, is proof of the high place which he occupied in the estimation of his contemporaries. On his part, he had never yet sat for a popular constituency, and he was to find the experience so stimulating that it was by no means without its influence upon his subsequent career. Liverpool has had every cause to be proud of its connection with Canning, but he owed much to Liverpool, for it was there that he came into contact with those commercial problems, the acquaintance with which was to stand him in such good stead when he was called upon to deal with the Americas. Liverpool can certainly claim to have played its part in making Canning a national figure.

The circumstances in which he was asked to stand may be gathered from a letter he wrote to Bootle Wilbraham on September 30th:

I received last night (by express) a letter from Mr. Litt, in London, enclosing one which he had received on Thursday from Mr. Gladstone,[1] of the same date with yours—i.e. Sat. the 26th. I confess to you (between ourselves) that I am not so sanguine of success as Mr. Litt is, or as, according to your account, Mr. Bolton[2] and Mr. Gladstone are—and you, I am sure, will be of opinion that I do right in not committing myself till I see the way close before me. I have stated in the most distinct and unequivocal terms to any person with whom I have had communication—to Mr. Cock, to Mr. Litt, and to Mr. Drinkwater—that I accept the seat if tendered freely and gratuitously. But being provided (as I am) with a seat

[1] Later Sir John Gladstone. Father of the Prime Minister.
[2] A leading Liverpool merchant who lived at Storrs on Windermere.

127

perfectly free and perfectly safe, it would be madness in one to engage in the expense of a contest for the mere *éclat* of representing Liverpool, at the risk of not succeeding, and with the certainty of all the trouble and precariousness of such a test.

On the other hand, it would be a very honourable seat on honourable terms.

Now Mr. Gladstone says that £10,000 will be wanted. They cannot start with less. About £2,000 is subscribed. He thinks by the end of this week the subscriptions may amount to £6,000 or £7,000 in Liverpool. The remainder they must have in London. But how? If it is meant that I am to subscribe under other names—it is plain that they do not believe the sincerity of my declaration that I will not be at expense—and only think that I mean to avoid the appearance of subscribing. But I really mean to be at no expense at all. There are some gentlemen, Mr. Litt for instance, connected with Liverpool who will subscribe in London : but a subscription among " private friends "—which is what Mr. Gladstone pointed at—I cannot hear of—at least I can not stir a step towards it.

Possibly after all the subscriptions at Liverpool may go on more rapidly than Mr. Gladstone calculates. He desires Mr. Litt to inform me that the Committee " look forward to the hour when they may be enabled to afford themselves the high gratification of giving me the invitation with a competent purse in their possession ". This implies, I hope, that I shall not receive the invitation, nor of course be called upon for any declaration—much less to go down to Liverpool, until they have a purse in their opinion competent to the object.

I am here, it is true, at 300 miles distance from Liverpool, but in London I should be at upwards of 200 miles distance, and I do not think it worth while to travel 200 miles to London —in order to be only 100 miles nearer to Liverpool. I shall therefore wait the arrival of the Invitation quietly here (my other seat requiring, as you may suppose, no personal attendance), holding myself ready to set out, upon receiving it at a moment's warning. . . .

Of course in all that you had occasion to say to Mr. Bolton you discouraged any notion of my giving anything like a pledge of support to Government. I would not give such a pledge for 50 seats. If Government should exert themselves or should intimate a wish against me—what would Mr. Bolton do? I do not suspect that they will—at least openly —but they are opposing Charles Ellis (in vain) at Seaford, and Huskisson (perhaps to more purpose) at Howick.[1]

When Canning wrote this letter to Bootle Wilbraham, who was exerting all his influence in South Lancashire to further his friend's candidature, he was staying at Saltram, near Plymouth, with Lord Boringdon, who had been a contemporary at Christ Church. Boringdon was, through Canning's influence, later given an earldom, and became Earl of Morley. He was a strong supporter of his benefactor, but voted with the Whigs after 1830.[2] Among the other guests was a Mr. Cyrus Redding, who has left an account of the impression that Canning made upon him:

I met for the first time Canning, then in the prime of life, just before his departure for the election at Liverpool. In private society he fully sustained that superiority which he showed in the House of Commons . . . neat in dress . . . Canning had nothing of the stiffness, arrogance or ordinary person of Pitt. He exhibited no extremes. His evening dress was in the plainer fashion of the time. There seemed to me about him, too, something of the character of his eloquence, classical, tasteful, candid, and conscious of innate power. A handsome man in feature, compact in person, moulded between activity and strength, although I fancied even then he exhibited marks of what care and ambition had done for him. His countenance indicated firmness of character, with a good-natured cast over all. He was bald as " the first Caesar ".

In the dining-room or drawing-room little of that theatrical manner was visible which was perceptible in the delivery of his Parliamentary speeches. His gait as he paced the drawing-room I even now see, his well-fitted blue ribbed silk stockings and breeches with knee-buckles fitting well-turned limbs . . . he spoke with a full, clear intonation. . . . Eight or nine years after, when I returned from the Continent, this eminent statesman had changed much in appearance.[3]

[1] Bagot, J., *op. cit.*, vol. I, pp. 392–394.
[2] His first wife, who was a daughter of the 10th Earl of Westmorland, left him for Sir Arthur Paget, and her story is said to have given Mrs. Henry Wood the plot of *East Lynne*.
[3] *Fifty Years' Recollections*, vol. I, pp. 177–178.

I

In Liverpool the supporters of Canning were extremely active, and on September 25th they had held a meeting at the Golden Lion, where, we are told, " a committee was immediately nominated to conduct the election, and the friends of Mr. Cannng entered into the most liberal subscriptions to give efficacy to their resolutions ".   On October 1st they sent him the following letter :

> Entertaining, as we do, the highest respect for, and the fullest confidence in, your talents, integrity, and public conduct, we feel a strong and anxious desire that this loyal and ancient borough should possess the high advantage of being represented by you in Parliament; and we, therefore, do most earnestly invite you to offer yourself as a candidate at the ensuing election.
>
> Should you favour us by your compliance, we beg to assure you of our utmost zeal and exertions in your behalf; and, from the knowledge we possess of the very favourable sentiments generally entertained of you by the freemen and other inhabitants of this large and populous borough, we cannot permit ourselves for a moment to doubt your being returned to Parliament by a large majority, notwithstanding any opposition that is or may be contemplated by others on the occasion.

Presumably the financial position was soon adjusted to meet the wishes of Canning, for he accepted the invitation at once:

> *Mamhead House, near Exeter,*
> *Sunday, October 4, 1812.*
>
> GENTLEMEN,
>
> In returning from a more distant part of the country, upon intelligence of the dissolution of Parliament, I am met here, this day, by your flattering invitation to Liverpool.
>
> I have not words to express my sense of the honour thus tendered to me.   It is one which, unconnected as I am with the town of Liverpool, I should certainly never have presumed to think of soliciting; nor can I forbear, even now, entreating you to reflect, whether any advantage or satisfaction which you can hope to derive from choosing me one of your representatives can compensate the trouble which (I am led to apprehend) you may have to encounter in accomplishing that object.

Having said this, if it be, nevertheless, your pleasure to call me to that distinguished situation, my services are at your command; I put myself into your hands; relying confidently upon the exertions which you will employ to give effect to your own wishes, and to vindicate your choice by making it triumphantly successful.

Had I presumed, uninvited, to solicit your suffrages, it would have been incumbent upon me to address to you some profession of my public principles, and some exposition of my public conduct.

As it is, you allow me to flatter myself that to your indulgent and favourable construction of those principles and that conduct (by which alone I am known to you) I am indebted for the invitation which I have this day received from you.

I am not likely to swerve from principles which have procured to me so signal and gratifying a distinction.

My conduct in Parliament will always be governed by the best judgment which I am able to form of what is conducive to the welfare or essential to the honour of the country.

I have only to add that gratitude, as well as duty will insure my unwearied attention to every thing that may affect the peculiar interests of the town of Liverpool, or which can contribute to its prosperity.

I have the honour to be,

> With the highest respect and acknowledgment,
> Gentlemen,
> Your most obliged and faithful servant,
> GEORGE CANNING.[1]

The election lasted from October 8th to 16th, and in addition to Canning the candidates for the two seats were Generals Gascoyne and Tarleton in the Tory, and Brougham and Creevey in the Whig, interest. Gascoyne had sat for Liverpool since 1796, and lived just outside the city at Childwall Hall, while Tarleton had first been elected in 1790, but his representation had not been continuous since that date, though at the dissolution in 1812 he and Gascoyne were the sitting members. Never before had the Whigs brought forward candidates of the calibre of Brougham and Creevey. How strenuous was the ensuing contest

---

[1] Therry, R., *op. cit.*, vol. I, pp. 94–98.

can be gathered from an extract from a letter which Brougham wrote to Grey.

> You can have no idea of the nature of a Liverpool election. It is quite peculiar to the place. You have every night to go to the different clubs, benefit societies, etc., which meet and speechify. This is from half-past six to one in the morning at least; and you have to speak to each man who polls, at the bar, from ten to five. It lasted eight days. I began my canvass three whole days before, and had nine nights of the clubs, besides a regular speech each day at close of the poll. I delivered in that time 160 speeches and odd.[1]

Stratford Canning returned from his mission to Constantinople in time to take part in his cousin's election, and his account of the contest confirmed that of Brougham:

> On reaching Liverpool we found the town in an uproar. Party ran high; bitter speeches were exchanged on the hustings, and mobs were violent in the streets. Windows were broken, candidates pelted, and for more effective missiles resort was had without ceremony to the pavement and the area rails. Fortune finally declared in favour of Mr. Canning, who was cheered, chaired, and feasted to the top of his bent. I cannot venture to say how many dinners were given to him and his friends by the Tory capitalists of Liverpool. I know that they were enough, with the help of turtle and punch, to imperil health far more than any riotous assaults in the street. It was an uninterrupted jubilee of two or three weeks, succeeded by a shorter but not less convivial ovation at Manchester, which as yet had neither a member of Parliament to plead its interests, nor a bishop to watch over its morals.[2]

The final state of the poll was as follows:

Canning	1,641
Gascoyne	1,532
Brougham	1,131
Creevey	1,068
Tarleton (retd.)	11

---

[1] Brougham and Vaux, Lord: *Life and Times*, vol. II, p. 62.
[2] Lane-Poole, S., *op. cit.*, vol. I, pp. 185–186.

At first, however, it had appeared as if the Whigs were carrying everything before them, and in these circumstances Canning and Brougham were said to be not unwilling to jettison their respective partners in the contest; at any rate Creevey suspected his colleague of some such intention. Canning soon established himself very firmly in Liverpool, which remained loyal to him until in 1823 the pressure of his duties at the Foreign Office compelled him to seek a less exacting constituency, as well as one nearer London, and he was returned for the Treasury borough of Harwich, which had once been represented by Samuel Pepys.

The election of Canning for Liverpool marked, as has been said, an important step in his career, though the full effect of it was not realized either by himself or others until some years afterwards. Almost from his entry into the House of Commons he had been regarded as one of the foremost Parliamentarians of the day, while *The Anti-Jacobin* and *The Quarterly Review* had taught him how the Press might be utilized as an organ of propaganda. Now his experiences in Liverpool showed him how the platform, too, might be made to serve the same purpose. Canning was, with the possible exception of Chatham, the first British statesman to appeal from the House of Commons to the electorate and the nation beyond its walls; and it was undoubtedly his success in Liverpool that showed him how, so far as the platform was concerned, it could be done. When he returned to the Foreign Office ten years later he displayed such a skill in mobilizing public opinion in support of his policy that he was enabled to overcome, almost single-handed, the opposition not only of foreign diplomats, but of the King and his own colleagues, and thus to succeed where a man with a lesser aptitude for conducting a campaign of propaganda must have failed. The Liverpool election of 1812, although it took place at a time when Canning's political career was under a cloud, thus contributed very materially to his future success, while it also brought him into personal contact with Brougham, with results that later affected both men considerably.

Nevertheless Canning's victory at Liverpool had been a personal rather than a political triumph so far as his position at Westminster was concerned, for never since he had been first returned to the House of Commons nearly twenty years before had his fortunes been so low as on the morrow of his triumphant return for the second city in the kingdom. Nor is the reason far to seek. The Government, although its head was an old friend, was firmly seated in the saddle, and, with Napoleon at last going down to defeat, it was under no necessity to make any further overtures to the man who, for one reason or another, had refused every suggestion that he should join it. Canning's own personal following in the Commons numbered between fifteen and twenty, but so strong was the ministry that it had little weight in the new Parliament, and it derived what small importance it possessed from the brilliance of its chief and the sound knowledge of Huskisson. As the months passed Canning came to realize the hopelessness of his position, and in the summer of 1813 he dissolved his group.

During this period he by no means ceased to play a part in the proceedings of the House of Commons. There was an autumn session in 1812, but it was a brief one, and Canning is not recorded as having spoken; when, however, Parliament re-assembled in the following year he intervened on several occasions. In February he supported the Government in the war with the United States, whose hostile attitude he believed to be in no small measure due to sympathy with France, and he told the House that " it is not paradoxical to say that we shall stand right, at no distant time, in the eyes even of our enemies in the United States; for by a singular anomaly, upon the issue of this struggle in which America is attempting to cripple our resources, depends not only the independence of Europe, but perhaps ultimately, the freedom of America herself ". In July, 1813, Canning spoke in support of the vote of thanks to Wellington for his victory at Vittoria, and he dwelt upon the influence of the campaign in the Peninsula on the progress of events in Central Europe:

It was not to Spain alone that the effects of the late victory will be confined. Spain had been the theatre of Lord Wellington's glory, but it would not be the boundary of the beneficial result of his triumph. The same blow which has broken the talisman of the French power in Spain, had disenchanted the North. How was their prospect changed! In those countries, where at most a short struggle had been terminated by a result disastrous to their wishes, if not altogether closing in despair, they had now to contemplate a very different aspect of affairs. Germany crouched no longer, trembling at the feet of the tyrant, but maintained a

balanced contest. The mighty deluge by which the Continent
had been overwhelmed began to subside. The limits of
nations were again visible, and the spires and turrets of
ancient establishments began to re-appear above the subsiding
wave. It was this victory which had defined these objects,
so lately involved in overwhelming confusion. To whom,
under God, were they indebted for this? To the man to
whom they were this day voting their thanks.[1]

Canning also brought forward the claims of the Catholics
when opportunity arose, while in 1814 he was largely instrumental
in persuading his old friend the Princess of Wales to adopt a more
reasonable attitude in her strained relations with her husband
than would otherwise have been the case, and to take up her
residence abroad. These various activities, however, could not
conceal the fact that politically Canning was isolated. It was
the nadir of his career, and he would have been a bold man who
would have prophesied the recovery which in less than a decade
was to raise Canning once more to the Foreign Secretaryship.

In addition he and his wife were increasingly worried about
the health of their eldest son, George; the boy had always been
delicate, and he was now ordered abroad by his doctors. About
the same time the Foreign Office was informed by Lord Strangford, then ambassador in Brazil, that the Prince Regent of
Portugal would like to return to Europe under British protection.
Liverpool and Castlereagh felt that no one would be more suitable
to receive the Portuguese monarch at Lisbon than Canning, who
had been so largely instrumental in persuading him to quit it.
The appointment, too, would enable him to leave the English
political scene for a time, as well as to be with his son while the
boy was abroad. The offer was accordingly made, and by the
end of the year Canning was settled in Lisbon as Ambassador
Extraordinary and Minister Plenipotentiary, but before he left
it had been agreed between Liverpool and himself that he should
have the refusal of the first vacancy in the Cabinet. That he did
not accept the mission with any particular enthusiasm is obvious
from his own account:

I consider my having accepted the Lisbon embassy as a
great political mistake; in all probability I should have had

[1] Therry, R., *op. cit.*, vol. III, pp. 422–423.

the most influential post in the Government in the House of
Commons long before, had I not fallen into that error. I
laboured hard to avoid accepting the appointment, but it
was so urged upon me by the King's Government, that I
thought I had not the moral right, as a public man, to refuse
it. If, therefore, the thing were now, with past experience,
to be done over again, I should act the same part, and,
conscious of right, I must brave the consequences.[1]

Canning's sojourn in Lisbon was politically quite unimportant,
but it was not without effect upon himself. In the first place it
brought him into contact with the British community in Portugal,
which was in the main commercial, and thus further impressed
upon him the close connection between British trade and British
diplomacy, while, secondly, it enabled him to gain an insight into
the Continent from within, which the long war had denied to him
and his contemporaries. He took advantage of the delay in the
Prince Regent's return to pay a protracted visit to France, and
for the rest of his life, whether in or out of office, he spent as much
time as he could afford on the mainland of Europe, time which
was certainly not wasted as his conduct of the country's foreign
policy abundantly proved. Last, but by no means least, during
this period of absence from the political scene he learnt to curb his
impatience. For the rest Canning found Lisbon a by no means
unpleasant post, as is shown by a paragraph from a letter which
he wrote in July, 1815, to Bagot, who was then British minister
at Washington:

George is at the baths of Caldas, where I am going on
Sunday to spend a few days with him and to take his brother
to join him. Our other children, Toddles and the little one,
are at Collares, near Cintra, where Mrs. Canning joins them
to-morrow. Lisbon is hardly tenable, this weather, and
Caldas is hotter still, but the heat appears to agree with George
prodigiously. I do not mind it; but it is too much for Mrs.
Canning and for the younger children otherwise in good
health. Collares and Cintra are as cool as a grotto and
beautiful beyond anything that I ever saw, except perhaps
the Lakes; and at the Lakes, last summer, Southey told me
that he thought them more beautiful than anything he had

[1] Stapleton, A. G.: *op. cit.*, p. 210.

ever seen except Cintra. Charles [1] has a house within 200 yards of ours at Collares.[2]

Indeed, it may be said that the time which Canning spent in Lisbon was far from having been wasted since it afforded him leisure to see many things in a truer perspective than had been the case in the past, while the Prime Minister in a series of letters kept him fully informed of what was happening at Vienna, where his old opponent, Castlereagh, was playing so prominent a part in the re-settlement of Europe.

It is not without interest to note that in the same year, 1815, a vacancy occurred in the representation of Oxford University, and Canning, who was beginning to wonder whether his prolonged absence abroad was quite fair to his Liverpool constituents, was not unwilling to come forward. His candidature, however, was hopeless from the start. " You must have forgotten English politics ", wrote Wellesley Pole to Bagot, " to suppose that Canning could have a chance for Oxford. Nothing but a violent, unrelenting Protestant would be tolerated by that sage University, and Mr. Peel was invited (I believe without any intrigue of his) and returned unanimously in consequence of his speech, which was a very good one, on the Catholic Question last Session."

Early in 1816 it became clear that the Prince Regent of Portugal had no immediate intention of returning to Lisbon, and Canning's mission accordingly came to an end. In these circumstances the Opposition was not slow to denounce his appointment as having been a " job " from the beginning, but when the matter was subsequently debated in the House of Commons his defence silenced the critics. At this point, and shortly before his return to England, the death of the Earl of Buckinghamshire created a vacancy at the Board of Control: Liverpool was in this way enabled to carry out his promise, and Canning at once accepted the Presidency which, of course, carried with it a seat in the Cabinet.

[1] Charles Ellis.
[2] Bagot, J., *op. cit.*, vol. II, p. 6.

CHAPTER VII

THE BOARD OF CONTROL

THE administration in which Canning at last found a place had been formed four years before on the murder of Perceval, and in the interval it had added to its prestige by the part which Britain had played in the overthrow of Napoleon. First of all Wellington's victories in the Peninsula, and then Castlereagh's diplomacy at Vienna, had raised its popularity to an unprecedented height; so that when Canning, for the first time for seven years, took his seat upon the Treasury Bench, his colleagues were still elated by their triumphs in the field and in the council-chamber, and, with the exception of a small minority of Whigs, the governing classes were prepared to accept the Cabinet at its own valuation.

The Prime Minister was still Liverpool, whose name has appeared so often in these pages. He was posthumously to incur the formidable displeasure of Disraeli, who has handed him on to posterity deprived of every shred of reputation for statesmanship. The unfortunate Liverpool was satirized as the "Arch-Mediocrity", and sneering references were made to his " meagre diligence ". The Government " fell into a panic ", Disraeli declared, " having fulfilled during their lives the duties of administration, they were frightened because they were called upon, for the first time, to perform the functions of government. Like all weak men, they had recourse to what they called strong measures. They determined to put down the multitude. They thought they were imitating Mr. Pitt, because they mistook disorganization for sedition." [1] Disraeli himself, it may be remarked, never had to deal with problems of anything like the magnitude of those which confronted Liverpool. The poets were even more bitter; Byron loaded the Foreign Secretary in particular with abuse, and Shelley

> . . . . met Murder on the way—
> He had a mask like Castlereagh.

Yet there was another side to the picture, and no man who was the incompetent functionary depicted by Disraeli could have controlled a team which, in his later days, contained such personalities as Canning, Castlereagh, Eldon, Huskisson, Vansittart,

[1] *Coningsby*, bk. II, ch. 1.

Palmerston, and above all, Wellington; beside these names the members of Disraeli's own ministries appear dwarfs indeed. Rather, surely, must one agree with Mr. Keith Feiling that " this over-worked Prime Minister has been pilloried long enough for the faults of millowners and justices; for severities in which he was overborne by Eldon, for omissions which he shared with Peel ".[1] When all is said and done, his Government was returned to power at four successive General Elections, so that if it was as bad as its critics alleged then some of the responsibility must rest with the electorate which kept it in office.

On the other hand there were in various parts of the country ominous signs of that depression which so often follows the conclusion of hostilities. Unemployment began to make its appearance, and with the rapid reduction of the naval and military establishments it quickly increased until it reached serious proportions. The Continent no longer required the war material which the enemies of Napoleon had been purchasing from Britain, and it was, for the moment, too impoverished to be a market for her normal products. Accordingly, there was a decline of 16% in British export trade, and of nearly 20% in the import trade: this was followed by increased unemployment and by wide-spread bankruptcies. In addition, there were other causes of distress, such as over-speculation, the impossibility of finding work for the returned soldiers, and the continual substitution of machinery for hand labour. Furthermore, the failure of the harvest resulted in a rise of the price of wheat from 52s. 6d. a quarter in January, 1816, to 103s. 1d. twelve months later, while by the middle of the following year it had reached 111s. 6d. In these circumstances it was small wonder that the working classes confused the sources of the evils from which they were suffering, and that while the Government was still wearing at Westminister the halo of Waterloo and Vienna, the murmurs of discontent else-where were already becoming distinctly audible.

The Government undoubtedly made a mistake in not dis-criminating more carefully between the different classes of re-formers, but their fault was the same as that of every admini-stration in similar circumstances: Pitt had been no wiser, and even in more recent times panic-stricken measures have been adopted towards those who were suspected of harbouring designs inimical to the safety of the state. Liverpool had witnessed the

[1] *Sketches in Nineteenth Century Biography*, p. 31.

storming of the Bastille with his own eyes, and he and his colleagues had at any rate the excuse that they had seen in France the effect of looking on helplessly while the agitation grew. The Government might have pursued a different policy had they received any support in the matter from the Opposition, but although in private the Whigs might deplore the more violent excesses of the Radicals, in public they did nothing to discourage, but much to stimulate, them. It must also be remembered that there was still no police force, and that a minor disturbance could easily assume dangerous proportions before it was checked.

The year in which Canning returned to England, that is to say, 1816, saw the beginning of the trouble. In May there was rioting in the counties of Cambridge, Essex and Suffolk, while at Littleport, in Cambridgeshire, the troops were compelled to open fire, with the result that two of the rioters were killed, and five more were subsequently executed for their share in the outbreak. Rick-burning began in many districts, and there was a distinct revival of Luddism, which had given so much trouble to the authorities during the war. There can be little doubt that the influence of Cobbett, exerted through *The Weekly Register*, had not a little to do with fanning the flames of revolt, though it must be admitted that Cobbett himself never advocated recourse to actual violence, and some of his opinions were definitely Tory in character. Yet his plea for sweeping reforms reached the ears of many who were none too scrupulous as to the means by which they might be attained. All over the country there were revolutionary clubs which demanded, like the Chartists of later years, universal suffrage and annual Parliaments. Before the end of 1816 the spirit of discontent had spread to London, where a rising took place with the seizure of the Tower for its object; it failed owing to the personal courage of the Lord Mayor, but not until some blood had been spilt. In January, 1817, the Regent was insulted in the streets on his return from the opening of Parliament.

These events not unnaturally alarmed the Legislature, and both Houses called upon the Government to put down what appeared to be a definite conspiracy against public order and private property. In consequence a Bill was introduced for the suppression of seditious meetings, and the Habeas Corpus Act was suspended until July 1st, 1817. Nor was this all, for Sidmouth sent a circular letter to the Lords Lieutenant of the counties for the information of the magistrates in which he said that, in the opinion of the Law Officers, persons charged on oath with seditious libel might be apprehended and held to bail. For this he was violently attacked, and his critics declared that it was unbecoming for the Home Secretary to interpret the law, while Cobbett, feeling himself at the mercy of informers, fled to the United States. All the same, those accused were only put on their trial, and one of the most notorious, Hone, was three times acquitted on the charge of uttering blasphemous libels. The Midlands and North still remained disturbed, and the so-called march of the Blanketeers took place in Manchester, while in Nottinghamshire a formidable gang armed with pikes was dispersed by the troops. The suspension of the Habeas Corpus Act was extended for a further period of six months.

The following year, 1818, witnessed a temporary improvement in the economic condition of the country, and a consequent diminution in the amount of unrest, but before it closed a strike of cotton operatives in Manchester was marked by the usual incidents of brutal violence towards those who refused to participate in it, and the soldiers were compelled to open fire. August of 1819 witnessed the so-called " Manchester Massacres " in the same city, though this particular disturbance was political rather than economic. A monster reform meeting was convened for the 16th of that month, and the magistrates foolishly decided to arrest the ringleaders in the middle of the demonstration. For this purpose they had at their disposal several companies of infantry, six troops of the 15th Hussars, and a body of Yeomanry, as well as a number of special constables. The Chief Constable declared that he could not effect the necessary arrests without the aid of the military, and a detachment of Yeomanry was ordered to advance, only, however, soon to be isolated in the middle of a surging crowd. At this point one of the magistrates, thinking that the Yeomen were in danger, asked the officer in command of the Hussars to rescue them, and to disperse the mob. Four troops of Hussars, and a few of the Yeomanry, thereupon charged, and people fled in all directions. Some of the demonstrators were cut down, and others were trampled on, but the talk of " several mounds of human beings " lying where they had fallen was mere political propaganda. In actual fact the loss of life did not exceed five or six, and there were a number of injured. Such was the famous Peterloo Massacre, which did so much to aggravate panic in one quarter, and resentment against the existing order in another.

Hardly had the noise of these events in Manchester begun to die down than the Cato Street conspiracy took place. Its author was one Arthur Thistlewood, and his plan of murdering the assembled Cabinet in a private house, after which a Provisional Government was to have been proclaimed, would probably have been successful had it not been detected by the aid of an informer. What actually happened was that twenty-four conspirators armed themselves in Cato Street, near Edgware Road, for the purpose of assassinating the ministers as they sat at dinner in Lord Harrowby's house in Grosvenor Square, while some of their associates were posted near the door of the house to summon them when all the guests were assembled. As a result of the information which had been given the dinner was not held, but the watchers were deceived by the arrival of carriages for a party next door, and thus failed to warn their co-conspirators in Cato Street. The plans of the authorities, too, miscarried, for the troops who were to have supported the police did not arrive in time, as the officer in command did not know the district, and no one had thought to provide him with a map; in consequence Thistlewood and a good many of his men escaped, though he himself was captured the next morning. In the following April an outbreak in Scotland was put down without much difficulty at Bonnymuir, though not before a treasonable proclamation had spread consternation in Glasgow; and the whole affair bore such a resemblance to the Cato Street conspiracy as to increase the alarm which that attempt had aroused.

Much of this is, of course, to anticipate, but it shows that the Liverpool administration was not " called upon to deal merely with merry peasants and innocuous idealists ";[1] nor were Canning's views at variance with those of his new colleagues. At the end of December, 1816, for example, when Sidmouth was about to propose the suspension of the Habeas Corpus Act, W. H. Lyttelton [2] wrote to Bagot, " Everybody agrees that the Doctor has done his part well. . . . By the bye, Canning is now very intimate with this self-same Doctor, which gives one a strange notion of the shortness of their memories, or excellence of their tempers. We are, however, not without our hopes that your old friend is collecting fresh materials for epigrams, and is reconnoitring in disguise."

---

[1] Feiling, K., op. cit., p. 27.
[2] Later the third Lord Lyttelton.

Lyttelton was, however, mistaken, for Canning's support of Sidmouth was perfectly genuine. In spite of his sympathy with all attempts to secure Roman Catholic Emancipation he wished to preserve the established order, and he opposed Parliamentary Reform as tending to upset the delicate balance of the Constitution. The founder of *The Anti-Jacobin* was hardly likely to view with favour the agitators who were urging the working classes to burn ricks and to wreck machinery, and the attempts that have been made to dissociate Canning from the domestic policy of the Liverpool administration are based upon a complete misconception of his character. He was very far from being a politician of the sentimental type who believes in the divinity of discontent, and objects to the use of force in any circumstances. He certainly wished to remove all real grievances, which some of his colleagues did not, but he had no hesitation in giving his support to the enforcement of order. Above all, if Canning had not agreed with the policy of the Government he would most assuredly never have accepted a seat in the Cabinet.

However, before discussing Canning's attitude towards the general politics of the day, some account must be given of his administration of his department, to which he was not, of course, an entire stranger, having been one of the Commissioners sixteen years earlier.

When he took office in 1816 the Governor-General was Lord Moira, soon to be created Marquess of Hastings, who, as one of the Whig leaders, had been a political opponent of Canning in the past. India, however, had wrought a great change in the erstwhile confidant of the Regent, and few Governors-General or Viceroys have worked so hard or so unselfishly. The length of his administration, although he was fifty-eight when he received his appointment, was surpassed only by that of Warren Hastings, while some idea of his devotion to duty can be gathered from the fact that he never went to the hills, and that he was always at his desk by four o'clock in the morning. Such a man was bound, whatever their differences in the past, to agree with Canning, and friction between the Board of Control and the Governor-General was reduced to a minimum. Hastings, to give him the name by which he is best known, had been three years in office in 1816, and the laurels of the war in Nepal were still fresh upon his brow.

In Central India, however, the situation was far from reassuring, for a large tract of country was being systematically ravaged by

Pathans, Mahrattas, and Pindaris. The pressure of the Peninsular War had caused the British Government to enforce a policy
of strict neutrality upon the East India Company, with the result
that for more than ten years the atrocities had continued unchecked.
In 1816 the Pindaris began to turn their attention to British territory, and during an incursion into the Northern Sarkars they
plundered over three hundred villages in twelve days. In these
circumstances, as Canning told the House of Commons, " the
Government in India could not longer have forborne; unless it
had forgotten what it owed to its subjects, and had been contented
to forfeit its good name throughout the territory of Hindustan ".
Hastings was firmly supported by Canning in his determination
to put an end to the Pindari menace, and both the Governor-
General and the President of the Board of Control arrived,
independently, at the decision to commence military operations for
this purpose.

The situation was a complicated one, as Canning showed the
House:

> It is obvious . . . that a war once excited in India might
> draw into its vortex many whom fear of our power only kept
> at peace. With respect to the Pindaris themselves, the diffi-
> culty was to find an opportunity of striking a decisive blow.
> Attacked, routed, scattered in all directions, they would
> speedily collect and congregate again; as a globule of quick-
> silver, dispersing for a moment under the pressure of the
> finger, re-unites as soon as that pressure is withdrawn. But
> the Pindaris had also chances of external support. They
> had, many of them, been trained to arms in the service of
> Scindia, the greatest among the native princes who maintain
> an independent rule; in the service of Holkar, long the rival
> of Scindia for the preponderance in the Mahratta confederacy;
> and in that of Meer Khan, a Mohammedan adventurer, who,
> originally employed as an auxiliary by Holkar, had the
> address to render himself, for a time, master of the govern-
> ment which he was called in to support, and to carve out for
> himself, in return for his abdication of that influence, a sub-
> stantial and independent sovereignty. However contemptible
> therefore in themselves, when compared with the numerous
> and well-trained armies of the British Government, yet, as the
> fragments of bands that had been led by formidable chieftains,

to whom they still professed allegiance, these vagrant hordes might be the means of calling into action powers of greater magnitude and resources—Scindia, Holkar, and lastly, Meer Khan, himself essentially a predatory power, and the leader only of more regular and disciplined Pindaris.

Nor was this the utmost extent of danger to be apprehended. Suspicions might also be naturally entertained that the other Mahratta powers were not displeased to see the British authority, against which they had more than once combined with all their forces in vain, weakened in effect and in opinion by the unavenged attack of such despicable antagonists; and that when the occasion should ripen, they might not be disinclined to revenge and retrieve their former defeats. But whatever might be the chances of future danger to be calculated, the case was one which did not admit of doubt. The most beneficial acquisitions of territory would not have justified the incurring either the expense or the hazard of a war; but no hazard and no expense could be put in competition with the vindication of national honour, and the discharge of national duty.[1]

There is no need to enter into details of the actual campaign which followed. In a little more than two years' fighting the Pindaris and the Pathans were crushed, and the pretensions of the Mahrattas were curbed. To impress upon the native rulers the consequences of a breach of faith the office of Peishwa was abolished, though the last holder was granted a pension, and it was his heir, Nana Sahib, who was to give so much trouble to Canning's son. The result of these wars was to establish the position that lasted for a century, namely that the general peace of India should be secured under the avowed paramount control of Great Britain, with the minimum of interference in the internal affairs of states allowed to retain their autonomy.

In this connection, Canning's own views upon British commitments in India are not without interest :

Anxious as I am for the prosperity and grandeur of our Indian empire, I confess I look at its indefinite extension with awe. I earnestly wish that it may be possible for us to remain stationary where we are, and that what still exists of substantive and independent power in India, may stand un-

[1] Therry, R., *op. cit.*, vol. IV, pp. 86–87.

K

touched and unimpaired. But this consummation, however much it may be desired, depends . . . not on ourselves alone. Aggression must be repelled, and perfidy must be visited with its just reward. And while I join with the thinking part of the country in deprecating advance, who shall say that there is safety for such a power as ours in retrogradation? [1]

Two other events worthy of note took place while Canning was at the Board of Control; one of them was the occupation of Singapore, and the other was the abolition of the censorship upon the Indian Press.

By the Treaty of Vienna the British Government restored Java, which had been occupied during the war, unconditionally to the Dutch, and although Hastings had disapproved of this proceeding, he had been powerless to interfere. Canning, however, appreciated as fully as did the Governor-General the importance of securing the route to the Far East, and in 1819 he authorized the occupation and retention of Singapore in spite of the annoyance aroused at The Hague. The abolition of the censorship of the Press could not permanently be maintained, but it is not without interest that the first newspaper in the vernacular appeared during these years with the full support of the Government.

Canning's work at the Board of Control is too often regarded as a mere incident in his career, and one hardly worthy of mention. It was, of course, overshadowed by his achievements at the Foreign Office, and by the Governor-Generalship of his son, but it is worth more than a passing notice, for it showed that the years which he had spent in the political wilderness had not in any way weakened his powers. He dealt with the Pindaris and the Mahrattas with the same vigour as that with which he had forestalled Napoleon, and his support of Hastings probably saved British India from a serious invasion. Canning was always quick to appreciate the issues at stake in any crisis, and he showed this ability in his treatment of Indian affairs just as fully as he had done, and was soon again to do, at the Foreign Office. Furthermore, the cordial relations which he maintained with Hastings show that he was always prepared to support his country's representatives provided their competence was proved, whatever had been their previous political affiliations.

Active as was the interest which he took in the work of his

[1] Therry, R., *op. cit.*, vol. IV, p. 105.

department, Canning was more occupied in defending the general policy of the Government in the House of Commons than in administering India, and he was not slow in calling attention to the demands made upon ministers:

> They shrink from no just responsibility; they neglect no attendance; they shirk no discussion in this House; but it ought to be borne in mind how great a change has taken place of late years in the business of the House of Commons—a change which has thrown a burden of business upon ministers, which no physical or mental constitution can adequately sustain. I call upon those members of the House of Commons who recollect the good old times when the destinies of the Empire were swayed in Parliament by Mr. Pitt, or Mr. Fox, to say whether the labours of an administration in those days were to be compared with what they are now. The ministers were not then harassed and perplexed by a complication of daily business, with the whole details of which, however trifling, it was expected that they should be intimately and accurately acquainted.

Of this burden Canning undoubtedly bore the major part. The Leader of the House of Commons was Castlereagh, who was not only a poor speaker but in the state of Europe he was naturally occupied mainly with his work at the Foreign Office. The Chancellor of the Exchequer was quite ineffective in debate; Huskisson confined his activities to those subjects of which he had special knowledge; while Peel and Palmerston, although men of great promise, did not yet carry the weight of the older ministers. In these circumstances the chief spokesman of the Government in the Lower House was Canning, and his task would have been more onerous still had not the Opposition been so divided that it was only rarely their leader, Tierney, could persuade them to combine for a frontal attack on the ministry. Rather had Canning to deal with the sniping of Brougham and Burdett, but this necessitated a constant alertness, and also a minute acquaintance with every detail of the suppression of the various disorders which were taking place, for the Opposition was always taxing ministers with undue severity in this respect.

Such being the case it is not surprising that Canning became very clearly identified with the policy of repression which the Opposition, or rather the Radical section of it, so hotly attacked, and on more than one occasion his attitude caused him to become the centre of controversy. The most notable instance was in connection with the petition of one Ogden. A professional agitator of this name had been imprisoned, and although during his incarceration he had been cured of an old complaint, on his release he at once posed as a martyr, and declared that far from having been cured his infirmity had actually been caused by the weight of his chains. He was an old man, and his defence was taken up by the Opposition both in and out of Parliament. During the debate on the Indemnity Bill in March, 1818, Canning poured scorn on Ogden and his sympathizers. After alluding to other examples of alleged cruelty which had been brought forward by Opposition speakers, he said :

> . . . Next, with all the pomp of eloquence, and all the flexibility of pathos, was introduced the revered and ruptured Ogden; his name was pronounced with all the veneration belonging to virtuous age and silver hairs; and yet, on enquiry, what did his case turn out to be, but that he had been cured of a rupture at the public expense? The greater part of the petition of this ill-used personage consisted of a nice and particular description of the manner in which his extruded bowels writhed round the knife of the surgeon; and it is impossible to forget the general shudder felt by the House when that part of the petition was read : yet the plain truth was that this man had laboured under this affliction (asserted in the petition to have been produced by the severity of his confinement) many years; and that he took advantage of his imprisonment to have it cured gratis, expressing afterwards to his friends and relatives the comfort and delight which he experienced on being made a new man again. His case might be a very fit case for the Rupture Society; but to require the decision of Parliament upon it was such a daring attempt upon its credulity as would probably be never again attempted.[1]

The phrase " revered and ruptured " was somewhat unfortunate, and it let loose a storm of abuse upon Canning's head : an anonymous pamphlet was published in the form of an open letter to him, full of the most scurrilous accusations, and the principal

[1] Therry, R., *op. cit.*, vol. IV, pp. 32–36.

charge was that he made fun of the sufferings of the people. To this Canning, hot-tempered as ever, replied as follows:

Gloucester Lodge, April 10th, 1818.

SIR,

I received, early in the last week, the copy of your pamphlet, which you (I take for granted) had the attention to send to me.

Soon after I was informed, on the authority of your publisher, that you had withdrawn the whole impression from him, with the view (as was supposed) of suppressing the publication.

I since learn, however, that the pamphlet, though not sold, is circulated under blank covers.

I learn this from (among others) the gentleman to whom the pamphlet has been industriously attributed, but who has voluntarily and absolutely denied to me that he has any knowledge of it, or of its author.

To you, Sir, whoever you may be, I address myself thus directly, for the purpose of expressing to you my opinion that you are a liar and a slanderer, and want courage only to be an assassin.

I have only to add, that no man knows of my writing to you; that I shall maintain the same reserve so long as I have an expectation of hearing from you in your own name; and that I shall not give up that expectation till to-morrow (Saturday) night.

The same address that brought me your pamphlet will bring any letter safe to my hands.

I am, Sir,
Your humble servant,
GEORGE CANNING.

For the Author of "A Letter to the Right Hon. George Canning ".

(Mr. Ridgway is requested to forward this letter to its destination.)

It was widely rumoured at the time that the author of the pamphlet was Sir John Cam Hobhouse, later Lord Broughton, the friend of Byron, but whoever he was he deemed discretion to be the better part of valour, and, while acknowledging Canning's letter, refused to disclose his identity.

The unhappy reference to Ogden's infirmities was also the indirect cause of a quarrel between Canning and *The Times*, for in June, 1819, that paper reported Joseph Hume as having said in the House of Commons that the President of the Board of Control had risen above the sufferings of others by laughing at them. As a result, Bell, the publisher, was summoned to the Bar of the House, and the reporter concerned was committed to the custody of the Serjeant-at-Arms; indeed, he very narrowly escaped imprisonment in Newgate, but was finally let off with a reprimand. Canning wrote a letter to Hume which practically amounted to a challenge, but an explanation was forthcoming, and no fight took place. *The Times*, however, never forgave Canning for the indignity that he had caused to be inflicted upon it, and was his enemy for the rest of his life. In 1821, it may be added, Canning came within an ace of having a duel with Sir Francis Burdett over some allusions to himself in a speech made by the Radical leader.

These incidents throw considerable light both upon the hot temper of Canning and upon the embittered political life of the period which followed the overthrow of Napoleon. To the end Canning was his own worst enemy, and although the disappointments of earlier years had forced upon him the advisability of curbing his impatience, the old Adam would out, and it caused him to be involved in these heated controversies. At the same time the dislike of Canning which was obviously so general upon the Opposition benches is the more remarkable in view of the rapidity with which it was changed into admiration as soon as he returned to the Foreign Office. He certainly never went out of his way to conciliate an opponent, but in spite of this the man who was accused of sneering at the sufferings of Ogden was to be, in less than ten years, at the head of a coalition administration which included more than one of his bitterest critics when he was at the Board of Control.

The real explanation of Canning's attitude at this time, it cannot be too often repeated, lies in the fact that, like his colleagues, he sincerely believed in the danger of revolution. If further evidence of this be required it is to be found in a paragraph from a letter which he wrote to Bagot in August, 1818, on the morrow of the General Election:

This year I could not write immediately after the termination of the session, because the election for the new Parliament followed close upon it, and called me to Liverpool almost as soon as I was released from the House of Commons. Newspapers will have enabled you to form a judgment of all that passed there, with which I had good reason to be satisfied. It was indeed more flattering, if possible, and more decisive than 1812,[1] and the rather as I have every ground for believing that my position, as a minister, had nothing to do with the result. I am afraid, therefore, that—however gratifying to me personally—it is not a set-off against failures and unpopularities elsewhere. I fear the general complexion of the returns is very unfavourable, and I fear still more that the general state of the publick mind is as (adverse I will not say), but as indifferent as at any period of our history. The dangers, in my conception, are greater than in 1793; the means of resistance, and the sense of the necessity of resistance, comparatively nothing.[2]

Holding these views it was only to be expected that Canning should have supported such measures as the Government thought necessary for the maintenance of law and order.

During these years of political strife Canning's family was growing up, and his second son, William, had, after some hesitation on the part of his father, been allowed to join the Navy. On the other hand the health of the eldest boy grew steadily worse. Very early in his life he had developed an incurable lameness, and neither the sojourn in Portugal nor the medical skill of the day was able to effect a cure. He became a helpless invalid, unable to move from his chair, until, in April, 1820, death at last released him from his sufferings. The blow to Canning was a severe one, for the child had always been very dear to him, and the measure of his grief may be gathered from the verses which he wrote for the boy's tombstone :

Though short thy span, God's unimpeached decrees,
Which made that shortened span one long disease,
Yet, merciful in chastening, gave thee scope
For mild, refreshing virtues, faith and hope,
Meek resignation, pious charity;
And since this world was not the world for thee,

[1] The actual figures were: Canning, 1654; Gascoyne, 1444; Earl of Sefton, 1280. 2,876 electors voted.
[2] Bagot, J., *op. cit.*, vol. II, p. 82.

> Far from thy path removed, with partial care,
> Strife, glory, gain, and pleasure's flowery snare,
> Bade earth's temptations pass thee harmless by,
> And fixed on Heaven thine unreverted eye,
> Oh! marked from birth, and nurtured for the skies!
> In youth, with more than wisdom's bearing wise;
> As sainted Martyrs, patient to endure;
> Simple as unweaned infancy, and pure;
> Pure from all stain (save that in human clay,
> Which Christ's atoning blood hath washed away).
> By mortal suffering now no more oppressed,
> Mount, sinless spirit, to thy destined rest!
> While I—reversed our nature's kindlier doom—
> Pour forth a father's sorrows on thy tomb.

Earlier in the year, in the last days of January, there had been another death, namely that of the King, which was also to affect Canning closely. George III had not exercised the royal power for nearly a decade, and in these circumstances it might have been supposed that his demise would make but little difference. This, indeed, would probably have been the case but for the action of the new Queen, who, in June, 1820, insisted on returning to England, and thereby precipitated a crisis which very nearly resulted in the overthrow of the monarchy itself.

Neither George IV nor his consort had anything approaching clean hands where the other was concerned, but they were not private citizens, and the Government had to take the nation's interests into account. These were well served by Caroline's absence on the Continent. Whether she would in any case have stayed there after her husband's succession to the throne is a moot point, but the omission of her name from the Litany drove her to fury, and she determined to return to England to secure her rights. Before she left the Continent she was warned that proceedings for adultery would be taken against her if she came back, and that the basis of the prosecution would be the report of commissioners who had been sent to Milan two years before to investigate her conduct. Caroline had undoubtedly been ill-used during her earlier days, but she was not one to learn from adversity, and her original impetuousness and lack of balance had been accentuated by her misfortunes. In addition, she was very badly advised, notably by one Alderman Wood, M.P., and she interpreted the plaudits of the mob, due to dislike of her husband, as evidence of her own popularity.

In this controversy Canning soon became inextricably involved. The Queen was an old friend, and had been godmother to the child he had so recently lost, while, it will be remembered, it was in no small degree due to his own representations in 1814 that Caroline had been induced to take up her residence abroad. It was not that he believed in her guilt, but rather that, to use his own words, " faction had marked her for its own ", and he declared that in similar circumstances he would have given the same advice to his nearest relative. Such being the case, the Queen's return, in spite of his disapproval of it, placed Canning in an extremely difficult position; and when his colleagues in the Cabinet decided to introduce a Bill to deprive her of her title, and to dissolve her marriage, he felt that the time had come when he could no longer remain silent. In effect, he was torn between considerations of private feeling which prevented him from co-operating with the Government of which he was so prominent a member and a sense of public duty that deterred him from opposing the measures which had been adopted. Accordingly, he placed his office at the King's disposal, but the monarch refused to allow him to resign, and gave him full liberty of action: Canning availed himself of this by going abroad, without resigning the Presidency of the Board of Control, early in August before the proceedings against the Queen began.

During the time he was away the Bill of Pains and Penalties was introduced in the House of Lords, where it was hotly debated. On the third reading, in the middle of November, the Government majority dropped to nine, and Liverpool, realizing the impossibility of getting the measure through the House of Commons, thereupon announced its abandonment. The Queen, however, foolishly refused to accept this decision in her favour, and tried to press her advantage by making further demands. At this point Canning returned to England, and as it was clear that Caroline's affairs were likely to be the leading topic of the day for some months to come, he decided to resign from the Government. His reasons are set out in his letter to the King:

India Board Office,
Dec. 12, 1820.

SIR, .

According to your Majesty's gracious permission, I now take the liberty of humbly addressing myself to your Majesty on the subject which your Majesty was so good as to allow me to open to you when last I had the honour of an audience.

Although I am bound to confess that Lord Liverpool, with whom I have in the interval had the fullest communication upon the subject, does not appear to be convinced of the necessity of the step which I am taking, I must also say that discussion and reflection have tended to confirm me in the opinion which I have already submitted to your Majesty.

When, in the month of June, I presumed humbly to represent to your Majesty the impossibility of my taking any part in the proceedings against the Queen, and in consequence laid at your Majesty's feet the tender of my resignation, your Majesty had the goodness and condescension to command me to continue in your service, abstaining from any share in those proceedings. And your Majesty was farther pleased to grant me full authority to plead your Majesty's express commands for so continuing in office.

That authority I have not abused. And I have persevered in obedience to your Majesty's commands (the generosity of which I can never sufficiently acknowledge) until a state of things has arisen to which they cannot be considered as applying.

The proceedings in the House of Commons, which was then in contemplation when your Majesty's commands were laid upon me, was one which would have been conducted (as that in the House of Lords) apart from all other matters. The absenting myself from that separate proceedings would have required no other explanation than that which your Majesty had so indulgently authorized me to furnish: nor need such partial absence from the House of Commons have created any embarrassment in the general conduct of Parliamentary business.

But the discussions respecting the Queen, which may now be expected in the House of Commons, will be so much intermixed with the general business of the session, that a minister could not absent himself from them without appearing virtually to abandon the Parliamentary duties of his station. On the other hand, to be present, as a minister, taking no part in the discussions, must produce not only the most painful embarrassment to himself, but the greatest perplexity to his colleagues, and the utmost disadvantage to the conduct of your Majesty's affairs.

From these difficulties, Sir, I see no remedy, except in the renewal to your Majesty of my humble, but earnest, request that your Majesty will be graciously pleased to approve of my retiring from the situation which I have now the honour to hold in your Majesty's Government. Entreating your Majesty to believe that I shall carry with me out of office an unabated zeal for the prosperity of your Majesty's reign, and an unalterable sense of gratitude for the kindness which I have uniformly experienced at your Majesty's hands from the moment of my entrance into your service. I am, with profound veneration and attachment,

Your Majesty's
Most dutiful and most obedient Subject and Servant,
GEORGE CANNING.

This time Canning's resignation was accepted, and it is pleasant to note that among the expressions of regret which he received were letters from Sidmouth and Castlereagh. Sidmouth wrote of an " irreparable " loss to his colleagues, and went on to say " your kind, cordial, and honourable conduct has made a strong and lasting impression on my mind "; while the Foreign Secretary thanked the retiring minister " for the uniform attention with which you have followed up, and the kindness with which you have assisted me, in the business of the department of which I am more immediately responsible ".[1] So Canning went out of office once more, and in February, 1821, he was writing to Bagot from Paris:

I am here in a state of idle existence long unknown to me, dividing with my wife the duty of chaperon to Harriet in the evenings, and passing my mornings in the Chamber of Deputies instead of all night long in the House of Commons.[2]

During the next eighteen months Canning rarely appeared at Westminster, and he spent much of his time on the Continent, particularly in France, where he contracted a personal friendship with Chateaubriand; he also obtained a great deal of firsthand knowledge that was to prove invaluable to him in the years to come. The death of the Queen early in 1821 in reality removed the only obstacle to him rejoining the Government, and during that year no less than four series of negotiations took place be-

[1] Stapleton, A. G., op. cit., pp. 316–319.
[2] Bagot, J., op. cit., vol. II, p. 110.

tween Canning and the Prime Minister with this end in view. The King, however, could be just as obstinate as his father, and he had taken offence at Canning's attitude in the Queen's case; in the face, therefore, of George's refusal to have him in the ministry, the negotiations all broke down.

The only business that brought Canning to the House of Commons was that connected with the problems of Parliamentary Reform and Roman Catholic Emancipation, for he was as convinced an opponent of the one as he was an advocate of the other. Few statesmen in recent times have believed so firmly in the balance of the Constitution as did Canning, and it was because in his opinion Parliamentary Reform would upset this balance he opposed it so strenuously. Indeed, his attitude on this question provides a clue to his whole political philosophy.

In the spring of 1822 Lord John Russell moved " That the present state of the representation of the people in Parliament requires the most serious consideration of the House ", and this gave Canning an opportunity of dealing with the whole subject of Parliamentary Reform from every point of view. During the course of his speech in support of the motion Lord John had admitted that in the past the House of Commons had proved both a jealous and an efficient custodian of the public liberties, and in particular he had gone so far as to declare that the Revolution of 1688, an event which in those days was generally approved, was essentially a Parliamentary, rather than a popular, movement in any sense of the term. This admission gave Canning an opening of which he was not slow to take advantage :

Surely these admissions of the noble lord are in no small degree at variance with his motion. Surely such admissions, if not ample enough of themselves to over-balance the direct arguments which the noble lord has, in the subsequent part of his speech, brought forward in the support of that motion, do at least relieve me from much of the difficulty and odium which might otherwise have belonged to an opposition to Parliamentary Reform. If I contend on behalf of the constitution of the House of Commons, such as it is, I contend at least for no untried, no discredited, no confessedly pernicious establishment. I contend for a House of Commons, the spirit of which, whatever be its frame, has, without any forcible alteration, gradually, but faithfully, accommodated itself to the progressive spirit of the country; and in the frame of which, if an alteration such as the noble lord now proposes, had been made a hundred and thirty years ago, the House of Commons of that day would, by his own confession, have been disabled from accomplishing the glorious Revolution, and securing the fruits of it to their posterity.

Lord John Russell had, however, quoted Pitt in support of his proposals, and Canning, in view of his claim to be Pitt's political heir, felt the necessity of explaining how he found it possible to oppose the motion without thereby being disloyal to his old chief. The difference, in his opinion, between the schemes of reform that Pitt had sponsored, and those that the Whigs were now putting forward, lay in the fact that the element of coercion was wholly lacking in the former, while it was an integral part of the latter.[1] On these grounds he felt that there was nothing inconsistent in a disciple of Pitt voting against the motion of Lord John Russell.

> Here then, I repeat it, is a difference of the most essential kind between the two propositions of Mr. Pitt and of the noble lord; a difference, not superficial, but fundamental; as complete indeed as the difference between concession and force, or between respect for property and spoliation. I am not, however, bound nor at all prepared to contend for the intrinsic or absolute excellence of Mr. Pitt's plan; and still less to engage my own support to such a plan, if it were to be brought forward at the present time. But placing it in fair comparison with the noble lord's, I must entreat the House to bear in mind that Mr. Pitt never lost sight of the obligation to preserve as well as to amend; that he proposed not to enforce any reluctant surrender; nor to sacrifice any other than voluntary victims on the altar of practical improvement.

Having thus, as it were, cleared the ground of the points which had been raised by the supporters of the motion, Canning proceeded to state the principles upon which his opposition to Parliamentary Reform was based, and the first of these was his

[1] Pitt had proposed to establish a fund of £1,000,000 to be applied to the purchase of franchises from such decayed boroughs as should be willing to sell them. Russell wished to deprive each of the smaller boroughs of one half of the elective franchise they then enjoyed, and to increase by a hundred the representatives of the counties and the larger towns.

conviction that any step in the direction of democracy must lead to uniformity of a very undesirable type.

For my part, Sir, I value the system of Parliamentary Representation for that very want of uniformity which is complained of in this petition [*i.e.* of 1793]; for the variety of rights of election. I conceive that to establish one uniform right would inevitably be to exclude some important interests from the advantage of being represented in this House.

Furthermore, Parliamentary Reform would upset the whole balance of the Constitution:

If it [*i.e.* the House of Commons] were to add to its real active governing influence such an exclusively popular character and tone of action as would arise from the consciousness that it was the immediately deputed agent for the whole people, and the exclusive organ of their will, the House of Commons, instead of enjoying one-third of the power of the state, would, in a little time, absorb the whole. How could the House of Lords, a mere assembly of individuals, however privileged, and representing only themselves, presume to counteract the decisions of the delegates of the people? How could the Crown itself, holding its power, as I should say, for the people, but deriving it altogether, as others would contend, from the people—presume to counteract, or hesitate implicitly to obey, the supreme authority of the nation assembled within these walls?

A few sentences later he defined the functions of the House of Commons as follows:

. . . Which functions are, not to exercise an undivided, supreme dominion in the name of the people, over the Crown and the other branch of the legislature, but checking the one and balancing the other, to watch over the people's rights and to provide especially for the people's interests.

Then, in a peroration which must be quoted in full, partly as a specimen of his superb oratory and partly as illustrative of his political views, Canning adjured the House to reject Lord John's motion:[1]

---

[1] The motion was rejected by 269 votes to 164.

Dreading therefore the danger of total, and seeing the difficulties as well as the unprofitableness of partial, alteration, I object to this first step towards a change in the constitution of the House of Commons. There are wild theories abroad. I am not disposed to impute an ill motive to any man who entertains them. I will believe such a man to be as sincere in his conviction of the possibility of realizing his notions of change without risking the tranquillity of the country, as I am sincere in my belief of their impracticability, and of the tremendous danger of attempting to carry them into effect; but for the sake of the world as for our own safety, let us be cautious and firm. Other nations, excited by the example of the liberty which this country has long possessed, have attempted to copy our constitution; and some of them have shot beyond it in the fierceness of their pursuit. I grudge not to other nations that share of liberty which they may acquire: in the name of God, let them enjoy it! But let us warn them that they lose not the object of their desire by the very eagerness with which they attempt to grasp it. Inheritors and conservators of rational freedom, let us, while others are seeking it in restlessness and trouble, be a steady and shining light to guide their course, not a wandering meteor to bewilder and mislead them.

Let it not be thought that this is an unfriendly or disheartening counsel to those who are either struggling under the pressure of harsh government, or exulting in the novelty of sudden emancipation. It is addressed much rather to those who, though cradled and educated amidst the sober blessings of the British Constitution, pant for other schemes of liberty than those which that Constitution sanctions—other than are compatible with a just equality of civil rights, or with the necessary restraints of social obligation: of some of whom it may be said, in the language which Dryden puts into the mouth of one of the most extravagent of his heroes, that,

" They would be as free as nature first made man,
Ere the base laws of servitude began.
When wild in woods the noble savage ran."

Noble and swelling sentiments!—but which must be reduced into practice. Grand ideas!—but which must be qualified and adjusted by a compromise between the aspirings of individuals and a due concern for the general tranquillity;

must be subdued and chastened by reason and experience, before they can be directed to any useful end! A search after abstract perfection in government may produce, in generous minds, an enterprise and enthusiasm to be recorded by the historian and to be celebrated by the poet: but such perfection is not an object of reasonable pursuit, because it is not one of possible attainment: and never yet did a passionate struggle after an absolutely unattainable object fail to be productive of misery to an individual, of madness and confusion to a people. As the inhabitants of those burning climates, which lie beneath a tropical sun, sigh for the coolness of the mountain and the grove; so (all history instructs us) do nations which have basked for a time in the torrent blaze of an unmitigated liberty, too often call upon the shades of despotism, even of military despotism, to cover them—

> " O quis me gelidis in vallibus Haemi
>   Sistat, et ingenti ramorum protegat umbra! "

A protection which blights while it shelters; which dwarfs the intellect, and stunts the energies of man, but to which a wearied nation willingly resorts from intolerable heats, and from perpetual danger of convulsion.

Our lot is happily cast in the temperate zone of freedom: the clime best suited to the development of the moral qualities of the human race; to the cultivation of their faculties and to the security as well as the improvement of their virtues: a clime not exempt indeed from variations of the elements, but variations which purify while they agitate the atmosphere that we breathe. Let us be sensible of the advantages which it is our happiness to enjoy. Let us guard with pious gratitude the flame of genuine liberty, that fire from heaven, of which our Constitution is the holy depository; and let us not, for the chance of rendering it more intense and more radiant, impair its purity or hazard its extinction

The noble lord is entitled to the acknowledgments of the House for the candid, able, and ingenuous manner in which he has brought forward his motion. If in the remarks which I have made upon it there has been anything which has borne the appearance of disrespect to him, I hope he will acquit me of having so intended it. That the noble lord will carry his motion this evening, I have no fear; but with the talents which he has shown himself to possess, and with (I sincerely hope) a long and brilliant career of Parliamentary distinction before him, he will, no doubt, renew his efforts hereafter. Although I presume not to expect that he will give any weight to observations or warnings of mine, yet on this, probably, the last,[1] opportunity which I shall have of raising my voice on the question of Parliamentary Reform, while I conjure the House to pause before it consents to adopt the proposition of the noble lord, I cannot help conjuring the noble lord himself, to pause before he again presses it upon the country. If, however, he shall persevere, and if his perseverance shall be successful—and if the results of that success shall be such as I cannot help apprehending—his be the triumph to have precipitated those results—be mine the consolation that to the utmost, and the latest, of my power, I have opposed them.[2]

Canning's hostility to Parliamentary Reform was only equalled in its intensity by his zeal on behalf of Roman Catholic Emancipation. Both during his term of office as President of the Board of Control, and afterwards, he made several speeches in the House of Commons on this subject, but as their interest was naturally more ephemeral than his opinions upon the balance of the Constitution, quotation from them would hardly serve any useful purpose. Suffice it to say that Canning adopted the line, which he had always taken, that the disabilities upon Roman Catholics had originally been imposed for political, rather than for religious, reasons, and that as these reasons were no longer operative the disabilities should be removed. In particular, he pleaded in April, 1822, for the admission of Catholic peers to the House of Lords, a step in this direction having been taken when George IV invited them to be present at his coronation.

Canning has been accused more than once of inconsistency in opposing Parliamentary Reform and the repeal of the Test Act on the one hand, and in supporting Roman Catholic Emancipation on the other, but to bring such a charge against him is completely to misunderstand the whole basis of his political faith. During a debate in the House of Commons in 1810 he gave clear expression of his views upon the nature of the Constitution:

[1] Canning was at this time on the eve of his projected departure for India.
[2] Therry, R., *op. cit.*, vol. IV, pp. 330–381.

L

The temper and practice of the British Constitution is to redress practical grievance, but not to run after theoretical perfection. It loves to set the subjects of the realm at ease in point of conscience, and it abhors practical oppression; but it cares little whether the theory of every part of its system squares exactly with that of every other part.

In these two sentences is to be found the key to Canning's conduct throughout the whole of his public life, and judged by this test he cannot be convicted of inconsistency.

Where he was persuaded that any section of the community was suffering under a real grievance he was the champion of reform, but he was not prepared to throw the Constitution into the melting-pot in pursuit of " theoretical perfection ". Canning supported Catholic Emancipation because he believed that the existing disabilities were a definite injustice, and that this could only be remedied by their abolition. On the other hand, he did not favour the repeal of the Test and Corporation Acts, for he considered that the measure which was passed annually, rendering them a dead letter, gave Nonconformists all the security that was necessary, while repeal would inevitably weaken the whole position of the Church of England, and so threaten that balance of the Constitution in which he so firmly believed. This readiness to remedy a grievance was never more fully shown than when Lord John Russell brought forward a motion for the disfranchisement of the borough of Grampound on the score of corruption, and the allocation of its two members to the county of Yorkshire. Canning, without abating one jot of his hostility to the principle of Parliamentary Reform, supported this proposal because it dealt with a particular grievance which required to be remedied.

If, then, Canning can be described as a moderate Tory, both his moderation and his Toryism were based upon a set of definite principles, and not upon any desire to elaborate a programme which should attract votes and support from both parties in the state— from the Tories because he was nominally a Tory, and from the Whigs on the ground of the liberality of his views. The two planks in his platform were the remedying of any practical grievance and the maintenance of the balance of the Constitution, and from this policy he never swerved, though it must be admitted that during his opposition to the ministries of Addington and "All the Talents " he had occasionally been guilty of a factiousness which did him little credit.

Canning was not happy out of office, but the attitude of the King seemed to preclude any early return to the Government, and he accordingly began to look for employment in other directions. In the last days of 1821 he had been asked to allow his name to be proposed to the Court of Directors of the East India Company as Governor-General in succession to Hastings, and in the spring of the following year he gave his acceptance for reasons which he explained to Huskisson: " I preferred India, opening to me in a certain way—that is, through an undoubted voluntary vacancy, and by the unsuggested solicitation of the Court of Directors—to—not office—but a struggle for office, liable to end either in second rejection—or in the breaking-up of the Government ". Once he had decided to go to India, with the promise of a peerage at the close of his service there, Canning became enthusiastic over the idea; nor is this in any way remarkable, for " apart from the splendour of the position as ruler for a time of the most extensive and populous dominion in the world, the field which it offers for the display of almost every kind of ability and the acquisition of almost every kind of fame, presents great attractions to a man of energy and ambition such as were at all times the leading features of Canning's character ".[1] It is, however, idle to speculate upon the possible result of his tenure of that high office which destiny had reserved for his son, for at the very moment that Canning was taking leave of his constituents in Liverpool, preparatory to his departure for the East, came the news that the Foreign Secretaryship was vacant.

Castlereagh had been continuously in office since 1812; he had worked for twelve to fourteen hours a day; and his official correspondence filled seventy volumes. Yet he was easily, though quite undeservedly, the best-hated member of the Government, and slowly but surely the iron entered into his soul. Nevertheless, as late as 1821 contemporaries noticed no change, and Croker was writing, " Londonderry [2] goes on as usual, and . . . like Mont Blanc, continues to gather all the sunshine upon his icy head. He is better than ever; that is colder, steadier, more *pococurante*, and withal more amiable and respected. It is a splendid summit of bright and polished frost which, like the travellers in Switzerland, we all admire, but no one can hope and few would wish to reach." In the following year the signs became visible that Castlereagh, to give the name by which he is best known, was no longer his former

---

[1] Yonge, C. D., *op. cit.*, vol. III, p. 156.
[2] He had succeeded as 2nd Marquess of Londonderry in April, 1821.

self. First of all he became a prey to profound melancholy, and he expressed doubts whether he would be able to attend an impending congress at Verona. Then he developed persecution mania, and imagined plots against his life. The doctor was called in, and matters were made worse by the usual bleeding and lowering drugs. The sick man, still believing in the plots against him, asked for, but was refused, his pistols, and his razors were taken from the room. On the morning of August 12th, 1822, he was heard to moan, " My mind, mind is, as it were gone ", and on being left alone for a few minutes he cut his throat with a small knife which he had managed to secrete in a drawer. Popular hate pursued him to his grave in Westminster Abbey. The funeral procession, reported *The Times*, " reached the great western door of the Abbey exactly at a quarter after nine o'clock. The assemblage of persons in that vicinity was so dense that the space unoccupied was merely sufficient to allow the procession to pass along it. On the arrival of the hearse among them, a most discordant yell displayed the animosity which they felt for the deceased nobleman."

At first there was complete uncertainty as to the dead man's successor, and the name of Wellington, though against his own wish, was freely canvassed. The King was in Scotland, and he did not hesitate to make his views clear by at once giving instructions that there should be no delay in the departure of the new Governor-General. Liverpool, however, realized the weakness of his Cabinet, and was determined to have Canning back in it; all the same it required the utmost firmness on his part to overcome the royal objections, and on September 8th, nearly a month after Castlereagh's death, Canning could write to Huskisson, " I have heard nothing. I know nothing." Within a week, however, the King had given way, and Canning was writing to Bootle Wilbraham:

> *Foreign Office,*
> *September* 16, 1822,
> ¼ p. 6.
>
> MY DEAR B. W.,
>
> Though a little too late for the purposes of information . . . I cannot refrain from letting you see by the evidence of a date that the Proposal [1] was that which, as you know, I could alone have accepted; that I have accepted it; and that in consequence here I am.

[1] The Foreign Secretaryship combined with the Leadership of the House of Commons.

CHAPTER VIII

THE FOREIGN OFFICE AGAIN

THE European situation was very different in the autumn of 1822 from what it had been when Canning left the Foreign Office thirteen years before. Then, he had been confronted by one of the greatest figures in the history of the world, and one whose subsequent overthrow was in no small measure due to the policy which he had pursued when Foreign Secretary. Now, he was called upon to play a leading part in the liquidation of that titanic conflict which had raged during the greater part of his adult life. On both occasions his truly remarkable power of seeing things as they really were, and not merely as he would have liked them to have been, stood him in good stead, and he had not long returned to the Foreign Office before he gave clear proof that he was as capable in time of peace as he had shown himself to be in that of war.

The existing order in Europe was based upon the Treaty of Chaumont of March, 1814, and the subsequent arrangements which had been made at the Congress of Vienna. Briefly, these placed upon Great Britain, Austria, Prussia, and Russia the responsibility for a period of twenty years of defending the territorial settlement effected after the overthrow of Napoleon, and also of preventing the restoration of the Bonaparte dynasty to the French throne. Furthermore, there were to be periodical re-unions of sovereigns and ministers to discuss the more important problems of the day. It will be remarked that the Treaty of Chaumont was purely an arrangement between the victorious Allies, and that it was, in certain circumstances, definitely directed against France; but, at the congresses which became so prominent a feature of the years following the conclusion of peace, that Power was treated as an equal; and after the foreign armies of occupation had been withdrawn in 1818 she had little to fear from any possible concentration against her.

It was obvious from the beginning that the Treaty of Chaumont and its corollary might mean much or little, according to the interpretation put upon them by the signatories. Until France had settled down under the rule of Louis XVIII, and while there was consequently danger of further trouble in that quarter, the

Quadruple Alliance served a very useful purpose. Before long, however, it became clear that Louis was a good deal more firmly established than were some of his victorious contemporaries, and Austria, Prussia, and Russia showed an increasing disposition to stretch the terms of the settlement in a way that was never intended. As members of the Holy Alliance, which Great Britain had refused to join, they declared that the *status quo* could only be maintained by the ruthless suppression of all revolutionary movements, and this, in its turn, naturally implied a right to interfere, by force if necessary, in the internal affairs of any country in which revolution showed its head. To this Castlereagh had been firmly opposed, and he said:

> We shall be found in our place when actual danger menaces the system of Europe, but this country cannot and will not act upon abstract and speculative principles of precaution. The alliance which exists [1] had no such purpose in view in its original formation. It was never so explained to Parliament, and it would be a breach of faith to Parliament now to extend it.

In 1820-21 revolution broke out both in Italy and in Spain, and it was at once apparent that Great Britain and her allies in the struggle against Napoleon were at the parting of the ways.

The Treaty of Vienna had restored the *ancien régime* in the Italian Peninsula in its entirety with the exception of the republics of Genoa and Venice, which were attributed to Piedmont and Austria respectively. At the same time the whole country in reality came under the domination of Vienna to an extent unknown before the French Revolution. Bourbons of the Spanish branch of that family still reigned at Naples and Lucca, but Spain herself had grown so weak that it was to Vienna rather than to Madrid that they had come to look for support; while the male line of the Estensi at Modena had died out, and an Archduke ruled there, as at Florence in the place of the vanished Medici. In effect, Italy was an Austrian protectorate in all but name, and a revolution there was as alarming to Metternich as if it had broken out in Hungary or Bohemia.

In Spain the situation was somewhat different. The war against Napoleon had, as we have seen, been carried on in the name of the absent Ferdinand by bodies unknown to the law, and

---

[1] *I.e.*, the Quadruple Alliance of Great Britain, Austria, Prussia, and Russia.

before it was over the whole system of government had been changed by the adoption of the so-called Constitution of 1812. Ferdinand had brusquely restored the old order as soon as he returned from exile, and although he treated both Liberals and *afrancesadas*, as those who had supported Joseph Bonaparte were called, with considerable severity, there is no reason to suppose that his rule was unpopular with the mass of his fellow-countrymen. Unfortunately for himself, however, he proved to be not only tyrannical, but hopelessly incompetent, and the revolt which had broken out in America accordingly began to make considerable headway. In 1820, some troops, under orders to cross the Atlantic, mutinied, and before long the whole country was in full revolution. On the other hand, Spain was unquestionably an independent, if decayed, Power, and was not the client of any other state. Moreover, France alone was in a military position to exercise any effective influence upon the progress of events in the Iberian Peninsula, for in the case of other Powers access was only possible across the sea, and this could not be effected without the permission of Great Britain, whose consent was almost certain to be refused.

Nevertheless the position of the British Government was not an easy one. Castlereagh was far from approving of the doctrine of intervention so popular with the members of the Holy Alliance, but it was not to the interest of Great Britain, as it was certainly beyond her power, to interfere where Italy was concerned. Nor did he wish to imperil the European equilibrium, so painfully re-established only a few years before, by encouraging movements which he knew to be doomed to failure, and with which he was in any case fundamentally out of sympathy. Furthermore, he realized that Austria had special rights in Italy, and her intervention in Naples, which soon took place, was covered by an agreement of June, 1815, between her and the Neapolitan Government, according to which the latter promised not to introduce constitutional changes other than those allowed in the Austrian dominions in Italy. At the same time he was quite firmly resolved that he would not give even a tacit consent to the employment of the same methods in respect of the Spanish revolt. Finally, Castlereagh believed in the congress system, since it provided an opportunity for the statesmen of Europe to come into personal contact, and he was reluctant to take any step which might accelerate the end of that system.

There was thus no such breach between the policies of Castlereagh and Canning as is sometimes alleged. Canning was by nature more downright than his predecessor, and he had not long been in office when he wrote to Bagot, " You know my politics well enough to know what I mean—when I say that for ' Europe ' I shall be desirous now and then to read ' England ' ";[1] yet the difference was in pace rather than in direction. In any event it is always easier for a new minister than for an old one to lead his country along a fresh path in international matters. Old friends and associates among the representatives of foreign Powers inevitably exercise a restraining influence, and even the most determined of men finds it difficult to turn his back upon those with whom he has been associated in good fortune and ill for a number of years. So it was with Castlereagh. He might entertain few illusions concerning the policy of Alexander or of Metternich, but he had worked with them, first of all to defeat Napoleon, and then to re-cast the map of Europe at Vienna. However much he might disapprove of their later conduct, it was in these circumstances but natural that he should tarry for a space at the parting of the ways, even if he had no doubt in his own mind that further co-operation was neither possible nor desirable.

For Canning the situation was very different. He saw in Alexander merely Napoleon's accomplice at Tilsit, and there was little in the memory of those days to recommend the Tsar in his eyes. With Metternich he had not had any earlier relations, so he was under no special obligation to consider the Austrian Chancellor's feelings. In effect, all that Canning did during his first few months at the Foreign Office was to pursue rather more vigorously the policy of detachment from the Holy Alliance which had been initiated by Castlereagh. To speak of any violent breach is to ignore the fact that there had been no change of government in Great Britain, and that Canning was not a dictator, but a minister in the Liverpool administration. " Our business is to preserve ", he said, " so far as may be, the peace of the world, and therewith the independence of the several nations which compose it." That is not a definition to which his predecessor would have taken exception, and the difference between their conduct of affairs was dictated by changing circumstances rather than by any fundamental conflict of principle.

The first problem with which Canning was confronted was the

[1] Bagot, J., *op. cit.*, vol. II, p. 138.

attitude to be adopted at the coming congress of Verona. The situation in Spain had gone from bad to worse, and Ferdinand VII was now little better than a prisoner in the hands of the revolutionaries. Wellington was selected as the British representative, and his instructions were those which Castlereagh had, with the approval of the King and the Cabinet, drawn up for his guidance.

The main subjects to be discussed were three; namely the Eastern Question, for the War of Greek Independence was in full swing; Spain and her colonies; and the affairs of Italy. In respect of the last of these the duty of the British representative was merely to keep himself informed, and to see that nothing was done " inconsistent with the European system and the treaties ". So far as the Eastern Question was concerned, the successes of the Greeks and " the progress made by them toward the formation of a government, together with the total paralysis of the Ottoman naval power in the Levant ", pointed to the fact that sooner or later Great Britain would be forced to recognize the Greek insurgents as belligerents. In the matter of Spain, which was clearly to be the chief topic at the congress, there was to be " a rigid abstinence from any interference in the internal affairs of that country ". As for the Spanish colonies, they had, as will be shown, already been in part recognized by Great Britain *de facto*, and Wellington was to draw attention to British commerce with them, which it was impossible to interrupt. On the other hand there was no immediate hurry to give *de jure* recognition " so as to create a certain impediment to the assertion of the rights of the former occupant ".

Wellington travelled to Italy by way of Paris, and he had not long arrived in the French capital before he became aware that Louis and his ministers were determined to intervene in Spain. Before, therefore, proceeding upon his journey, the Duke asked Canning for further instructions, which he immediately received, and couched in no uncertain terms:

If there be a determined project to interfere by force or by menace in the present struggle in Spain, so convinced are His Majesty's Government of the uselessness and danger of any such interference, so objectionable does it appear to them in principle, as well as utterly impracticable in execution, that when the necessity arises, or (I would rather say) when the opportunity offers, I am to instruct your grace at once frankly and peremptorily to declare, that to any such interference, come what may, His Majesty will not be a party.[1]

On the other hand it must be admitted that the French Government had very good reasons for intervention in Spain. The Tsar had already expressed a wish to send his Cossacks against the Spanish revolutionaries, and as Great Britain controlled the seas the only route from Russia to Madrid lay through France. Louis had little love for Alexander, while his subjects had too lively a memory of the habits of Cossacks ever to wish to see them in France again either as friends or foes; thus it did not take the French Government long to make up its mind that if intervention was to take place in the Peninsula it should be effected exclusively by French troops. In short, the only way of keeping a Russian army out of France was to send a French army into Spain. Furthermore, the evident differences between Great Britain and the Holy Alliance on the whole subject of intervention gave every hope that France would recover entire liberty of action, and the Duc de Montmorency, the French Foreign Minister, thus went to Verona with some very strong cards in his hand.

If these considerations of public policy induced the French Government to regard intervention in Spain in a favourable light, Louis himself had reasons of his own for being by no means opposed to it. In the first place, although his personal opinion of Ferdinand was none of the highest, yet he had no wish to see revolution triumph at his very door, or a democratic Spain become the refuge of every opponent of the French monarchy. More important still, in his opinion, was the need for securing a military triumph under the *drapeau blanc*. The army was steeped in Napoleonic traditions, and was generally considered to be none too loyal to the Bourbons; but a success in the very country where Napoleon had met with disaster would inevitably produce a reaction, and would thus constitute an important victory for that policy of national consolidation which Louis had pursued unflinchingly ever since he ascended the throne. Above all, he knew that he had no time to lose. He was an old man, and he was under no illusions as to the mistakes which his brother and heir would make when he inherited the crown. The one hope of Louis was to establish the throne so securely that it would survive Monsieur's reign, for he had every reason to suppose that his

[1] Therry, R., *op. cit.*, vol. V, pp. 6–7.

nephew, the Duc d'Angoulême, would follow in his own footsteps. Such being the case it was only natural that the French King should have come to the conclusion that the interests both of France and of the monarchy would be best served by sending an army into Spain with the Duc d'Angoulême at its head.

The Congress of Verona met at the beginning of October, 1822, and of the principal European monarchs only the Kings of England and France were absent. Montmorency opened the proceedings by asking for a definition of the attitude which the other Powers would adopt if France found herself compelled to intervene in Spain. To this Austria, Prussia, and Russia replied that they would support such action by withdrawing their representatives from Madrid, but they hesitated to promise any material aid, which suited Montmorency's purpose very well indeed, for that was the last thing he wanted. Wellington, however, took the opposite line, and gave it as his opinion that there was no chance of the revolutionary movement in Spain spreading to other countries. He declared that the British Government would not be committed in advance to approval of the attitude of any other Power, and before it could express an opinion it must know " the exact ground of complaint and the exact cause of war ". This attitude, of which Canning highly approved, convinced both Paris and the Holy Alliance that nothing was to be hoped for from Great Britain, and when Wellington further declared that the British minister at Madrid would confine himself to allaying the ferment which the communications of the other Powers must inevitably excite, they excluded the Duke from their more private deliberations. Finally, the Holy Alliance gave France a free hand in Spain, of which she was not slow to avail herself. A large army under the Duc d'Angoulême swept through the country, and within a brief space the revolution was crushed.

These events represented a notable triumph for Louis and his ministers: seven years before their country had lain prostrate at the feet of its enemies; now, with the approval of the leading Continental Powers, its armies had triumphed in the very land where the great Napoleon had met with disaster. This approval, too, had removed all possibility of such a threat on the Rhine, while the French armies were fighting elsewhere, as was to paralyse the action of Napoleon III in Italy a generation later. On the other hand Great Britain had proved powerless to prevent the invasion of Spain, and in these circumstances it would be

difficult to deny that Canning displayed remarkable skill in saving
his country from a serious diplomatic reverse which would have
lowered her prestige in the eyes of the whole world. A lesser
man would have made Europe ring with his denunciations of
French villainy, but in that case he would soon have been confronted with the alternative of giving way or fighting: as Britain
had neither the means nor the will to adopt the latter course, the
former would have been inevitable, and that would, in its turn,
have isolated her in Europe, since it would automatically have
thrown France into the arms of the Holy Alliance. Instead,
Canning allowed Metternich, who continued to work for the
preservation of the old system of alliances at all costs, to paper over
the cracks in the wall of European solidarity. Decisions were
therefore reached at Verona on such matters as the Slave Trade,
Latin America, Greece, and Italy that allowed a semblance of
unity to be maintained, and it was thus made to appear as if Great
Britain had separated herself from the other Powers on the question
of Spain alone.

The Opposition accused Canning of undue subservience to
France, and the criticisms of Lord Folkestone in particular stung
him to a fury reminiscent of his earlier days. " The Lacedae-
monians ", Canning retorted, " were in the habit of deterring
their children from the vice of intoxication by occasionally
exhibiting their slaves in a state of disgusting inebriety. But, Sir,
there is a moral as well as a physical intoxication. Never before
did I behold so perfect a personification of the character which I
have somewhere seen described as ' exhibiting the contortions of
the Sybil without her inspiration '. Such was the nature of the
noble lord's speech."[1]

Canning's real defence of his policy in respect of the French
invasion of Spain is contained in the most famous of his speeches :

> It would be disingenuous, indeed, not to admit that the
> entry of the French army into Spain was, in a certain sense, a
> disparagement—an affront to the pride—a blow to the
> feelings of England: and it can hardly be supposed that the
> Government did not sympathize, on that occasion, with the
> feelings of the people. But I deny that, questionable or
> censurable as the act might be, it was one which necessarily
> called for our direct and hostile opposition.

[1] Therry, R., *op. cit.*, vol. I, p. 136.

Was nothing then to be done? Was there no other mode of resistance than by a direct attack upon France, or by a war to be undertaken upon the soil of Spain? What, if the possession of Spain might be rendered harmless in rival hands —harmless as regarded us—and valueless to the possessors? Might not compensation for disparagement be obtained by means better adapted to the present time? If France occupied Spain, was it necessary, in order to avoid the consequences of that occupation, that we should blockade Cadiz? No, I looked another way: I sought materials for compensation in another hemisphere. Contemplating Spain, such as our ancestors had known her, I resolved that if France had Spain, it should not be Spain with the Indies. I called the New World into existence to redress the balance of the Old.[1]

In short, he was reverting to his policy of sixteen years earlier.

While Canning was, so to speak, finding his feet once more amid the tangled politics of Europe, at home he was beginning to encounter opposition both from the King and from certain elements in his own party.

His earlier relations with the royal family had, as we have seen, been uniformly friendly, and his political attitude towards the monarchy left nothing to be desired. For George III he clearly entertained very considerable respect, and during the negotiations for his return to office in 1812 he always expressed himself in a most appreciative manner of the attitude of the Prince Regent. It was not until the proceedings against the Queen were instituted that George IV appears to have begun to regard Canning with dislike, and it is probable that for his attitude at that time the King never really forgave him, for the monarch's reluctance to appoint Canning a successor to Castlereagh was certainly based upon private rather than upon public grounds. Canning realized not only that he had fallen into disfavour, but also the difficulties which he would inevitably encounter as a result, and one of his first steps after his return to the Foreign Office was to appoint Lord Francis Conyngham, the son of George's then mistress, as his Under-Secretary in succession to Lord Clanwilliam, who had resigned on the death of Castlereagh. For the moment, this resulted in a reconciliation, and George sent Canning his portrait,

[1] Therry, R., *op. cit.*, vol. VI, pp. 110–111.

as well as walking along the front at Brighton with his arm round the Foreign Secretary's neck.

During the Congress of Verona and its immediate aftermath all went well, though on one occasion the King took exception to the presence of Canning at a banquet given by the Lord Mayor of London, who had been a supporter of Caroline. Soon, however, differences of opinion in matters of foreign policy began to make their appearance, and Canning braced himself for the inevitable struggle—a struggle that was complicated by the King's dual position as ruler of Great Britain and of Hanover, and by the existence of a small coterie behind the throne.

The King of England was a constitutional monarch who governed through his ministers, but the King of Hanover was a despot, with representatives, responsible to himself alone, in every European capital. The position of a Foreign Secretary in these circumstances was extremely difficult, for the King possessed both a policy and a secret service of his own with which his British ministers were not necessarily acquainted. In fact much the same situation existed as in France under Louis XV, when the official ambassadors were liable to find themselves circumvented by the monarch's personal representatives. The difficulty was further increased by the aforesaid growing difference of opinion between George on the one hand, and Liverpool and some of his colleagues on the other, in matters of foreign policy. The King had long discarded the Whig sentiments—they could hardly be described as principles—of his youth, and now desired nothing better than to see Great Britain an active member of the Holy Alliance, while in spite of the revolutionary origin of his own throne he entertained strong legitimist sympathies. For a time he allowed Castlereagh to have access to the Hanoverian correspondence, but when British policy began to diverge from that of Austria and Russia, he placed obstacles in his way, and Canning naturally inherited his predecessor's difficulties. The King of Hanover set himself out to thwart the ministers of the King of England.

It was only natural that Alexander and Metternich should avail themselves to the full of the opportunity to fish in these troubled waters, and Canning soon found himself faced with the determined opposition of a small clique that pulled the strings behind the throne. First and foremost in this group were the Russian ambassador and his wife, the Count and Countess Lieven, of whom the latter was by far the more important. This extraordinary woman, for whom history contains few counterparts, was then in the fullness of her charms, and had come straight from the bed of the Austrian Chancellor to beguile the idle moments of the English King. Then there were the Austrian and French ambassadors, the Princes Esterhazy and Jules de Polignac, with Lady Conyngham and Sir William Knighton, the King's doctor, while the presence of the Duke of Wellington was by no means unknown. When Canning proceeded to advocate the recognition of the revolted Spanish colonies, a policy to which, as will be seen in the succeeding chapter, the Holy Alliance was strongly opposed, this clique at once set to work to get him out of office, and the year 1823 was not far advanced before George's enthusiasm for his Foreign Secretary began perceptibly to cool as a result of these manœuvres. Canning now realized that an indispensable preliminary to success in the diplomatic field was the conquest of the King, and he accordingly applied himself to the task.

As the breach between Great Britain and the Holy Alliance widened, the representatives of the latter redoubled their pressure upon George, and there was what Canning called a definite " plot to change the politics of the Government by changing me ". His reply was to deliver, in April, 1823, two speeches in the House of Commons in defence of his policy, which evoked so much enthusiasm in the country as momentarily to dismay his enemies at Court; in the following month, however, *The Times* reported that the King had wished success to the French invasion of Spain, and added that if this were true he must he mad. In July a remarkable scene took place at a ball at Carlton House, when George interrupted a conversation between Canning and the Vicomte de Marcellus, the French *chargé d'affaires*.

" What are you talking about to the representative of France? ", the King asked Canning, who replied, " Sire, I spoke to him of the excellence of representative government and of forced labour in the Commons. M. de Marcellus cannot be an orator at home, and he is an auditor abroad."

" I see ", observed George. " This year, M. de Marcellus, you have been an auditor under painful circumstances. I have made a complaint to you that it was necessary you should hear, and if you had not kept your mouth shut, and if Parliament could have heard you, you would have had great difficulty in answering."

" Sir ", said Marcellus, " the sailor forgets the storm when the calm returns."

" Very good," replied the King, " but don't be carried away by our system of government which is said to be so reasonable. If there are advantages, there are inconveniences, and I have never forgotten what a witty King once said of it to me, ' Your English Government ', he assured me, ' is only good to protect rascals and to intimidate honest men '. What do you think of that, Mr. Canning? Is there not a great fund of truth in it? "

Canning did not reply, so George continued, " We are still alone in our kind of government, and for the good of the world we ought not to desire our institutions for any other people. What is almost good with us would not be so with others. Every land has not the same fruits above, or minerals below, its surface. It is thus with nations, with their manners, and with their character. Remember this, M. de Marcellus; it is my opinion, fixed and unalterable."

After the King had moved away Canning remarked to the French diplomat, " Representative government has still one advantage that His Majesty has forgotten. Ministers have to endure, without answering back, the epigrams by which a King seeks to avenge himself for his impotence."[1]

This incident has been related in detail, not because it is important in itself, but rather that it shows the footing upon which Canning stood with the King when it took place. No contemporary British statesman was a more convinced monarchist than the Foreign Secretary, but he was not prepared to take his orders from a group of foreign diplomats sheltering behind the throne.

During the whole of the year 1824 he was thwarted, whenever possible, in his efforts to secure the recognition of the independence of the Latin American states, and towards its close there took place an incident which determined him to put an end to this type of opposition once and for all. In October he had proposed to pay a personal visit to Paris for the purpose of discussing American affairs with the new King of France, Charles X, and his ministers. On hearing of this, George instructed Wellington to write to Canning to the effect that the visit would be inopportune. Unfortunately for the King and the Duke, another member of the Cabinet, the Earl of Westmorland, the Lord Privy Seal, had recently had an interview with the French monarch, and had returned to London without informing the Foreign Office of what

---

[1] Temperley, H. W. V.: *The Foreign Policy of Canning, 1822–1827*, pp. 244–245.

he had done. Canning did not fail to make the fullest use of this breach of etiquette, and an acrimonious correspondence ensued between Wellington and himself. Finally, Canning sent the letters to the Prime Minister, who always supported him, and stated his belief that the original communication in respect of his proposed visit to Paris had been concocted between Wellington and the King, although the latter denied it. " Now this I hold not to be fair ", he wrote. " It is high time to look about one, and to beware of what Burke calls ' traps and mines '."

A subsequent chapter will show how Canning successfully carried through his policy of recognition, but it will be as well, in order not to break the continuity of the account of his relations with the King, to deal with its aftermath here. In February, 1825, he not only defended his attitude to George, but hinted by no means obscurely at the monarch's intrigues. This appears to have alarmed the King, who was under no illusions as to his own unpopularity, and was rightly apprehensive of the effect that would be produced were Canning to reveal his activities to the House of Commons. Moreover, the Holy Alliance was itself in process of dissolution owing to the growing differences between Russia and Austria in respect of the Near East, so that the Lievens and Esterhazy no longer spoke with the same voice. In these circumstances George, whose political sense was keen enough, decided to give way with as good a grace as possible, and his surrender—for it was nothing less—was arranged through Sir William Knighton. Canning, once his immediate object had been attained, was quite prepared to meet the King half-way, an attitude which his master fully appreciated. Before long the Hanoverian correspondence was again subject to the Foreign Secretary's supervision, and on November 8th, 1825, the representatives of the King of Hanover at foreign Courts were officially informed that their Sovereign could not support the Holy Alliance in any policy of interference in the internal affairs of other countries.

Whatever opinion may be held of Canning's differences with his colleagues upon more than one occasion, it can hardly be denied that he acted with commendable restraint in this struggle with the King. He had, for the policy that he was pursuing, the support not only of a large majority in the House of Commons, but also of all the more influential sections of public opinion in the country. There was, in effect, overwhelming force on his side, while against him was an unpopular monarch backed by a few foreign advisers. Yet, in spite of all these advantages, Canning held his hand, and as soon as George showed any signs of weakening, he went out of his way to enable the King to save his face. At the same time it cannot be too often stated that Canning by no means took exception to the fact of George's interference; it was to the manner of it that he objected. He denied the right of the King of Hanover to meddle with the affairs of the King of England, and his attitude was thus as orthodox as the most crusted old Tory could wish. There is no evidence that he resented the action of George III in 1800 much as he deplored the resignation of Pitt, and he most certainly did not believe that the King of England should be a mere figurehead; what he would not tolerate was dictation by a foreign clique who tried to utilize the throne for their own ends.

This contest with the King affords further evidence of Canning's growing determination not to tolerate the interference of one Power or group of Powers in the internal affairs of another. The gulf between Great Britain and the Holy Alliance which had been revealed by the discussions at Verona strengthened Canning in his resolve to have as little as possible to do with conferences and congresses in the future, for by this means alone did he see any hope of keeping in check what he described in the House of Commons as the " areopagitical spirit ". It was not, of course, that Canning wished to wash his hands of European affairs altogether, for he fully realized that England was in Europe whether her statesmen liked the fact or not, but he considered that after the differences which had been revealed at Verona, any further international gathering of this type was calculated to do more harm than good. When the questions to be discussed referred for the most part to the liquidation of the late war, conferences served a very useful purpose, but they became extremely dangerous when the Powers were not even in agreement among themselves on matters of principle. On the other hand, Canning was quite ready to offer the good services of Great Britain where he thought they might be of any use, and he had done so in the Franco-Spanish crisis for reasons that were quite consistent with his general policy, and he explained to the House of Commons:

We declined mediating between Spain and an alliance assuming to itself that character of general superintendence of the concerns of nations. But a negotiation between kingdom and kingdom, in the old, intelligible, accustomed, European form, was precisely the issue to which we were desirous of bringing the dispute between France and Spain. We eagerly grasped at this chance of preserving peace.[1]

In this particular instance the proffered mediation was declined by the French Government, but the fact that Canning had taken such a step, combined with the line which he had instructed Wellington to adopt at Verona, was a sufficient indication to the world of the principles by which British policy would be guided under the direction of the new Foreign Secretary.

[1] Therry, R., *op. cit.*, vol. V, p. 75.

CHAPTER IX

THE INDEPENDENCE OF LATIN AMERICA

IF Canning could not prevent the armies of Louis XVIII from marching in triumph from the Bidassoa to Cadiz, he was resolved that not even the intrigues of George IV, and the opposition of more than one of his colleagues in the Cabinet, should stop him from confining French action to Spain itself. The key to his views is to be found in the speech in which he defended his action in Parliament:

> I confess I think that the effects of the French occupation of Spain have been infinitely exaggerated. I do not blame these exaggerations; because I am aware that they are to be attributed to the recollections of some of the best times of our history; that they are the echoes of sentiments which, in the days of William and of Anne, animated the debates and dictated the votes of the British Parliament. No peace was in those days thought safe for this country while the crown of Spain continued on the head of a Bourbon. . . . Sir, is the Spain of the present day the Spain of which the statesmen of the times of William and Anne were so much afraid? Is it indeed the nation whose puissance was expected to shake England from her sphere? No, Sir, it was quite another Spain; it was the Spain within the limits of whose empire the sun never set; it was Spain with the Indies that excited the jealousies and alarmed the imaginations of our ancestors.[1]

In short, France might, temporarily at any rate, control Spain, since no vital British interest was affected thereby, but Spain with the Indies she should not have; and fortunately for Canning the progress of events in America was eminently calculated to further the end which he had in view.

The relations between Pitt and the Spanish colonists in the person of Miranda have already been noticed, and we have seen how only the Spanish rising against Napoleon prevented the dispatch of a British force to Venezuela under the command of the future Duke of Wellington. Two years later, in 1810, Bolivar

[1] Therry, R., *op. cit.*, vol. VI, pp. 108–109.

had himself come to London in the hope of enlisting the support of the British Government, but although he was received by Wellesley, then Foreign Secretary, he was told that nothing could be done in view of the alliance between Great Britain and Spain, but that consideration would be given to the just complaints and aspirations of Venezuela. The overthrow of Napoleon, and the manifest inability of Ferdinand VII to reduce his American subjects to obedience, modified the situation, and Castlereagh was able to pursue an independent policy. When, for example, in 1816 the Spanish Government attempted to play upon British suspicions of the United States he told Ferdinand's ambassador that " a long perseverance on the part of Spain in false notions of imposing by force a restrictive and exclusive system upon that country [*i.e.* Spanish America] had already alienated the minds of the people from her rule ", and " the only chance she had of success was to lose no time . . . to put her system there upon a national footing ".[1]

Spanish America was not Castlereagh's pre-occupation, and if he could possibly avoid it he was determined not to allow the progress of events there to constitute yet another difference between Great Britain and the Holy Alliance. At first he hoped to steer a middle course by encouraging the establishment, with or without the consent of Spain, of independent monarchies in the New World. Such a result would serve the double purpose of preventing the spread of republican principles—and this would appeal strongly to the Powers of the Holy Alliance—and of making British influence predominate over that of the United States. In 1818 the great Argentine patriot, San Martín, no lover of republics, had written to him suggesting that a representative monarchy should be set up in Buenos Aires, and two years later Castlereagh told the Colombian representative that the British Government would at once recognize any colony that adopted monarchical institutions.

Circumstances, however, began to force his hand, for in June, 1822, the Colombian minister was formally received by the President of the United States. Furthermore, there was the increasing strength of British public opinion in favour of recognition based mainly upon commercial arguments. In the eyes of Spain all South American vessels, and all vessels which traded with South America, were nothing else than pirates, and British merchants

---

[1] Webster, C. K.: *The Foreign Policy of Castlereagh*, vol. II, p. 411.

were not prepared any longer to tolerate such a state of affairs in respect of what had become one of the most important parts of their foreign trade. Castlereagh determined, therefore, to divide the commercial from the political problem. Commercial recognition must be given at once; political recognition could wait on circumstances, and if possible could be used as a means of encouraging monarchical rather than republican institutions in South America.

This policy was rendered the easier to effect owing to a recent change in the official British attitude towards colonial trade. Until 1815 the monopoly of the Mother Country, where colonies were concerned, had been maintained quite as vigorously as in the case of Spain, but more liberal ideas had lately begun to prevail. The Government was actually preparing the legislation necessary to admit the vessels of other nations to this trade, and to allow them to use British ports much more freely than before. It is not clear who first devised the scheme of extending the provisions of this measure to the vessels of the Spanish colonies, and of thus giving them a definite status. Anyhow, the Cabinet accepted it without demur on the proposal of the Foreign Secretary, and thus, in the summer of 1822, the Spanish colonial flags secured recognition.

A breathing-space had now been obtained, and the way was clear for a cautious approach to the thorny question of political recognition. At the end of July there was a debate on the subject in the House of Commons when the Opposition urged full recognition. Castlereagh would not agree, but he declared that " the whole was purely a British question, uninfluenced by foreign Powers and resting only upon the law of nations, and the character of generosity and prudence, which he trusted this country would ever maintain ". He obviously intended that the solution should be found at the forthcoming Congress of Verona, and in the instructions which he drew up, to which allusion has already been made, he wrote, " It will be the duty of the British Plenipotentiary to enter into discussion with the Allied Cabinets, endeavouring, as far as possible, to bring them to the adoption of common sentiments, but taking care, in every alternative, to leave to the British Government an independent discretion to act according to circumstances."

It is, indeed, by no means improbable that had Castlereagh lived recognition might have come more quickly than Canning was able to bring it about, for Castlereagh would not have been hampered as his successor was to be by the hostility of George IV and the suspicion of many of his colleagues in the Government. As Professor Webster has well said, " It would have been more clear to posterity that the independence of the Spanish colonies had been won and maintained by the enterprise and heroism of the South Americans themselves ".[1]

Such was the situation when Canning succeeded Castlereagh at the Foreign Office, and it was not, at first, rendered any easier of solution by the nature of the war that was taking place in Latin America. It is a mistake to assume that Bolivar and his colleagues were leading a national revolt, in which all classes of the population joined, against an alien and inefficient regime at Madrid. On the contrary, the conflict was very definitely a civil war, and the number of Spanish troops engaged was extremely small, for the bulk of the Royalist forces was composed of local volunteers. As for the Indians, they either held aloof from the contest altogether or fought on the Spanish side. There was no national uprising against Spain, but rather a fratricidal war which had for its counterpart the struggle that was going on in the Mother Country between Ferdinand and the Liberals : in America those who held the views of the latter advocated independence because previous experience had taught them that liberty was out of the question so long as Spanish rule continued. There was, however, a large body of opinion which was favourable to absolutism, and so supported the Spanish connection ; and, with a few exceptions, the clergy remained loyal to Madrid. In view of her weakness at home the wonder is not that Spain lost her American colonies so soon, but that she retained them for so long, and the explanation is that she received a great deal of support among the colonists themselves.

Of the Powers, apart from Great Britain and Spain, which were interested in these developments France pursued the policy that is the least easy to follow, and it is by no means improbable that Louis and his ministers were not of one mind on the subject. They were certainly not aiming, as is sometimes alleged, at placing French princes upon American thrones, for there were none available except the Duc d'Orléans, and he, to whom even the title of Royal Highness was denied, was the very last man whom Louis wished to see upon any throne, European or American.

[1] Webster, C. K., *op. cit.*, vol. II, pp. 435–436.

What is more probable is that the French Government wished Ferdinand to adopt the scheme that Aranda had suggested to his grandfather forty years before, namely that the American Vice-Royalties should become kingdoms with Infantes to rule them, while the King of Spain should himself take the title of Emperor. Colour is lent to this supposition by the fact that in 1820 the French Government was in negotiation both with Madrid and Buenos Aires for the establishment of the Duke of Lucca [1] upon the throne of Argentina: a step against which Castlereagh protested vigorously. It is unlikely that Louis contemplated the use of force to achieve this object, though three years later it was suggested from Paris to Angoulême that he might spare a few troops, as well as some ships, to establish principalities in America, but he replied that he must first complete his work in the Peninsula itself.

At the same time there was nothing in the nature either of Louis or of the then Prime Minister, Villèle, to suggest that they were capable of such a gamble as that which prompted the Mexican expedition of Napoleon III. They had just scored a remarkable success in Spain, and were most unlikely to risk the loss of this prestige for the mere sake of placing Bourbon princes upon shaky thrones on the other side of the world. Such being the case there was probably a good deal of bluff in the French threat of interference in the Americas, as well as a determination not to become too dependent either upon Great Britain or the Holy Alliance.

So far as the United States was concerned the situation was also complex, for her policy was governed by several considerations. She was too weak to undertake any considerable military operations, though she was extremely advantageously placed to intervene with effect in the affairs of the old Vice-Royalty of Mexico, if she could raise the necessary men and money. In effect, the attitude of Washington was influenced by three main factors, namely the desire for expansion to the West, the wish to sever all connection between the Spanish and Portuguese colonies on the one hand and their Mother Countries on the other, and the determination to turn to the best possible account the commercial potentialities of the new Latin American market. These aspirations call for closer examination.

The growth of the United States had been rapid. It was only twenty years since its Western boundary was the Mississippi, and—

[1] The Treaty of Vienna had temporarily dispossessed him of Parma in favour of Napoleon's widow.

although Napoleon had sold Louisiana in 1803 what was later
to be known as the Middle West was still practically an unknown
land. To the South, Florida had been in Spanish hands until
1819, while to the West of the Red River there stretched away to
the Pacific a vast territory that until yesterday had been the Vice-
Royalty of Mexico. Such being the case it behoved Washington
to walk warily, and President Monroe proved equal to the occasion. The anarchy in Mexico which had followed the overthrow
of Spanish rule in that country had tempted some citizens of the
United States to urge intervention, but Monroe set his face firmly
against any policy likely to displease Ferdinand until the sale of
Florida had been completed. Once that had taken place Washington began to regard the insurgent Spanish colonists with a much
more favourable eye, and the first steps were taken along the road
which twenty years later led to the annexation of Texas and the
war with Mexico.

In reality, the independence of Latin America was an unexpected
piece of good fortune for the United States. Instead of being, as
at the beginning of the century, hemmed in on all sides by the
colonial possessions of Spain, France, and Great Britain, she was
now in a fair way to becoming the mistress of the Northern part
of the American continent. The necessity of Napoleon and
Ferdinand had proved to be her opportunity to acquire Louisiana
and Florida, and now the Spanish colonies had followed her
example by severing the cord which bound them to Europe. As
soon, therefore, as the sale of Florida had been completed, it
became a cardinal point of policy at Washington that the revolted
colonies must be prevented from returning to their former status;
while if, in addition, they could be prevailed upon to adopt
republican constitutions, so much the better, for they would in
that case be more likely to rely upon the State Department than
upon the Foreign Office.

Above all, there were the almost limitless possibilities that were
opened up now that the shackles imposed on Latin American
trade by the Council of the Indies had been removed. These
advantages would, of course, come to an end if Spanish rule were
restored, while there was always the danger that if the new states
came within the British orbit their trade would go to Great Britain.
In these circumstances Monroe and Adams, the latter being his
Secretary of State, decided to lose no time, and as soon as they had
Florida safely in their pockets they proceeded to grant official

recognition to the now independent republics. The advantages of this step were considerable, for it provided the State Department with a direct channel of communication that was denied to the Foreign Office, while the appointment of consuls was a very great help indeed to the advancement of trade. On the other hand, the United States was not really in a position to reap the full harvest of her policy of recognition, for it was clear that one of the first needs of every Latin American country would be a loan, and she was far too poor to lend any money, while her naval and military strength was quite inadequate for any armed intervention in support of her policy. The position of the United States was thus that she was the first Power to stake out a claim in the former Spanish colonies, but it was uncertain whether she would be able to effect much in the way of its development.

Russia, through her possession of Alaska, was at this time an American Power, and that Alexander was determined to exploit the fact was proved by a decree which he issued in 1821 forbidding all save Russian subjects to fish, trade, or navigate over an enormous area lying between Siberia and North America. There were also rumours that the Tsar was endeavouring to induce Haiti to cede him the Isle des Vaches, and Russian agents were reported in Colombia, but Canning took little notice of all this, for he held that it was only with French aid that Russia could intervene effectively in Latin America. In the United States, on the other hand, Russian pretensions were taken much more seriously, and Adams conceived a personal distrust of the Tsar's representative at Washington that went far to promote the formulation of the Monroe Doctrine, though the President himself never regarded the threats of the Holy Alliance as serious, and he took the view that the prevention of their translation into practice would be a task for Great Britain, rather than for the United States.

From the very first Canning adopted the point of view that the old Spanish colonies must either come once again under the rule of the Mother Country, or they must become independent; in no circumstances could Great Britain tolerate their annexation, in whole or in part, by any other state. Having come to this decision, he made up his mind that he would not be a party to the holding of any conference that had for its end any interference in the affairs of the New World. A congress would provide an excuse for intervention to those who were in favour of such a policy, and the precedent of Verona was hardly encouraging. In fact Canning came to the conclusion that the right course for Great Britain was to hold the ring. If Ferdinand could subdue his rebels by himself, well and good; if not, then the Foreign Office would proceed to recognize their independence as soon as they had established some form of stable polity. The British mastery of the seas rendered the pursuit of such a policy eminently practicable, and it is in consequence not too much to say that for some time to come the destiny of the whole American continent lay in the hands of the British Government.

The question was not, however, by any means purely an academic one. For Austria and Prussia all that was at stake was the principle of legitimacy, and Russia, in spite of her possession of Alaska, was in much the same position. France, in view of her commitments in the West Indies and of French Guiana, was more directly interested in the progress of events in the old Spanish colonies, but even she was not concerned to the same extent as Great Britain, whose trade was at stake. Canning had not long returned to the Foreign Office before he was besought by the commercial interests, especially in his own constituency of Liverpool, to place them upon a more favourable footing. Spain was no longer able to give protection to the British merchant throughout vast areas of what were still nominally her colonies, and in the new states that were rising on the ruins of her empire he had no official *locus standi* at all. Furthermore, the sympathetic attitude towards the colonists adopted by Washington was enabling the citizens of the United States to obtain commercial advantages of which it would be very difficult to deprive them in years to come. In effect, the City wanted Canning to recognize the independence of the Latin American states, and thus to enable British commerce to steal a march on its rivals in the new market. Among those who urged this view was a young pamphleteer of twenty-one, Benjamin Disraeli, who declared that if the leaders of the revolt against Spain were " not pure and practical patriots, we know not what names should be inscribed on the illustrious scroll of national gratitude ".

There can be no doubt that to the end of his life Canning distrusted and disliked the United States, and he was determined that she should not obtain control of her Southern neighbours. In a memorandum to the Cabinet in the autumn of 1824 he said:

Sooner or later we shall probably have to contend with the combined maritime power of France and the United States.

The disposition of the new states is at present highly favourable to England.   If we take advantage of that disposition we may establish through our influence with them a fair counterpoise to that combined maritime power.   Let us not, then, throw the present golden opportunity away, which once lost may never be recovered.[1]

A few weeks later he returned to the subject in another memorandum:

The other and perhaps still more powerful motive is my apprehension of the ambition and ascendancy of the United States of America.   It is obviously the policy of that Government to connect itself with all the Powers of America in a general Trans-Atlantic league, of which it would have the sole direction.   I need not say how inconvenient such an ascendancy may be in time of peace, and how formidable in case of war.

I believe we now have the opportunity (but it may not last long) of opposing a powerful barrier to the influence of the United States by an amicable connection with Mexico, which from its position must be either subservient to or jealous of the United States.   In point of population and resources it is at least equal to all the rest of the Spanish colonies; and may naturally expect to take the lead in its connections with the Powers of Europe.   I by no means think it at present necessary to go beyond the mere relations of amity and commercial intercourse; but if we hesitate much longer, and especially if our commercial treaty with Buenos Aires should not take effect, all the new states will be led to conclude that we reject their friendship upon principle, as of a dangerous and revolutionary character, and will be driven to throw themselves upon the protection of the United States as the only means of security.[2]

Finally, when recognition was secured he wrote to Granville, " The deed is done, the nail is driven.   Spanish America is free; and if we do not mismanage our affairs sadly, she is English." [3]
That Canning's feelings were reciprocated is clear from a letter

[1] Temperley, H. W. V., *op. cit.*, pp. 145–146.
[2] *Ibid.*, p. 553.
[3] Stapleton, A. G., *op. cit.*, p. 411.

which Richard Rush, the United States minister in London, was one day to write to Henry Clay:

> Was it not he who discovered Erskine's arrangement, which, had it been sanctioned in England, might have prevented a war?[1] Was it not he who in 1823 infused the unfriendly tone into that long negotiation in London, almost refusing to listen to nine out of ten of our claims, obviously just as most of them were? And was it not he who in 1826 most abruptly closed the West Indian trade against us, upon pretexts the most unexpected and flimsy? . . . He esteems civil and political liberty no more than Lord Londonderry did, though circumstances have made him appear to be somewhat more their champion. . . . Mr. Canning never liked the United States nor their institutions, and never will. . . . He will watch all our steps with sharper and more active jealousy than perhaps any other English statesman living. Of all their public men, we have the least to expect from him.[2]

Adams held the same views, for as early as 1816 he had written that Canning had been " invariably noted for . . . bitterness . . . towards the United States ". When Canning died he observed, " May this event, in the order of Providence, avert the evils which he would, if permitted, have drawn down upon us! "[3] Such was the personal background of Canning's negotiation with the State Department.

As has been seen, one of Castlereagh's last acts had been to recognize the Spanish colonial flags, and Canning determined to utilize this precedent. Meanwhile, the capture of Quito by the insurgents at the end of May, 1822, strengthened his hand against those who, like the King and some of his colleagues in the Cabinet, wished to refrain from taking any action at all. At the same time reports were continually arriving in London of the damage done to British shipping by pirates who used Cuba as their base, and even the most convinced opponents of a forward policy were reluctantly forced to agree that the existing situation could not be allowed to continue. Accordingly, the British squadron in the West Indies was strengthened with the avowed intention of attacking the pirates on Spanish territory if necessary, while in December,

[1] *Vide supra*, ch. iv, p. 87.
[2] Colton, C.: *The Private Correspondence of Henry Clay*, pp. 165–166.
[3] *Memoirs*, vol. III, p. 437, and vol. VII, p. 328.

1822, Canning drew up a list of consuls for the chief towns in Latin America.

The result of the Congress of Verona, and the French invasion of Spain, caused the British Government to suspend any further action for a time, but when it became clear that the Duc d'Angoulême would soon have the whole kingdom at his mercy, Canning felt that the moment had arrived to give effect to his determination that the Spanish colonies should not share the fate of the Mother Country, and pass under the control of Paris. While, therefore, the French armies were occupying Cadiz, the British Foreign Secretary took three very important steps: he accredited the consuls, he sent a commission to Mexico and Colombia to report on the question of their recognition by Great Britain, and he asked the French ambassador for the views of his government upon the American situation.

The discussions, in October, 1823, with Polignac lasted several days, and the Frenchman strongly urged the convocation of a congress to deal with the whole question of Latin America. This was exactly what Canning did not want, so he outflanked Polignac by observing that he could not understand how a congress could discuss Spanish American affairs "without calling to their counsels a Power so eminently interested as the United States of America, while Austria, Russia, and Prussia, Powers so much less concerned in the subject, were in consultation upon it". This observation was peculiarly subtle, for Canning knew perfectly well that nothing would induce the United States, in the ears of whose citizens Jefferson's denunciation of "entangling alliances" was still ringing, to participate in a European conference, but the suggestion that an invitation should be sent to republican Washington would be sufficient to render the whole idea of a congress unpalatable to the Holy Alliance. Finally, Canning extracted from the ambassador an avowal that the French Government considered the recovery by Spain of her colonies to be out of the question, while he disclaimed any intention on the part of Paris to undertake armed intervention in America or to annex any part of it. In short, if Louis and Villèle had been bluffing, their bluff was now called.

This admission cleared the air considerably, and represented a definite success for Canning. It ensured that there should not be a repetition of the events of the previous year, when a European congress had authorized France to interfere in the internal affairs of another country, and it definitely separated the French Government from the Holy Alliance. The memorandum embodying these concessions, for such they really were, was not published until the spring of 1824, but its contents were known before the end of the month in which the conversations took place, and in a speech at Plymouth on October 28th the Foreign Secretary took care that its significance should not be lost abroad:

> But . . . let it not be said that we cultivate peace, either because we fear, or because we are unprepared for, war. . . . Our present repose is no more a proof of inability to act, than the state of inertness and inactivity in which I have seen those mighty masses that float in the waters above your town, is a proof they are devoid of strength, and incapable of being fitted out for action. You well know how soon one of those stupendous masses, now reposing on their shadows in perfect stillness—how soon, upon any call of patriotism, or of necessity, it would assume the likeness of an animated thing, instinct with life and motion—how soon it would ruffle, as it were, its swelling plumage—how quickly it would collect all its beauty and its bravery, collect its scattered elements of strength, and awaken its dormant thunder. Such as is one of these magnificent machines when springing from inaction to a display of its might—such is England herself: while apparently passive and motionless, she silently concentrates the power to be put forth on an adequate occasion.

The chancelleries realized that Canning meant what he said, but they had not lost hope of inducing Great Britain to participate in a conference, and the coterie behind the throne redoubled its efforts. Meanwhile, late in December, 1823, came the news of President Monroe's message to Congress, and the situation was thereby rendered the more acute.

The question to what extent Canning was responsible for the formulation of the Monroe Doctrine is not easy to answer, but the policy which he adopted towards France and the Holy Alliance in the early autumn of 1823 undoubtedly encouraged Monroe and Adams to make a stand which would not have been possible without the certainty of British support, given the weakness of the United States at the time. The fact was that Canning, before his interview with Polignac, had opened up negotiations with Rush, and had stated his views to him in the following terms:

Is not the moment come when our Governments might understand each other as to the Spanish American colonies? And if we can arrive at such an understanding, would it not be expedient for ourselves and beneficial for all the world that the principles of it should be clearly settled and plainly avowed?

(1) For ourselves we have no disguise. We conceive the recovery of the colonies by Spain to be hopeless.

(2) We conceive the question of the recognition of them as independent states to be one of time and circumstances.

(3) We are, however, by no means disposed to throw any impediment in the way of an arrangement between them and the Mother Country by amicable negotiation.

(4) We aim not at the possession of any portion of them ourselves.

(5) We could not see any portion of them transferred to any other Power with indifference.

If these opinions and feelings are, as I firmly believe them to be, common to your Government with ours, why should we hesitate mutually to confide them to each other, and to declare them in the face of the world?

If there be any European Power which cherishes other projects which look to a forcible enterprise for reducing the colonies to subjugation on the behalf or in the name of Spain, or which meditates the acquisition of any part of them to itself by cession or by conquest, such a declaration on the part of your Government and ours would be at once the most effectual and the least offensive mode of intimating our joint disapprobation of such projects. It would at the same time put an end to all the jealousies of Spain with respect to her remaining colonies, and to the agitation which prevails in those colonies, an agitation which it would be but humane to allay, being determined (as we are) not to profit by encouraging it.

Do you conceive that under the power which you have recently received you are authorized to enter into negotiation and to sign any convention upon this subject? Do you conceive, if that be not within your competence, you could exchange with me ministerial notes upon it?

Nothing could be more gratifying to me than to join with you in such a work, and I am persuaded that there has seldom in the history of the world occurred an opportunity when so small an effort of two friendly Governments might produce so unequivocal a good and prevent such extensive calamities.[1]

This letter was followed by further discussions between Canning and the minister, but before long it became apparent that although the two men agreed upon the main issue, differences existed between them on points of detail.   Rush was willing to sign a joint declaration provided that Canning would pledge himself to the immediate recognition of the revolted colonies.   Now this was just what the Foreign Secretary could not do, in view of the attitude of the King and several members of the Cabinet; and, in addition, he was still in hope that the new states would adopt monarchical constitutions, a possibility which would become very remote if Great Britain recognized their existing republican regimes.   Such being the case, the negotiations with Rush did not lead to any decisive result, but Canning's memorandum showed Washington exactly where Great Britain stood, and so precipitated action on the part of the United States.

There can be little doubt but that in these negotiations Canning was thinking not so much of initiating a policy of Anglo-American friendship as of making use of the United States in the game he was playing with the Continental Powers.   Accordingly, he wished to be quite sure of her attitude towards the whole question of the Spanish colonies before he communicated with Polignac.   Rush's comments convinced him that she was not prepared, to use a phrase of Adams, " to come in as a cock-boat in the wake of the British man-of-war ", but he found that the two Anglo-Saxon countries were sufficiently agreed for it to be safe for him to spike the guns of the Holy Alliance by insisting upon the admission of the United States to any proposed congress.   That Rush suspected this is shown by his letter to Clay, already quoted, and Adams certainly took the same view; if Canning made use of the United States in his negotiations with Polignac, Adams used his knowledge of the British attitude in the formulation of the Monroe Doctrine, for which he was more responsible than the President whose name it bore.   In effect, both Canning and Adams was trying to use the other for his own ends.

[1] Temperley, H. W. V., *op. cit.*, pp. 110–111.

N

The ultimate implications of Monroe's message were more important than the immediate, but the latter unquestionably strengthened the Foreign Secretary's hands against the Holy Alliance. At the time that Monroe spoke there were no illusions in the mind of himself, Adams, or Canning that the doctrine which he was formulating depended upon the British Navy, and it is in no way remarkable that the first thought of the chancelleries should have been that it was the result of an Anglo-American agreement. Canning was not slow to grasp the advantage of this from his point of view, and he wrote to Bagot, " The effect of the ultra-liberalism of our Yankee co-operators, or the ultra-despotism of Aix-la-Chapelle Allies, gives me just the balance that I wanted ".[1]

The year 1824 saw the international situation, at any rate so far as Latin America was concerned, still dominated by the British Foreign Secretary, but it took the whole twelve months to bring his opponents at home to agree to recognition. Wearisome as this undoubtedly was, Canning possessed one great advantage in that it was not possible for them to rely upon the arguments which were influencing the conduct of the Holy Alliance. Alexander and Metternich based their refusal to recognize the independence of the Spanish colonies on the ground that the origin of the new states was revolutionary, though in actual fact the Austrian Chancellor did not believe in legitimism, while the Tsar had ascended the throne over the body of his murdered father. Such an excuse could hardly be put forward by the man who owed his crown to the Revolution of 1688, so George IV, and those who thought with him, were forced back upon the argument of expediency, and in that connection events were decidedly favouring Canning.

In the first place, the position of the Spanish forces was precarious in the extreme everywhere save in Peru, where the battle of Ayacucho had still to be fought. The island of Chiloe, off the Chilean coast, and the castle of San Juan de Ulloa, which dominates the great Mexican port of Vera Cruz, were practically the only places in the Americas, apart from Cuba and Puerto Rico, that still held out for Ferdinand. Furthermore, there was always the danger that any delay in recognition would play into the hands of the United States. That Bolivar himself was favourable to Great Britain there could be no doubt, and it was only a few

[1] Bagot, J., op. cit., vol. II, pp. 217–218.

months later [1] that he made the following significant statement to Captain Maling:

> Of all countries South America is perhaps the least fitted for republican governments.   What does its population consist of but of Indians and Negroes, who are more ignorant than the vile race of Spaniards we are just emancipated from? A country represented and governed by such people must go to ruin.
>
> We must look to England for relief, we have no other resource.   And you have not only my leave but my request that you will communicate our conversation, and bring the matter under the consideration of H.B.M.'s Government in any manner which may seem best to you either officially or otherwise.   You may say I never have been an enemy to monarchies upon general principles; on the contrary, I think it essential to the respectability and well-being of new nations, and if any proposal ever comes from the British Cabinet for the establishment of a regular government, that is, of a monarchy or monarchies in the New World, they will find in me a steady and firm promoter of their wishes, perfectly ready to uphold the Sovereign England may propose to place and support upon the throne.
>
> I know it has been said of me, I wish to be a King, but it is not so; I would not accept the crown for myself, for when I see this country made happy under a good and firm government, I shall again retire into private life; I repeat to you, if I can be of service in forwarding the wishes and views of the British Cabinet in bringing about this desirable object they may depend upon my service.   I owe it to England, and I would infinitely sooner be indebted to England for its always generous and liberal assistance than to any other country. France or Spain would treat with me no doubt, were I to make similar proposals to them, but never will I submit to any interference with America on the part of those odious and treacherous nations.
>
> The title of King would perhaps not be popular at first in South America, and therefore it might be as well to meet the prejudice by assuming that of " Inca " which the Indians are so much attached to.   This enslaved and miserable country

[1] In March, 1825.

has hitherto only heard the name of King coupled with its miseries and Spanish cruelties, and a change of Vice-King has invariably proved a change of one rapacious oppression for another. Democracy has its charms for the people, and in theory it appears plausible to have a free government which shall exclude all hereditary distinctions, but England is again our example; how infinitely more respectable your nation is, governed by its King, Lords, and Commons, than that which prides itself upon an equality which holds out little temptation to exertion for the benefit of the state, indeed I question much whether the present state of things will continue very long in the United States. Indeed I wish you to be well assured I am not an enemy either to Kings or to an aristocratical government provided they be under the necessary restraints which your constitution imposes upon the three degrees. If we are to have a new government let it be modelled on yours, and I am ready to give my support to any Sovereign England may give us.[1]

Earlier still, Bolivar had, according to the British consul at Lima, shown himself " much prejudiced " against both the United States and France, and had expressed " dissatisfaction with the gentleman appointed by the United States to be Consul-General " there. Canning thus held some very strong cards in his hand, and he was fully determined to press his advantage home.

In the spring of 1824 he made a final effort to negotiate with Spain. He declined the suggestion of Madrid that he should participate in a conference on American affairs, but offered to guarantee Cuba to Spain if the Spanish Government would agree to a peaceful separation from the colonies on the mainland. This offer was promptly refused, and Canning then instructed the British minister at Madrid to inform the Spanish Government that " His Majesty reserves to himself the right of taking, at his own time, such steps as His Majesty may think proper, in respect of the several states of Spanish America, without further reference to the Court of Madrid ".[2]

Two events now took place which still further strengthened Canning's position, namely the reports of the commissioners that he had sent to Mexico and Colombia, and the evident desire of the

[1] Temperley, H. W. V., *op. cit.*, pp. 557–558.
[2] Temperley, H. W. V.: *Life of Canning*, pp. 184–185.

commercial interests in England that recognition should not be delayed any longer.

The commissioners reported very favourably on the prospects both of Colombia and Mexico, while in Buenos Aires the rule of Spain had not been effective for above a decade. Canning was disappointed that his agents had not been able to find any great evidence of monarchical sentiments, for he had no wish to see Spanish America become wholly republican, and he seems for a time to have believed that Itúrbide would be able to establish himself upon the Mexican throne. In spite, however, of his own views, which were also those of Bolivar, he was prepared to bow to the inevitable, and if the Americans wanted republics they should have them. To adopt any other course would merely be to play into the hands of the Holy Alliance.

In June, Sir James Mackintosh presented a petition, which bore the names of such City magnates as Baring and Montefiore, asking for the immediate recognition of such of the Spanish colonies as had established independent governments, and in particular Colombia, Buenos Aires, and Chile. This step was by no means unwelcome to Canning, for it enabled him to state his views in the House of Commons, while the interest which the City took in the matter weakened the resistance of the King and of his colleagues in the Cabinet. Ever since his first election for Liverpool in 1812 Canning had realized the value of public opinion, and since his return to the Foreign Office he had neglected no opportunity of mobilizing it in his support. Now he reaped his reward, and in the autumn of 1824 he began to circularize the members of the Cabinet with memoranda in favour of recognition. Wellington, Bathurst, Westmorland, and Eldon, with the connivance of the King, offered the most strenuous opposition, but the Prime Minister came down heavily on the side of his Foreign Secretary and old Oxford contemporary. On December 14th, 1824, Liverpool and Canning laid a minute before the Cabinet recommending the recognition of Buenos Aires, Mexico, and Colombia, and announced their intention of resigning if the proposal was not adopted. In the face of this threat their opponents in the ministry gave way.

Canning elaborated in a letter to Frere the views, quoted above, which he expressed to Granville:

> The thing is done . . . an act which will make a change in the face of the world almost as great as that of the discovery

of the continent now set free. The Yankees will shout in triumph, but it is they who lose most by our decision. The great danger of the time, a danger which the European system would have fostered, was the division of the world into European and American, Republican and Monarchical, a league of worn-out governments on the one hand, and of youthful and stirring states, with the United States, on the other. We slip in between and plant ourselves in Mexico. The United States have got the start of us in vain; and we link once more America and Europe. Six months more, and the mischief would have been done.[1]

The King's opinion was very different, and was conveyed in a communication to the Cabinet in which he declared that " the whole proceedings relative to this question are premature "; nevertheless he did not oppose his ministers' decision, and in the King's Speech at the opening of Parliament in February, 1825, there occurred the passage, " In conformity with the declarations which have been repeatedly made by His Majesty, His Majesty has taken measures for confirming by treaties the commercial relations already subsisting between this kingdom and those countries of America which appear to have established their separation from Spain." [2] Owing to the fact that he had misplaced his false teeth, George was unable to open Parliament in person, so, by the irony of fate, the Royal Speech was read by Eldon, one of the bitterest opponents of the policy it enunciated.

Canning's interest in Spanish America did not cease with the recognition of its independence, and to the end of his life he paid the greatest attention to British relations with the new states. From the beginning he had never sought any territorial gain, though it would have been easy to have carved an empire, hardly second to India either in wealth or in extent, out of the old Spanish dominions; and it was the commercial aspect of the problem that concerned him now. Once recognition had been granted, and Sucre had finally overthrown the Spanish power at Ayacucho, the threats of the Holy Alliance could be disregarded, and it was from Washington rather than from Vienna or Paris that danger was to be apprehended. In short, so far as Latin America was con-

[1] Temperley, H. W. V.: *Life of Canning*, p. 188.
[2] Aspinall, A.: *The Letters of King George IV*, vol. III, pp. 97–100. Before the end of the year there was, as has been shown, a reconciliation between the King and Canning.

cerned, the last years of Canning's life resolved themselves into a struggle for the goodwill of the new republics.

Adams had become President in 1825, with Henry Clay as his Secretary of State, and the new President's attitude towards the British Foreign Secretary has already been noted, while that of Clay can be gathered by the tone of Rush's communications with him. This did not make for particularly friendly relations between London and Washington, and in addition there was the fierce rivalry to secure commercial advantages in Latin America. Canning fully realized that her republican constitution and her early recognition of the new countries gave the United States an initial advantage, and it was the fear that she might utilize it that prompted him to define the British attitude so clearly in his instructions to his representative at the Congress of Panama in 1826:

> You will understand that to a league among the states, lately colonies of Spain, limited to objects growing out of their common relations to Spain, His Majesty's Government would not object. But any project for putting the United States of North America at the head of an American Confederacy, as against Europe, would be highly displeasing to your Government. It would be felt as an ill return for the service which has been rendered to those states, and the dangers which have been averted from them, by the countenance and friendship, and public declarations of Great Britain; and it would probably at no very distant period endanger the peace both of America and of Europe.[1]

The struggles which took place in every one of the new republics between the British and American representatives do not call for detailed treatment here, but that Canning was determined not to allow the New World to come under the hegemony of Washington is proved at every turn. For this reason he was particularly desirous that the new states should not pursue the same policy of isolation from the affairs of Europe that characterized the United States. In this he received the support of Bolivar and many of his followers, and for a time there was talk in Caracas, La Paz, and Lima not only of an attack on Cuba, but even on the Canary Islands and on Spain herself. That Canning

[1] Temperley, H. W. V.: *The Foreign Policy of Canning, 1822–1827*, p. 179.

was prepared to encourage these aspirations, provided that they were diverted into channels of which he approved, is clear from a message he sent in 1825 to be conveyed to the Sultan: "The Porte cannot doubt that all the inhabitants of both Americas to a man, are in their hearts favourers of the Greek cause, and might at no distant period become active co-operators in it. This is not the language of intimidation, it is that of truth." [1] The fact that such a situation did not materialize is no proof of its impossibility.

Canning sent, as we have seen, a representative to the Congress of Panama, and his act was welcomed by Bolivar, who did not hesitate to give it as his opinion that "the several states require to be upheld by the power and influence of Great Britain, without which no security can be expected, no consistency preserved, and no secret compact maintained ". There was, indeed, a considerable bond of sympathy between Canning and Bolivar, though the two men never met, and their personal relations were not without influence on the policy of their respective countries. [2] If the Congress of Panama was a failure, circumstances rather than Canning or Bolivar were to blame. Canning, however, was in no way discouraged, and almost his last act at the Foreign Office was to advise the creation of an independent Uruguay as a buffer between Brazil and Argentina; this suggestion was a tribute to his foresight, though it was not carried out until after his death.

Meanwhile, events were taking place in Portuguese America in which Great Britain, both for political and economic reasons, could not have failed to become implicated. The Prince Regent of Portugal, with whose career Canning had already been connected on two previous occasions, had in 1816 ascended the throne as John VI, without, however, abandoning Rio de Janeiro for Lisbon. Five years later he was persuaded to return to Europe, but before he left he appointed his eldest son, Pedro, Viceroy of Brazil, with secret instructions to proclaim himself Emperor if he found it impossible to maintain the Portuguese connection. Pedro lost no time in taking advantage of his father's advice, and in October, 1822, the Empire of Brazil came into existence with himself as its first monarch.

At once there developed a situation which found Britain and the Holy Alliance in opposite camps. Canning welcomed the

---

[1] Temperley, H. W. V.: *The Foreign Policy of Canning, 1822–1827*, p. 185.
[2] Rippy, J. F.: *Rivalry of the United States and Great Britain over Latin America, 1808–1830*, pp. 181–182.

new Brazilian Empire because it introduced the monarchical element into Latin America, while in Vienna, St. Petersburg, and Berlin there was some uncertainty as to the course to be pursued in view of the circumstances. Alexander, once again forgetful of the events attendant upon his own accession to the throne, fulminated against Pedro, but Metternich was more circumspect. For the Holy Alliance, too, the position was not made any easier by the fact that both Pedro and John proceeded to grant their subjects constitutions, a proceeding which rendered father and son equally obnoxious in the eyes of the Tsar and of the Austrian Chancellor.

All this placed Canning in a much more advantageous position than had been the case with regard to Spanish America, quite apart from the fact that Great Britain possessed treaty rights in respect of Portugal which she did not enjoy so far as Spain and her colonies were concerned. It is true that John and his Portuguese ministers by no means relished Pedro's precipitate act, but Canning knew that their acceptance of the inevitable was only a question of time. Accordingly, he watched with considerable satisfaction the progress of the campaign during which Lord Cochrane established the new throne, first by capturing the various Portuguese posts in the country, and then by suppressing a republican movement. When this had been done Great Britain concluded a commercial treaty with Brazil. The Portuguese Government was momentarily exasperated, but Canning began to exert all his influence to secure Lisbon's acknowledgment of Brazilian independence, just as he had worked unsuccessfully to secure a peaceful separation of the Spanish colonies from Spain. In this case he was more fortunate, and in August, 1825, Portugal officially recognized the independence of Brazil.

Canning's whole American policy is a tribute alike to his foresight and to his skill. Like Bolivar, he would have preferred the new states to have adopted monarchical constitutions as a guarantee of internal stability, and the history of the past hundred years has surely proved the two men to have been right. Monarchs chosen from among the reigning families of Europe would have gone a long way to prevent that isolation of Latin America from the rest of the world which has been so prominent a feature of its history, while the mere existence of a dynasty would have provided in each state that continuity of government which in the majority of them has been so conspicuous by its absence.

Brazil, which supported a monarchy until its growing pains were over, escaped the endless civil wars that dissipated the strength of its neighbours, and there is no reason to suppose that the form of government which ensured stability at Rio de Janeiro would not have performed the same function elsewhere.   Above all, had the revolted colonies become monarchies instead of republics, the theory of their government would at any rate have corresponded with the fact, for which there is always much to be said.   Had the monarchical rather than the republican principle prevailed in Spanish America, as Canning wished, some complications, which actually have been avoided, might have ensued, but in all probability they would have been as nothing to the advantages which would have accrued.

Furthermore, once the die had been cast in favour of republicanism it was no mean feat for monarchical and aristocratic England to rival successfully the democratic and republican United States. It is true that Canning did not always get the better of Adams and Clay, but in spite of the lead that Washington secured by its early recognition of the independence of the Spanish colonies there can be little doubt that by the date of Canning's death British influence and British trade were in the ascendant throughout the Latin portion of the New World.   At the same time, Canning was clever enough to use the United States, in spite of the fact that its ends were fundamentally different from his own, as a stick to beat the Holy Alliance.   The success he achieved is the more to his credit in view of the circumstances both at home and abroad which he had first of all to overcome.

CHAPTER X

PORTUGAL AND GREECE

ALTHOUGH Canning was only in the fifties, the protracted negotiations with regard to Spain and her colonies, as well as the intrigues to which they gave rise, gradually began to have an adverse effect upon his health. As early as August, 1823, he wrote to Frere, " You can have no conception of the labour which I undergo. The two functions of For. Sec. and Leader of the H. of C. are too much for any man—and ought not to be united; though I of course would rather die under them than separate them, or consent to have separation in my person." [1] In the following January he told Bagot, " You know that I have had a swingeing fit of the gout. I am afraid that you will think that my handwriting in my three private letters savours of it. In truth, however, it is not feebleness, but excessive occupation that has made me, as I find upon reading my letters over this morning I am, nearly illegible. I am tolerably well again, and by dint of the patience and long suffering with which I went through my last attack, I hope clear for the Session." [2]

That Canning worked hard is indisputable, and he impressed his contemporaries by his activity. Lord Dudley, who succeeded him at the Foreign Office in 1827, was among the number:

> His habits of industry must appear quite incredible to those who did not know him. I met him once at a country house, where he went for what he was pleased to call his holidays. He had his secretaries about him soon after eight, had despatches ready before breakfast, then wrote all day till six. At tea-time he established himself in a corner of the drawing-room to write his private letters; and this every day, only now and then with the exception of a ride, and even during that he talked eagerly and fully upon public affairs. [3]

On his visit to Paris in 1826 he kept the clerks there writing twelve hours a day, and Stapleton has left it on record that he could dictate three despatches at the same time.

[1] Festing, G., *op. cit.*, p. 260.
[2] Bagot, J., *op. cit.*, vol. II, p. 227.
[3] *Letters to Ivy*, pp. 326–327.

Sometimes, indeed, he was able to pay a visit to the haunts of his youth, and in the summer of 1825 he went to the Lake District, where he had stayed so long ago with Mrs. Crewe. On this occasion he was the guest of his late Liverpool constituent, John Bolton, at Storrs Hall, and the party included Sir Walter Scott, Charles Ellis, Wordsworth, and Southey. This gathering prompted Lord Strangford to write to Bagot, " I hear that Canning is in high force at the Lakes. I should have liked to have seen him and Southey together. How times are changed! It is now Southey who is the Anti-Jacobin, and Canning who scoffs at Kings and Priests. His South American and Roman Catholic policy is more archi-liberal than anything that poor Southey ever said or sang."

The local Press naturally gave great prominence to Canning's presence. " At the King's Arms at Kendal the statesman was received by the Mayor and a distinguished company, and entertained to a cold collation, at which, though there was punch and wine in abundance, Canning confined himself to soda water. He received an address, to which he answered in a most beautiful manner. . . . Mrs. Canning meanwhile drove on to Windermere. . . . The guests then proceeded in Colonel Bolton's carriage and four to Storrs, where they were joined by Scott, Wordsworth, and Southey." On one day there was a grand procession of boats to escort them on the lake, with Canning, Scott, and Wordsworth in the place of honour on Bolton's barge, " accompanied by the roar of cannon, the sound of bells, and the harmonious strains of two bands of music, while the shores re-echoed with the noise of cannon or the swelling note of the sonorous trumpet. . . . Mr. Canning and Sir Walter Scott were observed to sit opposite each other in the barge, both wearing white hats." During this visit Canning is described as having been much on horseback while he re-visited the scenes of earlier days.[1]

All the same, within two years Canning was dead, and Scott noted in his journal, " I saw with pain a great change in his health when I met him at Colonel Bolton's at Storrs ". The affairs of Portugal and Greece, quite apart from the perplexities of domestic politics, were hurrying him to a premature grave.

The problems of the Iberian Peninsula seemed destined to occupy the attention of Canning during the greater part of his official life, and he had hardly secured the peaceful separation of

[1] Bagot, J., *op. cit.*, vol. II, pp. 287–292.

Brazil from Portugal before, in March, 1826, John VI died, and the affairs of the House of Braganza were in the melting-pot once more. The crisis that followed the old King's death affected Great Britain very closely, in view of the treaties which bound her to Portugal, and the manner in which Canning handled it is not only one more proof of his genius as Foreign Secretary, but is eloquent testimony to the ascendancy that he had acquired in the counsels of the world.

The heir to the throne of Portugal was clearly the Emperor of Brazil; but John also had another son, Miguel, who had been implicated in various disorders which had followed his father's return to Portugal, and at this time he was living in exile in Vienna. The old King realized the danger of an attempt by Miguel to place himself upon the vacant throne, and almost his last act had been to appoint a Council of Regency from which his younger son was carefully excluded. Pedro did not long keep Europe in suspense as to his intentions, for in June he renounced the crown of Portugal in favour of his daughter, Maria, a child of eight, whom he proposed in due course to marry to her uncle, Miguel, and at the same time he endowed Portugal with a fresh constitution.

Canning heard this news with rather mixed feelings. His confidence in the Brazilian Emperor does not appear to have been unqualified, and he had no great faith in constitutions that were imposed from above. On the other hand, he saw nothing in what had occurred to justify any departure from the principle of non-intervention, and he realized that in view of Pedro's action the Holy Alliance would in the long run be bound to recognize the new order at Lisbon. Indeed, he seems to have taken a mischievous pleasure in giving Metternich a dose of his own medicine, and Esterhazy wrote ruefully to the Austrian Chancellor in July, 1826:

It would appear to hear him that there has never been a more zealous defender of the free exercise of the rights and prerogatives of sovereigns, since misfortune willed that he, whose acts cause so much embarrassment, has so strangely neglected the monarchical interests, whose existence he so strongly compromises in the states of Europe and America. The arguments in favour of absolute power in the mouth of Mr. Canning are not naturally such as to demand serious attention; and he even only uses them, I am sure, from a spirit of derision by which this minister is sometimes led away.[1]

Indeed, Vienna and St. Petersburg could hardly deny the right of a monarch to grant, as Louis XVIII had done, a constitution to his subjects, nor, such being the case, could they very well refuse to recognize it once it had been granted.

The Holy Alliance was not slow to appreciate the force of Canning's logic, and as the Portuguese authorities had taken the oath to the constitution, the new order was duly accepted, though with the proviso that the revolutionary contagion must not be allowed to spread beyond the frontiers of Portugal. Unfortunately, events soon began to take place which rendered it exceedingly doubtful whether this stipulation would be fulfilled. Miguel, in spite of an order from the Emperor of Brazil, had not yet taken the oath, and this delay, combined with his notorious dislike of Liberalism in any form, gave every opponent of the existing regime both an opportunity and an excuse to create trouble. In August, 1826, a regiment mutinied, and crossed the frontier into Spain, where it was not disarmed, but was welcomed with ill-concealed joy by Ferdinand and his supporters. This event made it quite clear that the Spanish Government had no intention of observing even the outward forms of neutrality towards Portugal, and as the French troops had not yet completely evacuated Spain it was obvious to Canning that the attitude of Paris must be of the first importance. For this reason, therefore, he visited the French capital in September.

At this date Charles X had been upon the throne of France for two years, and his personal inclinations were already beginning to influence French policy in directions very different from those of his brother's reign. His private character, at any rate in old age, was by no means unattractive, and Leopold I of the Belgians, wrote of him that " he was blinded by certain absolute ideas, but a good man, and deserving to be loved. . . . An honest man, a kind friend, an honourable master, sincere in his opinions, and inclined to do everything that is right." [2] Unhappily, however, the King did not combine with these excellent qualities of the heart any clarity of perception, with the result that in spite of all that he did for France he kicked away the props that supported

[1] Temperley, H. W. V.: *The Foreign Policy of Canning, 1822–1827*, pp. 368–369.
[2] *The Letters of Queen Victoria*, First Series, vol. I, p. 67.

the throne. He certainly intended to consolidate what Louis had begun, but owing to his inability to distinguish between the apparent and the real he brought the whole edifice down in less than six years. Nevertheless, the very fact that Charles felt his position to be secure at home made it the more necessary for the Foreign Office to take him seriously into account, for it rendered him prone to play a more spirited part abroad than his brother had done. Louis XVIII was not only cautious by nature, but the weakness of France after the fall of Napoleon prevented the adoption of a forward foreign policy; by 1826, however, the country had to a very large extent recovered, while her King was one of those whose taste for adventure is only stimulated by the passing of the years.

Canning spent over a month in Paris, where he discussed the problems of the Peninsula with Charles and Villèle. He was everywhere received with the greatest distinction, and the King asked him to dinner at the Tuileries, when the only other guests present were the Dauphin and the Dauphine, and the Duchesse de Berri. Of this dinner Canning wrote to George IV:

> It is said (Mr. Canning knows not how truly) that this honour has been conferred on no other individuals (not of Royal or reigning families) except the Duke of Wellington and Prince Metternich. The Duke of Wellington stands on grounds of his own, common to no other individual in Europe, or the world. But Mr. Canning . . . cannot admit that the Foreign Minister of the Emperor of Austria, or any other potentate, could be entitled to a distinction not com- municable equally to the individual (however personally un- worthy) who holds the same office under your Majesty. And he is satisfied that it is to this consideration solely that the determination of H.M.C. Majesty is to be ascribed.[1]

In spite of these courtesies, Canning's visit to Paris was not an unqualified success, for he did not manage to persuade the French Government to put pressure upon Ferdinand to observe the ordinary obligations of neutrality, but he did succeed in sowing so many doubts in the minds of Charles and his ministers as to the right course to pursue, that in the end they did nothing at all, which suited British policy excellently. Events, too, were not

[1] Aspinall, A., *op. cit.*, vol. III, pp. 175–176.

slow in justifying Canning's action in ascertaining the intentions of the French Government, for in November, 1826, the Portuguese insurgents invaded, in conjunction with Spanish troops, the province of Traz oz Montes, and Lisbon appealed to Great Britain for help in accordance with the provisions of the treaties guaranteeing her against invasion. What followed is best described in Canning's speech in the House of Commons:

> On Sunday, the 3rd of this month, we received from the Portuguese ambassador a direct and formal demand of assistance against a hostile aggression from Spain. Our answer was that although rumours had reached us through France, His Majesty's Government had not that accurate information, that official and precise intelligence of facts, on which they could properly found an application to Parliament. It was only on last Friday night that this precise information arrived. On Saturday His Majesty's confidential servants came to a decision. On Sunday that decision received the sanction of His Majesty. On Monday it was communicated to both Houses of Parliament, and this day, Sir, at the hour in which I have the honour of addressing you, the troops are on their march for embarkation. . . .
>
> Let us fly to the aid of Portugal, by whomsoever attacked; because it is our duty to do so; and let us cease our interference where that duty ends. We go to Portugal, not to rule, not to dictate, not to prescribe constitutions, but to defend and to preserve the independence of an ally. We go to plant the standard of England on the well-known heights of Lisbon. Where that standard is planted, foreign domination shall not come.[1]

It only remains to add that the presence of British troops in Portugal had the desired effect, and they remained there until after Canning's death.

These negotiations well illustrate both the firmness and the caution of Canning, and are further evidence against the charge of rashness which has so often been preferred against him. On the contrary, had any minister of more infirm purpose been at the Foreign Office it is not easy to see how a general war could have been avoided. The success of Canning's diplomatic strokes lay in the fact that they were very carefully prepared in advance,

[1] Therry, R., *op. cit.*, vol. VI, pp. 72 and 92.

and were only executed after allowance had been made for every contingency; but once the time had come to act, the blow was always delivered at some vital spot, and the dispatch of the troops to Portugal in 1826 can be paralleled by the seizure of the Danish fleet so soon as the details of the conversations at Tilsit reached London. Moreover, the allegedly aggressive foreign policy of Canning led to far less bloodshed in the long run than the pacifism which marked that of some of his successors. The reason, however, is not far to seek, for it lies in the fact that Canning never threatened unless he was prepared to use force, and then only when some vital British interest was at stake.

Meanwhile, another and even more intricate problem than that of the future of Portugal was occupying Canning's attention, namely the Eastern Question, which was re-opened by the Greek rising.

For three centuries after the fall of Constantinople in 1453 Greece and the Greeks hardly entered into the calculations of European statesmen; indeed, so completely had Hellas become part of the Ottoman Empire with its Oriental associations that men talked of going from Greece " into Europe ". The only foreign Power with which the Greeks came in contact during this period was Venice, who for a time held some of the Greek islands and part of the mainland, but with her they had nothing in common either in point of race or, what was of greater importance, of religion: they were certainly not prepared to take up arms against the Porte for the sake of the Republic of St. Mark. The accession of Catherine II to the Russian throne in 1762, however, marked the beginning of a new era, and henceforth Russia, rather than Venice, was the foreign Power that loomed most largely in the eyes of the Greeks. With her they shared a common religion, and the Tsarina did all she could to win their support in the hope of one day reviving the Eastern Empire. She formed a corps of Greek cadets, she caused her younger grandson to be christened Constantine, and during her first war with Turkey she sent into the Mediterranean in 1770 a fleet which actually landed Russian sailors in the Morea. It is true that only a few Greeks joined them, but the incident ushered in a new phase of the Eastern Question.

The next fifty years witnessed the steady growth of Russian influence in the Levant. By the Treaty of Kutchuk-Kainardji in 1774 the Tsarina not only obtained considerable territorial gains,

o

but also a pretext for claiming protective rights over members of the Greek Church living in the Sultan's dominions—a concession which might mean much or little according to the policy of St. Petersburg from time to time. The Treaty of Bucharest in 1812 gave fresh sanction to this provision, and it advanced the Russian frontier to the Pruth, thereby bringing the Tsar very much closer than before to those whose interests he claimed the right to protect. In these circumstances it was not so surprising as might otherwise appear that the first blow for Greek independence should have been struck by an officer in the Russian service and an A.D.C. to Alexander I, namely Prince Alexander Ypsilanti. In March, 1821, accompanied by a number of Greeks in the Tsar's army, he raised the standard of revolt in Moldavia, and called on the people to rise against the Sultan. The appeal met with no response from the Vlach peasantry who hated the Greeks worse than the Turks, but it was the signal for an insurrection in the Morea on April 2nd of the same year. The War of Greek Independence had begun.

From the beginning the fighting was characterized by atrocities on both sides, but it was the hanging of the Orthodox Patriarch in Constantinople, by order of Mahmud II, outside the gate of his own palace that did much to rivet the attention of Western Europe upon the struggle in Greece; though it is an interesting commentary upon Near Eastern politics that at least one of the Christian bodies in Constantinople sang a *Te Deum* to celebrate the death of the heretical ecclesiastic. Nevertheless, the anger roused by this savage act soon died away, or rather was damped down since it did not at the moment suit the policy of any Power to exploit it.

The attitude of Metternich towards the Greeks was the same as that which he was adopting towards the risings in the Iberian and Italian Peninsulas and in Latin America. To him, in effect, the Greeks were merely rebels against their ruler, the Sultan. It is true that the Austrian Emperor was considerably affected by the death of the Patriarch, but the record of recent Austrian campaigns against the Turks was not encouraging, and in any case Vienna could hardly ally itself with those who were not only rebels against constituted authority but schismatics as well. Metternich, therefore, was resolved upon a policy of strict neutrality so far as Austria was concerned, and he was also determined to enforce it upon the other members of the Holy Alliance. He was under no illusions as to the threat to the whole European system contained in the Greek rising; Prussia, having no interests at stake in the Near East, could be safely ignored, but the Tsar would obviously require very careful handling.

For Alexander the situation was very different from that which confronted him with regard to insurrectionary movements elsewhere. His subjects had no ties with those concerned in them, and he could afford to indulge his absolutist opinions as he wished, but this was far from being the case in the matter of Greece. His own Russians and the insurgents were members of the same church, and a wave of indignation had swept across his dominions when the death of the Patriarch became known. Nor was this all: ever since the Treaty of Kutchuk-Kainardji the policy of St. Petersburg had been to protect the Orthodox Christians in the Ottoman Empire, and if the Tsar now stood aside Russian prestige would be bound to suffer. Fortune favoured Metternich in that Alexander was not in Russia, but in Germany, when the news of the Patriarch's death reached him, so that Russian public opinion exercised little or no influence over him. Metternich was therefore the better able to play upon the Tsar's dislike of revolution to cure him of any sympathy he might have felt for his co-religionists, and after a moment of hesitation Alexander adopted the point of view of the Austrian Chancellor. The Russian representative at Constantinople was instructed to make a vigorous protest, and to withdraw, but hostilities were not to follow. Metternich could breathe freely, the more so since neither France nor England showed any disposition to stir.

Louis XVIII was the last man in Europe to be affected by a series of massacres in the Levant, quite apart from the fact that friendship with the Porte had been the traditional French policy since the days of Francis I. France had no interests of any kind to consider in Greece, and so long as it was Orthodox, not Roman Catholic, Christians who were being slaughtered, the concern was none of the Most Christian King or of his ministers. Great Britain, too, was at first only remotely interested; Castlereagh was the disciple of Pitt, and the Government was more interested in keeping in the good graces of the Sultan than in interfering on behalf of the Greeks. After all, there had been insurrections in plenty in the Ottoman Empire before, and they had come to nothing, so it was but natural for Castlereagh to fall in with Metternich's view that the Greeks were but another European complication which it would be wiser to leave alone. Indeed, so strongly was the British Foreign Secretary of this opinion that a proposal for a joint demonstration of the Powers at Constantinople, for the protection of Christians in the Sultan's dominions, failed owing to the strenuous opposition of the British ambassador, Strangford. So far as French and British public opinion was concerned, it as yet took little interest in the Greeks and their cause, for news travelled slowly, and there were problems of far greater importance much nearer home to attract the attention of the ordinary citizen.

Such being the case it is hardly remarkable that the Greek delegates were not received at the Congress of Verona, where Metternich succeeded in imposing his own views upon the other Powers. Nevertheless, it was not long before two events took place which forced the Eastern Question upon the attention of Europe; one was the British recognition of the Greeks as belligerents, and the other was the arrival of Lord Byron at the seat of war.

The act of recognition took place in March, 1823, and was inspired by exactly the same motives, namely a care for British commerce, that were influencing Canning in his attitude towards the Spanish colonies. The Turks, like the Spaniards, were no longer able to protect British subjects and their goods throughout wide areas of land and sea over which they nominally ruled. The Ottoman fleet had taken shelter in the Dardanelles, and the Greek naval commanders were increasingly resorting to frank piracy, taking into Nauplia as prizes of war the ships of all nations impartially. It was useless to hold the Sultan responsible for a state of affairs which he was powerless to control, and so the responsibility had to be fastened upon the *de facto* Government of Greece. " The recognition of the belligerent character of the Greeks ", wrote Canning, " was necessitated by the impossibility of treating as pirates a population of a million souls, and of bringing within the bounds of civilized war a contest which had been marked at the outset on both sides by disgusting barbarities." To Metternich's vehement protests Canning replied that he could only treat the Greeks as pirates or belligerents, and as they had acquired " a certain degree of force and stability " the latter course appeared preferable. The Austrian Chancellor was by no means converted by such reasoning, especially in view of the fact that much of the Turkish commerce was carried in Austrian

bottoms, and there can be no doubt that Wellington's remark—
" We pass in Europe for a Jacobin Club "—represented opinion
in Vienna at the time. All the same Canning was careful not to
proceed any further than circumstances rendered necessary, and
he persuaded the Admiralty and the War Office to strike off the
active list all naval and military officers who were serving with
Greek forces.

Byron arrived at Missolonghi in January, 1824, and on April
19th he died, after it had been whispered into his almost uncon-
scious ear that Canning, the only British statesman for whom he
had any respect,[1] was more favourable to the Greek cause. His
death first made the Greek cause popular in Western Europe. In
an age when to be educated was synonymous with an acquaintance
with the classics, Philhellenism was assured of many supporters in
advance, quite apart from the fact that Englishmen had not yet
learnt by bitter experience to be somewhat suspicious of nations
struggling to be free. In these circumstances the poet's death
came as a call to action, and Greek loans, with the most doubtful
security, were subscribed as soon as they were floated. This
demonstration of popular feeling was by no means lost upon
Canning, but he had not been President of the Board of Control
for four years without realizing the danger there would be of
arousing Moslem fanaticism in India if Great Britain gave open
support to the enemies of the Commander of the Faithful. For
the present, therefore, Canning was not prepared to depart from
his policy of neutrality, and he was confirmed in this attitude by
the obvious inability of the Turks to suppress the Greek rising,
which led him to expect that the independence of Greece was only
a matter of time, and of no long time at that.

For these reasons, as well as on account of his general dislike
of conferences, Canning refused throughout the year 1824 to
participate in any congress on the subject of Greece, and he maintained this attitude in spite of the pleadings of Alexander and
Metternich. Both the Russian and the Austrian desired a con-

---

[1] Yet something may remain perchance to chime
With reason, and what's stranger still, with rhyme.
Even this thy genius, Canning, may permit,
Who, bred a statesman, still wast born a wit,
And never, even in that dull House, couldst tame
To unleaven'd prose thine own poetic flame;
Our last, our best, our only orator,
Even I can praise thee—Tories do no more.
The Age of Bronze.

ference, though for very different reasons. The Tsar hoped that he would be authorized to intervene in the Ottoman Empire, just as France at Verona had been given a mandate to invade Spain, for he was becoming impressed by the volume of opinion in Russia in favour of the Greeks. Metternich, on the other hand, thought that at another congress he would be able to reaffirm his influence over Alexander, and prevent any departure by the Powers from the policy of complete neutrality.

While these negotiations were in progress the news arrived that the Sultan had called in the aid of Mehemet Ali, the Pasha of Egypt, and in February, 1825, the latter's son, Ibrahim, landed in the Morea. Before his arms the Greeks had to give way, and his methods of warfare were marked by further atrocities; indeed, he was credited with the intention of depopulating the Morea, and of re-peopling it with *fellaheen* from his father's pashalic. This intelligence was too much for a Europe by now permeated with Philhellenistic ideas, and it was clear that action of some sort by the Powers was inevitable in the immediate future.

In the meantime Canning was taking steps to avoid anything in the nature of a breach either with Vienna or St. Petersburg. He appointed Stratford Canning to succeed Strangford at Constantinople, and instructed him before taking up his post to interview both Metternich and the Tsar, while to St. Petersburg he also sent a new secretary to the embassy, whom he described as " my predecessor's brother-in-law; consequently acceptable to the Holy Alliance: and he is further peculiarly qualified for the cold and the glare of the snowy clime, by wearing a large brown wig and spectacles, probably green. He will have nothing to do . . . but to wear them in the manner most agreeable to the Emperor." [1]

At this point Alexander called a conference at St. Petersburg, at which the British Government finally refused to be represented merely " as a buffer between the colliding interests of Russia and Austria ", and which was in consequence only attended by the delegates of the Holy Alliance and France. This congress had not long been sitting before it was obvious that the points of view of Austria and Russia were not only incompatible, but actually irreconcilable, and by May, 1825, its sessions were suspended altogether. A conference that fails to agree nearly always leaves a situation worse than it found it, and so it was in this case. The Tsar took umbrage at the opposition of Austria to his plans, and

[1] Bagot, J., *op. cit.*, vol. II, p. 268.

when it came to his ears that Metternich had openly boasted of his ascendancy over him the Imperial anger knew no bounds. In August the Tsar wrote to his representatives abroad that he would work with Metternich no longer, and the Holy Alliance was at an end.

The residuary legatee proved to be Great Britain. By his adroit diplomacy Canning had avoided taking sides with Russia or with Austria, and now that they had quarrelled he knew that before long one or other of them would seek British support. At the same time he was under no illusions that Britain alone could enforce a settlement of the Greek problem. Ever since she had been a Great Power it had been proved that her action on the Continent was ineffective unless she had a reliable ally on the mainland of Europe, and the events of the War of American Independence had provided added confirmation of this. In Asia and America it was different, for in that case sea-power came into play, as was being shown at that very moment in connection with the Spanish colonies; but Canning knew that he could no more prevent a Russian army crossing the Pruth, or an Austrian one marching down the Danube, than he had been able to stop the Duc d'Angoulême from invading Spain; if, therefore, Russian or Austrian armies must march, it was in every way desirable that they should do so in support of a policy agreeable to the British Government rather than of one to which it was opposed.

Such was the situation when, in the summer of 1825, Stratford Canning arrived at St. Petersburg with instructions to suggest to the Tsar a joint intervention of the Powers, but with the stipulation that no coercion should be used against the Sultan. This did not go far enough for the Russian Government which replied that " intervention, once begun, must continue till its end is gained ". All the same Lieven was instructed to listen to any " confidential communications " which Canning might make on the subject, and to draw him on by hinting that, if Great Britain finally refused to consider the use of force, Russia might be compelled to act alone. Each party now knew where the other stood, and at Seaford the outlines of the new policy were discussed.

An interruption to the negotiations was caused by the death, or disappearance, of Alexander on December 1st, 1825. There was for a time uncertainty as to the succession to the Russian throne, and there was an outbreak of mutiny among certain regiments whose officers had become infected with Liberal opinions. In addition, Strangford proved so maladroit a negotiator that he very nearly wrecked the whole of Canning's projects. A lesser man than the Foreign Secretary would have been daunted by this series of misfortunes, but Canning had learnt by bitter experience in home politics how to snatch victory from defeat, and he tenaciously adhered to his original purpose. The Grand Duke Nicholas ascended the throne with the consent of his elder brother, Constantine, and soon stamped out in blood the sedition among his troops. Canning realized that the new Tsar would be desirous of distracting the attention of his subjects from domestic to foreign affairs, and he determined to take advantage of the opportunity. With this end in view the Duke of Wellington was sent to St. Petersburg to congratulate Nicholas I on his accession, and to come to an understanding with him in respect of the Eastern Question. " I hope ", wrote Canning, " to save Greece through the agency of the Russian name upon the fears of Turkey without a war." Nicholas and Wellington were admirably suited to one another, and the Tsar was in any event anxious for a separate understanding with Great Britain. Negotiations were thus easy, and on April 4th, 1826, the Protocol of St. Petersburg was signed.

This document, the full import of which Wellington, who was a strong Turcophil, most assuredly did not understand, stipulated that mediation should be offered to the Porte in respect of Greece. If the Sultan accepted, Greece was to become a dependency of the Ottoman Empire, and was to pay tribute, though she was to enjoy liberty in all that concerned religion and commerce, while certain of her officials were still to be nominated by the Sultan. It was further agreed that the first effort at mediation was to be made by Great Britain alone, and it was only if this failed that the two Powers were to co-operate to bring pressure on the Porte, though the actual conduct of subsequent negotiations, and the delimitation of the boundaries of Greece, were to be undertaken by them jointly. Lastly, both Great Britain and Russia disclaimed any territorial or commercial designs upon the integrity of the Ottoman dominions, and they invited Austria, France, and Prussia to accede to the Protocol. The Tsar, indeed, went so far as to ask them to guarantee any settlement that might be reached, but the British Government, which would not give such a pledge itself, naturally refrained from requesting others to do so.

The terms of the Protocol were thus such that they could be claimed as a victory either for London or for St. Petersburg. The

Tsar congratulated himself that he had prevented British action in the Morea, and that he had committed Great Britain to a Turco-phobe policy of which several members of the Cabinet, including Wellington, most assuredly did not approve. To some extent this was certainly true, but Canning had merely allowed himself to be pushed along a road on which he was in any event only too willing to travel. He had no desire to take armed action of any sort in the Mediterranean, and by refusing to give a guarantee he had minimized the risk of becoming involved in hostilities. Furthermore, he had pledged the Tsar not to annex any Turkish territory, and in view of his fear that Nicholas had designs upon the greater part of the Ottoman dominions in Europe, this was a distinct gain. Although he had not got all he could have desired, nevertheless the continued separation of Russia from Austria was worth a few concessions.

The policy of moderating the Russian appetite for Ottoman vilayets by becoming the ally of Russia was a new departure in British diplomacy. The Younger Pitt had, unsuccessfully, en-deavoured to achieve the same end by frontal opposition, and later British Governments reverted to his methods rather than to those of Canning; the Crimean War and the crisis of 1877–78 were the consequence. It was not until the shadow of the Germany of Wilhelm II fell across Europe in the early years of the following century that Sir Edward Grey reverted to Canning's policy, and later still there were to be further deviations from it. Further-more, it is not without interest to note that while Canning kept the nation practically united behind him, Disraeli alienated a large section of British public opinion.

It soon became clear that although the Greeks, chastened by the reverses they had sustained since the landing of Ibrahim, were willing to accept the terms of the Protocol, the Porte was not, and so even the pacific Canning was compelled to envisage the possi-bility of having to use force. In the meantime he had, as we have seen, been paying a visit to Paris in the autumn of 1826, and he had thus had an opportunity of discussing with Charles X and Villèle the problems of the Near East as well as those of Spain and Portugal.

French pride had been severely wounded by the signature of the Protocol, and Paris did not consider that the request that France should associate herself with Great Britain and Russia made up for the original affront. At the same time, the French

Government fully realized that if it merely continued to sulk there was a real danger of isolation, for the final decision of Austria and Prussia was not yet known, and there was thus still a chance that they might come into line with London and St. Petersburg. Villèle, too, had nothing like a free hand in the matter. His ministry was by no means so strong as it had been, while Romanticism, which was undermining the throne, was creating a great volume of Philhellenic sentiment throughout France. The country had to a large extent recovered from the war, it had been flattered by the success of the national arms in Spain, and it was in a mood for adventures; so that it would have been decidedly unsafe for so weak an administration as that of Villèle to swim against the current. There was also the attitude of the King himself to be considered. It has already been shown that Charles lacked the caution of his predecessor, and he was as impetuous in his old age as he had been in his youth when he besought Louis XVI to let him fight in the War of American Independence, and when he had taken part in the siege of Gibralter. Thus it is not surprising that he should have come under the spell of Philhellenistic ideas, while his piety spurred him on to complete the task of Saint Louis. Many factors, therefore, were at work to range France by the side of Great Britain and Russia, provided that this could be accomplished without any loss of prestige.

Canning returned to London not only thoroughly conversant with the trend of opinion in France where the Near East was concerned, but, on the whole, by no means dissatisfied with it. He realized, however, that concessions would have to be made, for the French Government had given him clearly to understand that it would not sign the Protocol, as if it were bound to follow the bidding of Great Britain and Russia, but would require a definite treaty to be drawn up, and ratified by the Powers on an equal footing. Canning would have preferred something less definite, but his cousin was informing him from Constantinople that force alone would bring the Porte to its senses; and it was very important that Metternich should be isolated in his opposition to the Protocol, for although he had the support of Prussia, the attitude of Berlin was a matter of no importance in what related to the Near East.

In actual fact, some months elapsed before the French demands were met, and the Treaty of London, which embodied them, was signed. The delay was very largely due to Canning's succession to the Premiership, for the intrigues which preceded that event naturally distracted his attention from even the most pressing problems of foreign politics. Before the Treaty of London was concluded Canning had been succeeded at the Foreign Office by Lord Dudley,[1] but the document was in reality the work of the new Prime Minister, and formed a fitting conclusion to his four and a half years as Foreign Secretary.

In its final form, the treaty did not mention the Protocol in the preamble, and so saved the face of Villèle, whose ministry was by this time tottering to its fall. Article 1 required the immediate assent both of the Sultan and of the Greeks to an armistice. Article 2 put Greece under the suzerainty of the Porte, made her liable to pay a fixed tribute annually, but allowed her freedom in the matter of internal administration subject to Ottoman control. The treaty, however, did not contain any clause about freedom of religion and of commerce, but it provided for the expropriation of the Turkish landowners after compensation had been made. Article 4 pledged the Powers to open negotiations at once with the Porte. Article 5 was an avowal of mutual disinterestedness. Article 6 contained an optional guarantee of the settlement. Article 7 provided for the ratification of the treaty. There was also a secret clause pledging the three Powers, if the Porte did not accept the armistice, to accredit consuls to Greece, and to interpose between the Turkish and Greek forces with a view to the prevention of any further hostilities. The treaty was signed on July 6th, 1827, by Dudley, Lieven, and Polignac. Its sequel was the battle of Navarino and the independence of Greece; but by then Canning was dead, and lesser men had taken up a burden which was to prove too heavy for them.

As may be supposed, Canning left his mark upon the Foreign Office to no inconsiderable extent. Throughout the eighteenth century, and during the early years of its successor, the British representatives at foreign capitals were usually great nobles who had no special qualifications, beyond a long purse, for the posts to which they were appointed. This custom was not, of course, in any way peculiar to Great Britain, but its defects are obvious,

[1] John William Ward, succeeded in 1823 as Lord Dudley and Ward. He had a habit of talking to himself in two different voices, which was explained by his friends to be only Dudley talking to Ward. Samuel Rogers wrote of him:

Ward has no heart, they say, but I deny it,
He has a heart, and gets his speeches by it.

and not the least was the attempted remedy of special envoys who carried on the real negotiations, of which the ambassador himself often knew nothing. Louis XV had brought this latter system to a fine art, with results that were equally embarrassing to his ministers and to foreign Powers. Canning had little opportunity to initiate any reforms during his first term at the Foreign Office, but Castlereagh began to take the matter in hand as soon as the war was over, and his successor worked along the same lines; with the result that by the time of Canning's death the Foreign Service, to use the new phrase, was well on its way towards attaining the form in which we have it to-day.

Canning increased the staff at the Foreign Office, but he delegated very little of the more important work to other hands. It will, in this connection, already have become apparent from the record of his conduct of affairs that he left practically no latitude to British ambassadors and ministers abroad, and it was, in fact, he who began that policy of strict control from Whitehall which in more recent times has changed the whole profession of diplomacy. In the age of Canning the telegraph had not yet been invented, so that the regulation of details from London was impossible; but this tendency was already at work, and the time was fast passing when an ambassador had any say in the formulation of policy; strangely enough, it was his own cousin, Stratford, who was the last great diplomat of the old school. That Canning's more rigid discipline was not unnecessary is clear from the fact that the minister at Lisbon had to be reproved not only for his " slovenly penmanship ", but also for the objectionable practice of packing up tea in his official despatches. It had also become a habit with a great many ambassadors to introduce irrelevant and personal topics into their letters, and this, too, was censured. Canning made a rule of keeping private and official correspondence distinct, and of destroying the former. Those who did not conform to the new order suffered for their disobedience, however highly placed or well-connected they might be.

In nothing, however, was Canning's zeal for efficiency more marked than in his attitude towards the Consular Service, where he worked in close co-operation with his friend Huskisson. At the date of his return to the Foreign Office the standing of the vast majority of British consuls left a good deal to be desired. Some of them were, indeed, professional, and others merchants of substance, but too many were either adventurers, or bankrupt men of fashion like Beau Brummel, who was British consul at Caen. Canning, who may be said without exaggeration to have had the commercial interests of the country more closely at heart than any previous Foreign Secretary, realized that individuals of this type were worse than useless, and that he was most careful in the appointments he made in the old Spanish colonies is shown by the case of Mr. Staples. This gentleman had taken up a consular post at Acapulco, in Mexico, after promising, as all Canning's consuls were compelled to do, absolutely to renounce trade. It was not long, however, before it transpired that Staples had entered into a contract for a loan to the Mexican Government, and he was accordingly informed that there was no further occasion for his services. This action, it may be noted, was taken in spite of the fact that he was the brother-in-law of the Marquess of Ormonde.

Nevertheless, there were many flashes of the old Canning, and the most remarkable proof of this is to be found in the famous despatch which he sent to Bagot at The Hague to inform him that in consequence of the obstinate attitude of Falck, the Foreign Minister of the Netherlands, a 20% duty would be levied on Dutch shipping. The despatch was as follows:

Decypher, Separate, Secret, and Confidential.

Foreign Office,
January 31, 1826.

Sir,

In matters of commerce the fault of the Dutch
Is offering too little and asking too much.
The French are with equal advantage content,
So we clap on Dutch bottoms just 20 per cent.
(Chorus) 20 per cent, 20 per cent.
(Chorus of English Customs House Officers and French Douaniers)
(English) We clap on Dutch bottoms just 20 per cent.
(French) *Vous frapperez Falck avec* 20 *per cent.*

I have no other commands from His Majesty to convey to your Excellency to-day.
I am with great truth and respect, Sir,
Your Excellency's most obedient humble servant,
GEORGE CANNING.
His Excellency the Rt. Honble. Sir Charles Bagot, K.B.

The humour of the situation was heightened by the fact that Bagot did not possess the necessary cypher, and wrote that he hoped the " circumstances will not be productive of any public inconvenience ". Canning duly forwarded the cypher, and what ensued can best be gathered from Bagot himself.

You have fretted me to fiddle-strings, and I have a great mind not to give you the satisfaction of ever knowing how completely your mystification of me has succeeded. It was more than you had a right to expect when you drew from me that solemn and official lamentation which I sent you of my inability to decypher His Majesty's commands; but, as the Devil would have it, your success did not end here. The post which brought me the decyphers arrived at eleven o'clock at night, when I had only time before I sent off the other messenger to read your grave regret at what had occurred and to acknowledge the receipt of the mail. The next morning Tierney [1] and I were up by cock-crow to make out *la maudite dépêche*, and it was not till after an hour of the most indescribable anxiety that we were put " out of our fear " by finding what it really was, and " you Pyramus " were not Pyramus, but only " Bottom the weaver ".
I could have slain you! But I got some fun myself, for I afterwards put the fair decypher into Douglas's [2] hands, who read it twice without moving a muscle, or to this hour discovering that it was not prose, and returned it to me, declaring that it was " oddly worded; but he had always a feeling that the despatch must relate to discriminating duties ".[3]

This was Canning in his gentler moods, and well might Strangford, who had just incurred a severe reprimand for his maladroit diplomacy at St. Petersburg, write to Bagot, " Happy man, that you are, to swig your curaçoa in peace, and to be able to open your despatches without the fear of their actually exploding in your face ".
Canning was, of course, in a better position to control his subordinates than most Foreign Secretaries, for his apprenticeship had been a particularly long and varied one. He had not only

[1] Second Secretary at The Hague.
[2] First Secretary at The Hague.
[3] Bagot, J., *op. cit.*, vol. II, pp. 321–325.

served as Under-Secretary in times of great difficulty, and been Foreign Secretary for two eventful years, but he had actually represented his country abroad. It was doubtless due to this practical experience that he felt himself justified in relaxing some of the stricter of the existing regulations in the Foreign Office. His immediate subordinates, for instance, were summoned to his room by a messenger instead of by a bell, and were not required to stand in his presence except on official occasions, whereas Chatham had never in any circumstances allowed them to be seated. He had his reward, for if a few of the higher diplomats smarted under the lash of his rebukes, the opinion of the vast majority of those who served under him was probably expressed by the clerk who wrote, a few months after his death, " Alas, poor Mr. Canning. How we all miss him."

In nothing did the attitude of Canning as Foreign Secretary differ from that of his predecessors so much as in respect of the policy which he adopted towards the Press. In spite of his own journalistic activities in earlier years he was never its favourite, and to the day of his death it opposed him whenever it dared. To some extent he was himself responsible for this hostility, for he had supported the Six Acts, which had muzzled it, while his quarrel with *The Times*, for which that newspaper never forgave him, has already been related. That he was by no means opposed to a free Press is, however, incontestable, and was clearly shown by his attitude to the Indian newspapers while he was President of the Board of Control, for the man who gave direct encouragement to journalism in the vernacular could hardly be accused of desiring the suppression of the Press at home. Nor was he under any illusion as to its power, for in the year that he returned to the Foreign Office he made some observations on the subject in a speech at Liverpool:

> What should we think of that philosopher, who, in writing, at the present day, a treatise upon naval architecture and the theory of navigation, should omit wholly from his calculation that new and mighty power—new, at least, in the application of its might—which walks the water, like a giant rejoicing in his course; stemming alike the tempest and the tide; accelerating intercourse, shortening distances; creating, as it were, unexpected neighbourhoods, and new combinations of social and commercial relation; and giving to the fickleness of

winds and the faithlessness of the waves the certainty and
steadiness of a highway upon the land? Such a writer,
though he might describe a ship correctly, though he might
show from what quarters the winds of Heaven blow, would be
surely an incurious and an idle spectator of the progress of
nautical science, who did not see in the power of steam a
corrective of all former calculations.

So, in political science, he who, speculating on the British
Constitution, should content himself with marking the dis-
tribution of acknowledged technical powers between the
House of Lords, the House of Commons, and the Crown,
and assigning to each their separate provinces—to the Lords
their legislative authority, to the Crown its veto (how often
used?), to the House of Commons its power of stopping
supplies (how often, in fact, necessary to be resorted to?);
and should think that he had thus described the British
Constitution as it acts and as it is influenced in its action:
but should omit from his enumeration that mighty power of
public opinion, embodied in a free Press, which pervades,
and checks, and perhaps, in the last resort, nearly governs
the whole. Such a man would, surely, give but an imperfect
view of the government of England as it is now modified, and
would greatly underrate the counteracting influences against
which that of the executive power has to contend.[1]

Six years earlier he had defined his own attitude towards the
Press by the observation, " I acknowledge its power, I submit to
its judgment, but I will not be summoned to its bar ".

This independent attitude did not commend itself to the editorial
mind, especially as it was accompanied by a refusal to communicate information to particular newspapers. In fact, The Star was
the only organ that consistently supported him, and in respect of
it alone did he sometimes depart from his fixed policy, by providing it with inspired statements. The hostility of the Press to
Canning hardly reflects credit upon contemporary proprietors
and editors, and the fact that their attitude was due not only to
the machinations of his opponents, but also to the receipt of
bribes from abroad,[2] explains why Canning never took journalism
quite at its own valuation. He was ready to regard it as an organ

[1] Therry, R., *op. cit.*, vol. VI, pp. 404–405.
[2] Even *The Times* is alleged to have been in French pay for two years.

of public opinion, but he knew too much about its inner workings
to allow himself to " be summoned to its bar ".   Nevertheless, if
Canning cared little for Press criticism of his conduct, many of
his more fervent supporters took a different view, and an attempt,
with which Disraeli was associated, was made to found a new
paper, called *The Representative*, in support of Canning, but it
only ran for six months, when it was closed down after incurring
considerable losses.

The secret of Canning's indifference to hostile criticism in the
Press lay in the fact that he looked rather to the support of that
public opinion which no editor dared defy, and that he was justified in taking this attitude is proved by events, for *The Morning
Herald*, one of the organs of his opponents, was forced to admit
that " it strikes us that no minister, since the Revolution, excepting
only the great Lord Chatham, has acquired the same national
popularity which is at this moment possessed by Mr. Canning ".[1]
In the days of *The Anti-Jacobin* he had realized the need of
fighting his enemies, at that time the partisans of revolution,
elsewhere than merely on the floor of the House of Commons, but
it was not until his election for Liverpool, which had the same
influence upon his career that the Midlothian Campaign had upon
that of Gladstone, that he fully grasped the possibilities of mobilizing public opinion in his support.   As a contemporary wrote of
him, " Mr. Canning is, so far as our recollection serves, the first
British minister who has valued himself upon maintaining a
constant intellectual intercourse with his constituents, and has
seized every opportunity of personally inculcating . . . those
political opinions . . . which he had invariably advocated in the
Commons ".

Unquestionably this policy was to a very large extent forced
upon him, for Canning was no democrat at heart, and he was as
ready to defy public opinion as to court it, but the end which he
had in view admitted of no alternative.   Unless he could carry
the country with him he had little hope of making headway
against the King, his more intransigent colleagues, and the Holy
Alliance.   He succeeded only because at last George feared for
his crown, ministers for their offices, and foreign Powers for the
outcome of a struggle in which Britain was obviously united.   In
the pamphlet [2] which she published after Canning's death his

---

[1] January 28th, 1824.
[2] *An Authentic Account of Mr. Canning's Policy.*

P

widow went even further, and claimed that he also enlisted support on the mainland of Europe itself:

> While he was at the helm there was not one of the European governments who dared to provoke the vengeance of England, because they well knew that a war with England would be a measure too unpopular to hazard. Thus Mr. Canning was enabled to hold language and to carry measures in defiance of the principles and prejudices of some, and contrary to the orders of the governments of the great continental Powers. By these means he obtained over these governments an influence which he employed not only to promote the interests of England, but the general prosperity of the world.

In actual fact the clue to Canning's foreign policy is to be found in the instructions which he drew up for his cousin in 1824:

> To preserve the peace of the world is the leading object of the policy of England. For this purpose it is necessary in the first place to prevent to the utmost of our power the breaking out of new quarrels; in the second place, to compose, where it can be done by friendly mediation, existing differences; and thirdly, where that is hopeless, to narrow as much as possible their range; and fourthly to maintain for ourselves an imperturbable neutrality in all cases where nothing occurs to affect injuriously our interests or our honour.

In spite of a natural impetuosity which had often stood him in ill stead where domestic politics were concerned, Canning rarely came to a hasty decision on official matters, and then only when the circumstances of the case did not permit of delay. He had, too, an uncanny knack, not uncommon in the Irish, of foreseeing the line that Continental statesmen would take, and thus he was rarely confronted with unexpected situations. Furthermore, his genius was as conspicuous in peace as in war, and the man whose rapidity of thought after Tilsit had resulted in the frustration of Napoleon himself, was the same as he who displayed the patience of a Job during the long negotiations that preceded the recognition of the Latin American states. This ability to go to the heart of whatever problem was confronting him brought Canning to the conclusions which he outlined to Stratford, and it is proof of his skill that he made Great Britain the arbiter of the world without having recourse to arms. He knew that the domestic situation demanded peace, but he also realized that peace was more likely to be maintained by firmness than by timidity, and events proved him right.

It is sometimes objected that Canning was a Liberal abroad and a reactionary at home, but there is little substance in the charge, though the criticism was made by Metternich, who once sarcastically offered him Austrian troops to suppress disorders in Ireland. Canning was certainly no democrat in the modern sense of the term, but he did not believe in the legitimist doctrines that had become so fashionable in Vienna and St. Petersburg. Above all, he was susceptible to the logic of facts, and when Liberalism triumphed, he was not prepared to sacrifice British interests by a blind refusal to bow to the inevitable. Moreover, it was not until the King of Spain and the Sultan had shown themselves quite incapable of re-establishing their authority in America and Greece respectively that he began to take any notice of the new states that were coming into existence, thereby pursuing a policy very different from that of Paris and Madrid at the time of the War of American Independence. He actually delayed the recognition of the Latin American republics in the hope that they might adopt monarchical constitutions, and he did all that he could to consolidate the Empire of Brazil. In short, abroad as at home, he endeavoured to establish a balance, and like so many who strive after a happy mean he was accused of inconsistency.

Canning, like Chatham before him, realized that Great Britain was not solely a European Power. He admitted that her geographical situation precluded the adoption of any policy of isolation, splendid or otherwise, so far as Continental questions were concerned, and, as always, his aim was to strike a balance. In Canning's day the overseas possessions of Great Britain, with the exception of India and the West Indies, were too insignificant to be of much account in the eyes of the Foreign Office, though the man who sanctioned the occupation of Singapore was assuredly not blind to the possibilities of the future; and his attitude towards Latin America proves how close was his attention to all that concerned Britain's position in the world beyond the confines of Europe. If Chatham won Canada on the battlefields of Germany, Canning showed the impotence of the Holy Alliance in

the New World, and he finally broke it in the Near East.   He
displayed, too, an appreciation, rare in a civilian, of the benefits
to be derived from that unquestioned mastery of the sea
that Great Britain possessed in his day, and he used it to the
disadvantage of Napoleon himself.   In short, he envisaged his
country as a world-Power, which could never be indifferent to
European problems, but which necessarily viewed them from a
different angle from that of the purely Continental states.

Finally, he was the first Foreign Secretary to be guided to any
marked degree by the commercial needs of the country.   To some
extent this attitude may have been imposed upon him by the
necessity of seeking support in fresh quarters, but the influence
of Huskisson can also be traced.   Canning was not compelled to
subordinate every other consideration to the economic, for the
progress of the Industrial Revolution, in spite of the disorders that
accompanied it, was bringing to England a prosperity hitherto
unknown in her history.   Yet Canning realized that expanding
industries require expanding markets, and his attitude towards
Spanish America and Brazil was based as much upon economic
as upon political considerations.   Had he lived to old age it is
more than likely that he would have combined the interest in
foreign affairs that characterized Palmerston with that compre-
hension of the country's industrial and commercial needs which
was possessed by Peel, and so have prevented the creation of that
gulf between different points of view which so often weakened
British action during the nineteenth century.

CHAPTER XI

PRIME MINISTER

On February 17th, 1827, Liverpool, whose health had been none too good for several months, was found insensible in his breakfast-room as the result of a stroke, and for the first time for fifteen years the Premiership was obviously soon to be vacant. The qualifications of Liverpool for the high office which he held, and the vilification to which he has been subjected, have already been discussed, and the break-up of the Tory party the moment that his guiding hand was removed is an eloquent testimony to the value of his achievements. In these circumstances, it is not surprising that a new era in British politics began on that February morning when the Prime Minister was incapacitated from any further participation in the government of the country.

The Cabinet which thus found itself so suddenly deprived of the chief who alone had kept it together was a very different body from that which had taken office with him fifteen years before. Of the more important ministers, only the Lord Chancellor, the Lord Privy Seal, the First Lord of the Admiralty, and the Secretary of State for War remained the same as in 1812. Canning had succeeded Castlereagh at the Foreign Office and as Leader of the House of Commons, while Sidmouth at the Home Office had given place to Robert Peel. Huskisson and Wynn had also brought fresh blood into the administration during recent years, though the same observation can hardly be applied to the substitution of Robinson for Vansittart as Chancellor of the Exchequer. On the whole, however, the *personnel* of the Government was a great deal more imposing in 1827 than it had been in 1812, and its debating strength in both Houses was formidable in the extreme.

In policy the changes had been still more remarkable. The Government had assumed office in time of war, and had as its immediate object the conclusion of a victorious peace. That purpose had been accomplished, and it was at least as much the misfortune of ministers as their fault that they then embarked upon a course of repression at home. To this there succeeded, with the advent of Peel to the Home Office, a milder policy which undoubtedly regained for the Cabinet a good deal of the support that Sidmouth and his Six Acts had alienated. Huskisson, at the

Board of Trade, was winning the approval of the commercial classes, though in the early weeks of 1827 the landed interest was becoming seriously disquieted by the proposal to reduce the duty on corn. Nevertheless, to some extent the new ministers were in the nature of a patch on an old garment, and it cannot be too often stated that only the personal skill of Liverpool had held the Cabinet together. As we have seen, Wellington, Eldon, and Westmorland strongly disapproved of Canning's foreign policy, while the memory of the political crises earlier in the century prevented any very real co-operation between several of the ministers. Indeed, a less homogeneous administration it would be impossible to discover in recent British history, while the extent to which some of its members were prepared to push their intrigues was seen in Canning's relations with the King when the recognition of the Spanish colonies was under discussion.

Apart from the proposal to reduce the duty on corn, the two burning questions of the day were still Roman Catholic Emancipation and Parliamentary Reform, and upon the former the Cabinet was hopelessly divided. Reform had become the true line of division between Whigs and Tories, and none of the latter would hear of it, but so far as Emancipation was concerned there was considerable difference of opinion within the ranks of the Government supporters. Canning, Huskisson, Melville, and Robinson were in favour of a concession to the Roman Catholics, which was opposed by the rest of the Cabinet, including Liverpool himself. In the country at large the position was still much the same as that already described, and the Tory strongholds were the centres of opposition to any alteration in the existing laws. Whenever the subject was debated in Parliament it was left to a free vote of the House, but though the Commons usually showed a majority in favour of Emancipation the Lords were decidedly of the other way of thinking. The King, too, was known to be a " Protestant ", but the recent death of the Duke of York, the heir presumptive to the throne, had considerably weakened that interest in the Royal Family.

The division in the ministry on the subject of Roman Catholic Emancipation was repeated in the matter of Canning's foreign policy, with the important difference that on this issue the Prime Minister supported his old friend. The leading opponent of Canning was Wellington, for of late years the two men had drifted far apart, and the long series of reverses which the Iron Duke had suffered at the hands of the Foreign Secretary had naturally done nothing to heal the breach. While Liverpool was still at the head of affairs these various cracks could be papered over, but the closest observers had for some time realized that when he was gone the centrifugal tendencies in the Cabinet would triumph, and so it proved.

When the Prime Minister's illness overtook him, Canning was at Brighton, and was himself indisposed as the result of a chill which he had caught at the funeral of the Duke of York. On hearing the news, Peel came down from London to see him, and it was agreed that no change should be made for the present, as there was still a chance that Liverpool might recover. Before long this hope was at an end, but Canning advised the King not to act precipitately—advice which George was only too willing to adopt, for his choice was far from obvious. There seemed, however, to be four possible solutions—Canning, Peel, Wellington, or a figure-head under whom the existing ministers would be content to serve.

Canning's claim to the succession was based upon several grounds. Since 1822 he had been the Leader of the House of Commons, and he had been in Parliament for more than a generation. He was also incontestably the greatest orator of the day. Outside Westminster he was clearly the most popular member of the Cabinet, while the vigour and success of his foreign policy had made him an international figure. At the same time there were strong influences working against him. It is true that Canning had at last learnt to practise that restraint of which the lack had done him so much harm in the days of the Addington and Perceval administrations, but he was for various reasons unpopular among certain sections of the Tory party. His championship of Roman Catholic Emancipation alienated the more bigoted elements, while his foreign policy was an object of detestation to all who drew their inspiration from Wellington. Nor was this all, for there was every reason to suppose that Canning's accession to the Premiership would mean the refusal of several of Liverpool's ministers to serve under him, and so cause the disintegration of the party, which, except for twelve months, had been in power since 1783. In short, Canning was the man who was indicated by his experience, his genius, and his widespread popularity as the successor of Liverpool, but the opposition to him in his own party, combined with the King's personal views on the religious question, made it exceedingly doubtful if he would be appointed to the office where the vast majority of his fellow-countrymen undoubtedly wished to see him.

" Orange " Peel, as he was then called on account of his determined opposition to Emancipation, was eighteen years younger than Canning, but his career had been so brilliant that he was seriously considered by many Tories as the only possible successor to Liverpool. The son of a Lancashire manufacturer, though himself educated at Harrow and Christ Church, Oxford, Peel was representative of the new middle-class which had been called into existence by the Industrial Revolution. He had been hardly a year in the House of Commons when Perceval made him an Under-Secretary at the age of twenty-two, and in 1812 he became Chief Secretary for Ireland. Oxford University had preferred him to Canning as its representative, and he had become Home Secretary in the same year that Canning succeeded Castlereagh at the Foreign Office. Always a man of extreme circumspection, Peel had contrived so far to please every section of his party. The more extreme Tories supported the opponent of any concession to the Roman Catholics, though it was a marvel to Palmerston " how such a man as Peel, liberal, enlightened and fresh minded, should find himself running in such a pack ". On the other hand, he was obviously inclined towards a relaxation of the Navigation Acts and the abolition of slavery, and this won him a measure of popularity among the progressives.

Wellington was certainly favoured in many quarters, but it was generally agreed that his chances were fewer than they would have been had he not accepted the post of commander-in-chief in succession to the Duke of York; that appointment, it was felt, could hardly with propriety be combined with the Premiership in a constitutional monarchy like England.

Lastly, there was the suggestion that a way out of the difficulty might be found by placing some man of straw in the position that Liverpool had held. In theory this plan had much to recommend it, and it would probably have postponed the break-up of the Tory party, but the trouble was obviously going to be to find a figure-head at once sufficiently unambitious not to provoke jealousy, and yet capable enough to hold together a very heterogeneous administration. Various names, such as Bathurst and Melville, were at once bandied about in political circles, but this particular solution was never much more than a pious aspiration.

There was, however, an external force to be taken into consideration, and that was the attitude of the Opposition. The Whigs had been out of office for twenty years, and on a number of questions their views were identical with those of Canning and his friends, so that it is in no way remarkable that a large section of the party began to think in terms of a coalition as soon as the news of the Prime Minister's illness was received. In the forefront of this movement was Brougham, who saw clearly that a junction between Canning and Huskisson on the one hand, and the Whigs on the other, must split the Tories for ever. Once having arrived at this conclusion, he was not the man to let the grass grow under his feet, and " he started off with two important advantages: he had Lord Lansdowne, the leading exponent of coalition in the House of Lords, almost completely under his thumb; and he had the Whig Press on his side ".[1] A third asset was his close personal friendship with Canning. The Liverpool election of 1812 had left no bitter memories for either man,[2] and after Canning's resignation from the Board of Control they had stayed together at Bolton's house at Storrs, an event, incidentally, which fluttered the political dovecotes at the time very considerably. In spite, however, of the similarity of their opinions on so many subjects, there was clearly no foundation for Wellington's suspicions that Canning and Brougham had discussed the possibility of a coalition before Liverpool's seizure.

Three days after the crisis began *The Times* appeared with a leading article advocating the formation of a coalition between the Canningites and the Whigs, and further advising Lansdowne neither to insist upon any great number of ministerial posts nor to make the adoption of Catholic Emancipation as a Cabinet question an essential condition of his support. This article was almost certainly inspired by Brougham, and it was closely connected with a meeting of the Opposition members of the House of Commons held to discuss the situation. Among those who advocated the idea of a coalition was Lord John Russell, though he changed his mind a month later, and the meeting finally decided to support without reservation any administration of which Canning

---

[1] Aspinall, A.: *Lord Brougham and the Whig Party*, p. 141.
[2] It is related that one night when Brougham was due to dine with Canning, the latter noticed that his servants had placed in the centre of the dinner-table a piece of silver which had been presented to him by his constituents in Liverpool. Canning at once ordered it to be removed out of consideration for the feelings of his guest.

might be the head, whether or no he was in a position to further Emancipation. Canning was informed of this decision on February 22nd, so that in less than a week after Liverpool's seizure he was in a stronger position than any of his rivals for the Premiership.

On the other hand, the Whigs in the House of Lords were not so favourably disposed towards Canning as their co-religionists in the Commons, for if Lansdowne was under the influence of Brougham, Grey had abandoned none of his old distrust, and regarded " the son of an actress as being *de facto* incapacitated from being Premier of England ". Nevertheless, for a moment even he wavered, and wrote to his son, " If Canning was in health and vigour, and could establish his ascendancy, I think it would produce overtures to some of the Opposition, *nommément* to Lansdowne, which I do not think it would be discreditable for them to accept, if a fair assurance were given them of a determined and *bona fide* support of the Catholic question ; by which I mean that it should be brought forward as a measure of the Government ".[1]

While these negotiations were afoot the Cabinet had decided to meet Parliament, and to pass the Corn Bill, while the discussion of a motion relative to Catholic Emancipation which stood in the name of Sir Francis Burdett would provide an excellent opportunity of testing the feeling of the House of Commons upon a question that must gravely affect the choice of a successor to Liverpool. Canning, on February 22nd, informed the King, who was at Brighton, of this decision, and he agreed.

Canning returned to London on February 27th, and on the first day of the following month he moved the adoption of the Government's resolutions on the importation of corn, Huskisson being absent owing to illness. His speech was conciliatory in the extreme, and provided no weapon for his opponents to use against him. He took the line that the resolutions which he was moving represented the happy mean between the opinions of those who advocated the free importation of foreign corn and of those who desired its total prohibition. After pointing out the merits of the proposals he showed his appreciation of the fact, which many of his contemporaries did not realize, that there were now two Englands, one agricultural and the other industrial :

> These are some of the benefits which this plan presents to the House ; and if it should appear, upon trial, that interests,

---

[1] Trevelyan, G. M.: *Lord Grey of the Reform Bill*, p. 374.

which are now supposed as wide as the poles asunder, may thus be approximated more nearly than is now believed to be possible, such a result would be worth all the rest.   It will tend to sweeten the ill blood which has too long subsisted between two classes of the community looking with jealousy at each other, and to unite conflicting opinions as well as interests, which have appeared to be altogether irreconcilable.[1]

The resolutions were duly passed, and Canning's skill in handling a subject which was not his own certainly improved his prospects.

A few days later the debate on Burdett's motion took place, and it was marked by an acrimony which showed how conscious were the chief speakers of what was at stake.   Canning rose to address the House at 2.30 A.M. on March 6th, and his speech was very largely a record of his attitude on the Emancipation question, obviously given for the purpose of enlightening the new members whom the General Election of the previous year had sent to Westminster. It was, however, characterized by a passage of arms between Canning and the Master of the Rolls, during which the latter objected to his legal opinion being quoted.   Canning maintained his perfect right to do so, and then carried the war into his opponent's camp by suggesting that the speech of the Master of the Rolls was merely the repetition of a pamphlet written by Dr. Phillpotts, the Bishop of Exeter, adding, to complete his discomfiture, three lines adapted from a popular song:

> Dear Tom, this brown jug, which now foams with mild ale,
> Out of which I once drank to sweet Nan of the Vale,
> Was once Toby Phillpott's.[2]

Canning's peroration, however, as was his wont, raised the question to the highest plane, though it will be noted that he care-

---

[1] Therry, R., *op. cit.*, vol. VI, p. 137.
[2] The original song is in *The Poor Soldier*, a comic opera by John O'Keefe, and the music is by William Shield.   The opera was performed about 1785, and the song and the music were sold separately.   It ran as follows:

> Dear Sir, this brown jug that now foams with mild ale,
> Out of which I now drink to sweet Kate of the Vale,
> Was once Toby Filpot, a thirsty old soul,
> As e'er crack'd a bottle, or fathom'd a bowl;
> In boozing about, 'twas his praise to excel,
> And amongst jolly topers he bore off the bell.

Notes and Queries, Tenth Series, vol. XII, pp. 470–471.

fully refrained from committing himself to any particular line of action:

> The present system against the Catholics may be sustained a little longer, from year to year; but speaking of the age of a country, the time of its duration must be short indeed. The motion of the honourable baronet does not, however, call upon those who may still be attached to that system to abandon it: it is merely a declaration on the part of the House that the state of Ireland, and of the Roman Catholic people, require some consideration from the Legislature. To this proposition it is intended to propose a direct negative, imparting that Parliament does not think the state of Ireland, or the laws affecting the Roman Catholics, deserve consideration. It is upon this vote that the House is about to divide.
>
> This resolution goes no farther than to state that the House adopts the opinion of its predecessors, as to the propriety of considering the question; of those predecessors, who sent up to the House of Lords, three bills of relief to the Roman Catholics. By voting with the honourable baronet, I do not more than sanction this proposition; reserving to myself the power of acting or not acting upon it as hereafter I may think proper. On the other hand, if this Resolution be negatived; if the House of Commons shall decide that the consideration of the state of Ireland is not worthy to be entered upon, then is the House of Commons changed indeed; and I shudder to contemplate the consequences which from such a change may ensue.[1]

The debate was also marked by a fierce duel between Peel and Brougham, but when the division was taken it was found that Burdett's motion had been lost by four votes.

The debates on the Corn Bill and on Roman Catholic Emancipation had done little to solve the crisis. Canning's ability in piloting the first measure through committee had been both remarkable and remarked, but on the religious issue he had undoubtedly suffered a reverse, while feeling between the opponents and the supporters of relief had become more embittered than ever. On the other hand, the margin of four votes was certainly not sufficient to warrant the appointment of a " Pro-

[1] Therry, R., *op. cit.*, vol. VI, pp. 177–178.

testant " Premier, and the end of the first week of March saw the solution of the problem of Liverpool's successor transferred from Westminster to Windsor, whither the King had gone from Brighton.

From the beginning George had hoped that, as in 1812, after the murder of Perceval, the crisis would in due course be solved without the necessity of him making a choice between various aspirants to the vacant Premiership. He would himself have liked the Government to continue upon its previous footing, and he was far from pleased when he became aware that there was no statesman to be found who possessed the same qualifications as the late Prime Minister for preserving the outward semblance of unity in the Cabinet. It is difficult, indeed, to avoid the conclusion that he definitely shirked his constitutional responsibility. Fortunately for Canning, however, his opponents made a false move, for the Dukes of Buckingham, Newcastle, and Rutland protested to the Sovereign against the possible appointment of a " Catholic " Prime Minister. This act was rightly regarded by the King as an unwarranted interference with his prerogative, but he made one last endeavour to avoid a breach with the past. Peel came to Canning with the suggestion that they should both agree to serve under Wellington, but he was met with a blunt refusal. This settled the question, for it was quite clear that Wellington could not form an administration without Canning, and no other statesman was now in the running for the succession to Liverpool. Accordingly, on April 10th, the King sent for Canning, and told him to prepare a plan for the reconstruction of the ministry.

Whether by accident or by design George refrained from actually appointing Canning to be Prime Minister at this audience, and the result was to precipitate a final quarrel with Wellington. Canning had, upon leaving Windsor, got into touch with all his colleagues in the Cabinet, including Wellington, and offered to continue the Government upon the same lines as his predecessor had done. This elicited not only a complaint from the Duke with regard to the tone of the communication he had received, but also the question who was to be Prime Minister. To this Canning replied:

I believed it to be so generally understood that the King usually entrusts the formation of an administration to the individual whom it is His Majesty's gracious intention to place at the head of it, that it did not occur to me, when I communicated to your Grace yesterday the commands which

I had just received from His Majesty, to add that, in the present instance, His Majesty does not intend to depart from the usual course of proceeding on such occasions.

I am sorry to have delayed some hours this answer to your Grace's letter; but from the nature of the subject, I did not like to forward it without having submitted it (together with your Grace's letter) to His Majesty.[1]

On the receipt of this second communication Wellington for once in his life appears to have lost his head and his temper, and talked of a rebuke covered " with His Majesty's sacred name and protection ". In private his language was even stronger, for he described Canning as a " charlatan ", and referred to his conduct as " foolish, insulting, and indecent "; when, four months later, he heard that Canning was dead, he wrote, " I hear that Dr. Farr says it was Canning's temper that killed him ". He at once resigned both his office and the command of the army, generally behaving in so unreasonable a manner as to afford Tom Moore more than a little justification for the verses:

> Great Captain, who takest such pains
> To prove—what is granted—*nem. con.*
> With how moderate a portion of brains
> Some heroes continue to get on.

If Wellington was, fortunately, the only one of his old colleagues with whom Canning actually quarrelled on this occasion, the Duke was by no means alone in refusing to serve under him, for of Liverpool's Cabinet only Harrowby, Huskisson, Robinson, and Wynn did not send in their resignations, while Bexley withdrew his. The sentiments of the retiring ministers were described by Lyttelton in a letter to Bagot, where he said, " The greatest rancour is in Canning's old colleagues against him, and I assure you it often disgusts me ". On April 12th Canning saw the King again, and the Sovereign, on hearing of what had happened, expressed grave doubts whether he had sufficient support to enable him to form a ministry. Canning replied by informing George of the Whig offer, and added, " Sire, your father broke the domination of the Whigs. I hope Your Majesty will not endure that of the Tories." To which the King replied, " No, I'll be damned if I do ", and Canning left the room Prime Minister at last.

[1] Temperley, H. W. V.: *The Foreign Policy of Canning, 1822–1827*, p. 430.

The majority of the ministers who resigned were old opponents of Canning, and the course they took was in no way unexpected, but this was not the case with Peel. Why he should have parted company with the man with whom he had so much in common is something of a mystery, for it was understood that Emancipation, the only issue upon which they differed, was to remain an open question. Nearly twenty years later Peel's conduct on this occasion was made the subject of the most violent attack by Lord George Bentinck and Disraeli, and it was freely stated that he had no other end in view than to embarrass Canning. Indeed, the charge was made that he had already changed his mind on the subject of Emancipation and that at the very time he " told Mr. Canning in the House of Commons, that his unlooked-for opposition to that statesman was grounded on a difference of opinion on the Catholic question, he had in his desk a letter, in which, two years before, he had told Lord Liverpool that, in his opinion, the Catholic claims ought to be granted ". Perhaps, however, the best explanation is that of Disraeli: " Those who are well informed of the political history of this country know that between Mr. Canning and Mr. Peel there existed an antipathy. They disliked each other: Mr. Canning was jealous of Mr. Peel, and Mr. Peel was a little envious of Mr. Canning." [1]

The news that Canning was Prime Minister roused an enthusiasm in the country that had not been known since the days of the Pitts, for, like them, he had in reality been called to office by the voice of the nation. Even the King achieved a revival of popularity on account of the line he had taken, for the Tory magnates were now as much disliked as their Whig prototypes had been forty years before. The Press, for the first and last time, came out on Canning's side, and the resignation of the old ministers was greeted with something like a sigh of relief. " The Hundred Days of Canning ", as Metternich termed his Premiership, could hardly have begun under more favourable auspices.

His first appointment was a bold one, for it was nothing less than to revive the office of Lord High Admiral and to confer it upon the heir to the throne, the Duke of Clarence, though without, of course, a seat in the Cabinet. The other posts were temporarily awarded to the more outstanding of the progressive Tories, for it was clear that, if the Government were to stand, a coalition with

[1] For another point of view, cf. Lever, Sir Tresham: *The Life and Times of Sir Robert Peel*, pp. 92–93.

the Whigs was inevitable, and before very long. Canning himself took the Chancellorship of the Exchequer, and he left Huskisson and Wynn at the Boards of Trade and of Control respectively. Bourne became Home Secretary, and Dudley and Ward went to the Foreign Office, while the Master of the Rolls succeeded Eldon as Lord Chancellor. The future, however, depended upon the co-operation of the Whigs, and at first negotiations with them proceeded none too smoothly.

Brougham was away on circuit during these critical weeks, and as a result discussions were continued between Lansdowne and Canning. Somewhat reluctantly, the former agreed to shelve the questions of Parliamentary Reform and of the repeal of the Test and Corporation Acts, but he insisted as evidence of the Government's intentions that the Lord-Lieutenant and the Chief Secretary for Ireland should be " Catholics ". Canning was agreeable to this, but the King was not, and on April 20th the negotiations for the formation of a coalition broke down.

It was at this moment that Brougham exerted perhaps his greatest influence upon the course of English politics. Whether his advocacy of a coalition was entirely, or even principally, disinterested it would be better not to enquire too closely, for there can be little doubt that the *rôle* of king-maker strongly appealed to his vanity, but he was a good party man, and he was determined to prevent any reunion in the Tory ranks. When he learned that the conversations between Lansdowne and Canning were at an end he raised a storm in the Whig camp, and exerted all his pressure on Devonshire. That Duke refused to put himself at the head of those who were in revolt against Lansdowne's leadership, but he did use his influence, and, as a result, the negotiations were not only re-opened, but were brought to a successful conclusion. It was arranged that the Whigs were to have three seats in the Cabinet, namely Lansdowne the Home Office, Tierney the Mint, and Carlisle the Privy Seal; while the offices of Lord Chamberlain and Attorney-General were also given to members of that party, though it was not until July that the re-shuffle was complete. That the coalition ever came into being at all was due to Brougham, and his consciousness of the fact made him a veritable thorn in Canning's side, while he could not be silenced by office, for the King refused to have him as a minister, and Brougham declined any other form of employment.

Neither Brougham's eloquence nor Devonshire's powers of

persuasion could reconcile Grey to the coalition. He confessed to " a rooted distrust of Canning ", and he carried this, according to James Abercromby, later Lord Dunfermline, to the length of " vilifying his parentage and reproaching him with the frailties of his mother ".

The policy of the Government was defined by Canning in the House of Commons:

> But to come to the present condition of that question [*i.e.* Catholic Emancipation], I say again, it remains in this Government in the state it was truly described to be in by Lord Castlereagh in 1812; and precisely as it has been since repeatedly described by myself; in short, as it was described to be in 1825, in a debate which took place in the month of March upon the state of Ireland; and in the very last debate in the last session of Parliament, in the same year, upon Catholic Emancipation.

Canning then cited some words which he had employed on that occasion, and which gave him the same liberty of action as those that he had used in the debate on Burdett's motion a few weeks before. He continued:

> These were the words I used then, and my opinions are not in the slightest degree varied at the present moment. Such was the footing upon which this question stood when I was the colleague of my Right Honourable friend (Peel), and such is the footing on which it stands now. Let it be observed, therefore, by those with whom I have formerly acted, and from whose objections on this occasion I do not shrink, however the acknowledgment I have made may be attempted to be converted into matter of opposition, that, with those who form the present Cabinet, and some of whom formed part of the last, the Catholic question now stands on the same ground as it stood on under Lord Liverpool's Government: that is, it is a question which each member of the Government is at liberty, if he pleases, to bring forward in the Cabinet, or to propound to Parliament; but if any member of the Government shall so bring it forward in either House of Parliament, he is bound distinctly to state that he does so in his individual capacity only, and not as pledging his colleagues to his own opinions on the subject. This,

Q

Sir, is the position of the Catholic question now; it is the same in which it was placed in the year 1812; it is the same in which it has now stood for fifteen years successively.

Upon the other great problem of the day he was equally clear:

There have been one or two questions put to me. I trust the House will extend its indulgence to me, while I briefly answer them. I am asked what I mean to do on the subject of Parliamentary Reform. Why, I say, to oppose it, to oppose it to the end of my life in this House, as hitherto I have done. I am asked what I intend to do respecting the repeal of the Test and Corporation Acts. My answer is, to oppose it, too. It has happened by some accident that the Test Act is one of the few subjects upon which it has never yet been my lot to pronounce an opinion fully in this House; but I have an opinion upon it, and I do not hesitate to declare it. I think that the exertions of the Legislature ought to be directed to the redress of practical and not theoretical grievances. I think that any meddling with the Test Act, of which the alleged grievances are comparatively theoretical, might tend to prejudice that great question, which is attended with real practical and pressing grievances to those whom the present laws relating to it affect, and the success of which I have most truly at heart. I will therefore oppose the repeal.[1]

In spite of the few concessions which he made to their opinions Canning received the support of the larger section of the Opposition. Nevertheless, the late spring and early summer constituted a period of anxiety for the new Prime Minister, for his administration, being a coalition, had to meet attacks from both sides, that is to say from those who thought its programme did not go far enough, as well as from those who considered that it went too far. Of these two bodies of opinion the leaders were Grey and Wellington respectively, and unfortunately for Canning both were in the House of Lords where his Government was at its weakest, and where he was unable personally to reply to his critics.

Grey launched his attack at the beginning of May, and in a speech inspired by the technique of *suggestio falsi* he managed to achieve a considerable, if ephemeral, parliamentary triumph.

[1] Therry, R., *op. cit.*, vol. VI, pp. 204–231.

With the object of weakening the Whig support of the new Prime Minister he charged him, when at the Foreign Office, with neglecting to defend the Spanish Liberals against the armies of Louis XVIII. This so irritated Canning that for a moment he thought of taking a peerage in order to be able to deal in person with any further onslaughts on the part of the Whig leader. His wife, indeed, maintained that this attack shortened her husband's life, and although that is probably an exaggeration there can be no doubt that it was a source of considerable annoyance to him, more particularly in view of the fact that the Government did not possess a spokesman in the Upper House who could answer it properly.

Wellington had spoken with some bitterness on the re-assembling of Parliament at the beginning of May, when the various ex-ministers justified their respective resignations, but his dislike of Canning went so far as to allow him to propose a wrecking amendment, which was carried, to the Corn Bill, which was a legacy from the previous Government, and for which he was consequently just as responsible as the Prime Minister himself. The Duke's hostility was more irritating than dangerous, though his success on this occasion showed that Canning would have a difficult task before him in carrying Government measures through the House of Lords. The other ex-ministers did not cause him any particular anxiety, and Peel's speech on his resignation had passed off without any passage of arms between the late Home Secretary and his old colleagues.

On June 1st, Canning, as Chancellor of the Exchequer, introduced the Budget, and he displayed as intimate an acquaintance with the financial position of the country as with the details of its foreign policy. On the 22nd of the same month he made, on the Corn Amendment Bill, what was destined to be his last speech, and although he had only another six weeks to live he seems to have lost none of his old fire. Among those who heard him was the twenty-three year old Disraeli, who told the House of Commons in 1846, " I can recall the lightning flash of that eye and the tumult of that ethereal brow. Still lingers in my ear the melody of that voice."

Parliament rose at the beginning of July, and Canning refused to answer a question whether there would be an autumn session. His Government had, on the whole, come through very well, and on most divisions its majority in the Lower House had been over a hundred, though in the Lords, as we have seen, it was comparatively weak. The signature of the Treaty of London on July 6th was a further triumph for the Prime Minister personally, while the re-arrangement of seats in the Cabinet which took place about the same time was calculated to strengthen the coalition. It is true that the recess had hardly begun before Tierney said, " We cannot go on: the coach must all be unpacked and re-packed again ",[1] but it is difficult to see what ground he had for his pessimism. No doubt, as in all coalitions, there were bickerings between the two wings, and it is certain that they tried Canning sorely, but that there was any external or internal threat to the life of his administration at the end of July it is impossible to believe.

It was his own life that was drawing to a close, although his medical advisers told him in July that his constitution was unbroken, and that he had " stamina for several years to come ". He seems to have taken some time to shake off the chill which he had contracted at the funeral of the Duke of York, while the difficulties by which he was surrounded from the moment that Liverpool had his seizure undoubtedly affected his general health. Huskisson, who was going abroad, saw him about the middle of July for what proved to be the last time, and thought he looked ill, though Canning denied that there was anything wrong with him. Other observers, however, were of the same opinion as Huskisson, and Devonshire suggested that he should take a rest at his house at Chiswick. On July 20th he availed himself of the Duke's invitation, although that was where Fox had died. Years later, his host wrote, " Canning died in a room upstairs. I had a great foreboding when he came here, and would not allow of his being in the room below where Fox had died." [2] On the evening of August 2nd he was seized with the most violent pains, which Knighton, whom the King sent to examine him, diagnosed as due to inflammation of the liver. For the greater part of a week he lingered on in the greatest agony, and in the early hours of August 8th, 1827, he died.[3]

---

[1] Olphin, H. K.: *George Tierney*, p. 235.
[2] *Notes and Queries*, vol. CLXXIII, p. 332.
[3] Years later Frere wrote the following epitaph:

> I was destroyed by Wellington and Grey.
> They both succeeded. Each has had his day.
> Both tried to govern, each in his own way,
> And both repent of it—as well they may.

Canning was buried, privately at his own request, in Westminster Abbey near the grave of Pitt, and in the fullness of time there were erected by the side of his monument, the statues of his son, Charles, " Clemency " Canning, the first Governor-General of India under the Crown, and of his cousin Stratford Canning, Viscount Stratford de Redcliffe, the " Great Elchi ". Surely a unique testimony of a nation's gratitude to two generations of one family.

APPENDIX I

GENEALOGICAL TABLE

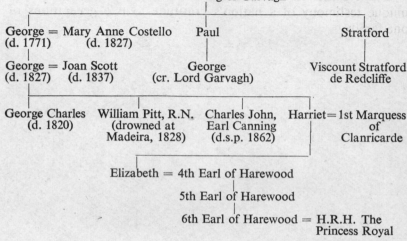

Stratford Canning of Garvagh

George = Mary Anne Costello   Paul   Stratford
(d. 1771)   (d. 1827)

George = Joan Scott   George   Viscount Stratford
(d. 1827)   (d. 1837)   (cr. Lord Garvagh)   de Redcliffe

George Charles   William Pitt, R.N.   Charles John,   Harriet = 1st Marquess
(d. 1820)   (drowned at   Earl Canning   of
             Madeira, 1828)   (d.s.p. 1862)   Clanricarde

Elizabeth = 4th Earl of Harewood

5th Earl of Harewood

6th Earl of Harewood = H.R.H. The
                          Princess Royal

APPENDIX II

BRITISH ADMINISTRATIONS, 1783–1827

Pitt, December, 1783.

First Lord of the Treasury and Chancellor of the Exchequer.	W. Pitt.
Home Secretary.	Earl Temple.
	Lord Sydney (1783).
	W. W. Grenville (1789).
	H. Dundas (1791).
	Duke of Portland (1794).
Foreign Secretary.	Marquess of Carmarthen.
	Lord Grenville (1791).
War Office.	H. Dundas (1794).
Lord President.	Earl Gower.
	Lord Camden (1784).
	Earl Fitzwilliam (1794).
	Earl of Mansfield (1794).
	Earl of Chatham (1796).
Lord Chancellor.	Lord Thurlow.
	Lord Loughborough (1793).
Lord Privy Seal.	Duke of Rutland.
	Earl Gower (1784).
	Earl Spencer (1794).
	Earl of Chatham (1794).
	Earl of Westmorland (1798).
Admiralty.	Viscount Hood.
	Earl of Chatham (1788).
	Earl Spencer (1794).
Ordnance.	Duke of Richmond.
	Marquess Cornwallis (1795).
Lord-Lieutenant of Ireland.	Duke of Rutland.
	Marquess of Buckingham (1787).
	Earl of Westmorland (1790).
	Earl Fitzwilliam (1794).
	Earl Camden (1795).
	Marquess Cornwallis (1798).
Secretary at War.	Sir George Yonge, not in Cabinet.
	W. Windham (1794), in Cabinet.

Addington, March, 1801.

First Lord of the Treasury and Chancellor of the Exchequer.	H. Addington.
Home Secretary.	Duke of Portland.
	Lord Pelham (1801).
	C. P. Yorke (1803).
Foreign Secretary.	Lord Hawkesbury.
War Office.	Lord Hobart.
Lord President.	Earl of Chatham.
	Duke of Portland (1801).
Lord Chancellor.	Lord Eldon.
Lord Privy Seal.	Earl of Westmorland.

248 GEORGE CANNING

Admiralty.	Earl St. Vincent.
Ordnance.	Earl of Chatham.
Board of Trade.	Lord Auckland.
Board of Control.	Viscount Lewisham.
	Viscount Castlereagh.
Lord Lieutenant of Ireland.	Earl of Hardwicke, not in Cabinet
Secretary at War.	C. P. Yorke, not in Cabinet.
	C. Bragg (1803), not in Cabinet.

Pitt, May, 1804.

First Lord of the Treasury and Chan-cellor of the Exchequer.	W. Pitt.
Home Secretary.	Lord Hawkesbury.
Foreign Secretary.	Lord Harrowby.
	Lord Mulgrove (1805).
War Office.	Earl Camden.
	Viscount Castlereagh (1803).
Lord President.	Duke of Portland.
	Viscount Sidmouth (1805).
	Earl Camden (1805).
Lord Chancellor.	Lord Eldon.
Lord Privy Seal.	Earl of Westmorland.
Admiralty.	Viscount Melville.
	Lord Barham (1805).
Ordnance.	Earl of Chatham.
Board of Trade.	Duke of Montrose.
Board of Control.	Viscount Castlereagh.
Duchy of Lancaster	Lord Mulgrave.
	Earl of Buckinghamshire (1805).
	Lord Harrowby (1805).
Lord-Lieutenant of Ireland.	Earl of Hardwicke, not in Cabinet.
	Earl of Powis, not in Cabinet.
Secretary at War.	W. Dundas, not in Cabinet.

Grenville, February, 1806.

First Lord of the Treasury.	Lord Grenville.
Home Secretary.	Earl Spencer.
Foreign Secretary.	C. J. Fox.
	Viscount Hawick (Sept.).
War Office.	W. Windham.
Lord President.	Earl Fitzwilliam.
	Viscount Sidmouth (Oct.).
Lord Chancellor.	Lord Erskine.
Lord Privy Seal.	Viscount Sidmouth.
	Lord Holland (Oct.).
Chancellor of the Exchequer.	Lord H. Petty.
Admiralty.	Viscount Hawick.
	T. Grenville (Sept.).
Ordnance.	Earl of Moira.
Chief Justice, King's Bench.	Lord Ellenborough, in Cabinet.
Lord-Lieutenant of Ireland.	Duke of Bedford, not in Cabinet.
Secretary at War.	R. Fitzpatrick, not in Cabinet.

Portland, March, 1807.

First Lord of the Treasury.	Duke of Portland.
Home Secretary.	Lord Hawkesbury.

Foreign Secretary.	G. Canning.
War Office.	Viscount Castlereagh.
Lord President.	Earl Camden.
Lord Chancellor.	Lord Eldon.
Lord Privy Seal.	Earl of Westmorland.
Chancellor of the Exchequer.	S. Perceval.
Admiralty.	Lord Mulgrave.
Ordnance.	Earl of Chatham.
Board of Trade.	Earl Bathurst.
	Earl of Harrowby (1809).
Lord Lieutenant of Ireland.	Duke of Richmond, not in Cabinet.
Secretary at War.	Sir J. Pulteney, not in Cabinet.
	Lord G. Leveson Gower (1809), in Cabinet.

Perceval, October, 1809.

First Lord of the Treasury and Chancellor of the Exchequer.	S. Perceval.
Home Secretary.	R. Ryder.
Foreign Secretary.	Earl Bathurst.
	Marquess Wellesley (1809).
	Viscount Castlereagh (1812).
War Office.	Earl of Liverpool.
Lord President.	Earl Camden.
	Viscount Sidmouth (1812).
Lord Chancellor.	Lord Eldon.
Lord Privy Seal.	Earl of Westmorland.
Admiralty.	Lord Mulgrave.
	C. P. Yorke (1810).
Ordnance.	Earl of Chatham.
	Lord Mulgrave (1810).
Board of Trade.	Earl Bathurst.
Lord Lieutenant of Ireland.	Duke of Richmond, not in Cabinet.
Secretary at War.	Viscount Palmerston, not in Cabinet.

Liverpool, June, 1812.

First Lord of Treasury.	Earl of Liverpool.
Home Secretary.	Viscount Sidmouth.
	R. Peel (1822).
Foreign Secretary.	Viscount Castlereagh.
	G. Canning (1822).
War Office.	Earl Bathurst.
Lord President.	Earl of Harrowby.
Lord Chancellor.	Lord Eldon.
Lord Privy Seal.	Earl of Westmorland.
Chancellor of the Exchequer.	N. Vansittart.
	F. J. Robinson (1823).
Admiralty.	Viscount Melville.
Ordnance.	Lord Mulgrave.
	Duke of Wellington (1819).
Board of Trade.	Earl of Cloncarty, not in Cabinet.
	F. J. Robinson (1818).
	W. Huskisson (1823).
Board of Control.	Earl of Buckinghamshire.
	G. Canning (1816).
	C. B. Bathurst (1821).
	C. W. Wynn (1822).

Master of the Mint.	Earl of Cloncarty, not in Cabinet.
	W. W. Pole (1814), in Cabinet.
	T. Wallace (1823), not in Cabinet.
Duchy of Lancaster.	C. B. Bathurst.
	N. Vansittart (1823).
Without Portfolio.	Earl Camden, in Cabinet.
Lord Lieutenant of Ireland.	Duke of Richmond, not in Cabinet.
	Viscount Whitworth (1813), not in Cabinet.
	Earl Talbot (1817), not in Cabinet.
	Marquess Wellesley (1821), not in Cabinet.
Secretary at War.	Viscount Palmerston, not in Cabinet.

Canning, April, 1827.

First Lord of the Treasury and Chancellor of the Exchequer.	G. Canning.
Home Secretary.	W. S. Bourne.
	Marquess of Lansdowne (July).
Foreign Secretary.	Viscount Dudley and Ward.
War Office.	Viscount Goderich.
Lord President.	Earl of Harrowby.
Lord Chancellor.	Lord Lyndhurst.
Lord Privy Seal.	Duke of Portland.
	Earl of Carlisle (July).
Lord High Admiral.	Duke of Clarence, not in Cabinet.
Board of Trade.	W. Huskisson.
Board of Control.	G. W. Wynn.
Master of the Mint.	T. Wallace, not in Cabinet.
	G. Tierney (May), in Cabinet.
First Commissioner of Woods and Forests.	G. Arbuthnot, not in Cabinet.
	Earl of Carlisle (May), in Cabinet.
	W. S. Bourne (July), in Cabinet.
Duchy of Lancaster.	Lord Bexley.
Without Portfolio.	Marquess of Lansdowne (May–July), in Cabinet.
Lord Lieutenant of Ireland.	Marquess Wellesley, not in Cabinet.
Secretary at War.	Viscount Palmerston, in Cabinet.

INDEX

A

Roman Catholic Emancipation, 51, 52, 54, 55, 56, 70, 113, 114, 122, 125, 137, 143, 156, 161, 162, 204, 230, 231, 232, 233, 234, 235, 236, 239, 241, 242
Romana, Marquess de la, 91, 92
Ross, Tyrell, 107
Roskilde, battle of, 79
Rügen, island of, 75, 76
Rush, Richard, 189, 191, 193, 199
Russell, Lord John, 156, 157, 158, 162, 233
Rutland, Duke of, 237

S

Salamanca, 97
Salmon, Agnes, 11
San Juan de Ulloa, castle of, 194
San Martín, 181
Sardinia, King of, 34
Sayer, James, 45
Schiller, J. C. F. von, 44
Scott, Joan. *See* Joan Canning.
Scott, Sir Walter, 11, 115, 204
Seaford, Lord. *See* Charles Ellis.
Shelley, P. B., 138
Sheridan, R. B., 15, 18, 26, 28, 30, 32, 34, 61, 80, 99
Sidmouth, Viscount. *See* Henry Addington.
Singapore, the occupation of, 146
Sneyd, Rev. John, 27, 35, 51, 53, 72
Southey, Robert, 46, 47, 136, 204
South Hill, 51, 69, 117, 118
Spanish Insurrection, the, 89, 90, 91, 94, 95
Spithead and the Nore, mutinies at, 40
Stapleton, A. G., 203
Star, The, 224
Stael, Madame de, 65
Storming of the Bastille, the, 139, 140
St. Petersburg, the protocol of, 216
Strachan, Sir Richard, 102
Strangford, Lord, 204, 214, 216, 222
Stratford de Redcliffe, Viscount. *See* Stratford Canning.
Sucre, A. J., 198

T

Talavera, battle of, 101
Talleyrand, Prince, 64, 75, 112
Tarleton, General, 131, 132
Temperley, Professor, 27
Temple, Lord, 99
Therry, R., 120
The Times, 150, 164, 175, 223, 233

Thistlewood, Arthur, 142
Thurlow, Lord Chancellor, 36, 55
Tierney, G., 42, 98, 147, 240
Tilsit, 76, 94; treaty of, 77, 78, 80, 82, 83, 87, 91, 168, 209, 226
Trafalgar, battle of, 68, 72, 77, 81
Traz oz Montes, invasion of, 208
Trifler, The, 17
Turner, Sharon, 115

V

Vaches, Isle des, 186
Vansittart, N., 120, 138, 229
Venezuela, 89, 180, 181
Verona, Congress of, 164, 169, 170, 171, 172, 174, 178, 179, 182, 186, 190, 212
Vienna, Congress of, 114, 165
Vienna, treaty of, 146, 166, 168
Villèle, 184, 190, 207, 217, 218, 219
Vimeiro, 92

W

Walcheren expedition, 101, 102, 121
Waterloo, battle of, 139
Weekly Register, The, 140
Wellesley, Henry, later Lord Cowley, 106
Wellesley, 1st Marquess, 98, 116, 122, 124, 181
Wellesley, Sir Arthur. *See* Duke of Wellington.
Wellington, 1st Duke of, 44, 71, 79, 89, 92, 95, 98, 101, 124, 134, 138, 164, 169, 171, 175, 176, 177, 179, 180, 197, 207, 213, 216, 217, 230, 231, 232, 233, 237, 238, 242, 243
Westmorland, 10th Earl of, 53, 71, 176, 177, 197, 229, 230
Whitbread, Samuel, 67
Whitworth, Lord, 64
Wilberforce, William, 68
Wilbraham, Bootle, 29, 83, 108, 109, 127, 129, 164
Wilkes, John, 25
Windham, William, 30
Wordsworth, William, 204
Worsley, Sir Richard, 29
Wynn, C. W., 229, 238, 240

Y

Yarmouth, 82
Yarmouth, Lord, 17, 105, 106
York, Duke of, 230, 231, 232, 244